3⁸⁰

W9-BCM-309

COMPARATIVE
POLITICS
A Developmental Approach

The Little, Brown Series
in Comparative Politics

Under the Editorship of
GABRIEL A. ALMOND

JAMES S. COLEMAN

LUCIAN W. PYE

AN ANALYTIC STUDY

COMPARATIVE POLITICS

A Developmental Approach

Gabriel A. Almond
Stanford University

G. Bingham Powell, Jr.
Stanford University

Boston
LITTLE, BROWN AND COMPANY

COPYRIGHT © 1966, BY LITTLE, BROWN AND COMPANY (INC.)

ALL RIGHTS RESERVED. NO PART OF THIS BOOK
MAY BE REPRODUCED IN ANY FORM OR BY ANY
ELECTRONIC OR MECHANICAL MEANS INCLUDING
INFORMATION STORAGE AND RETRIEVAL SYSTEMS
WITHOUT PERMISSION IN WRITING FROM THE
PUBLISHER, EXCEPT BY A REVIEWER WHO MAY
QUOTE BRIEF PASSAGES IN A REVIEW.

LIBRARY OF CONGRESS CATALOG CARD NO. 66–28124

THIRD PRINTING

Published simultaneously in Canada
by Little Brown & Company (Canada) Limited

PRINTED IN THE UNITED STATES OF AMERICA

To
DOROTHEA K. ALMOND
and
PATRICIA L. POWELL

Foreword

THE Little, Brown Series in Comparative Politics has three
main objectives. First, it will meet the need of teachers to
deal with both western and non-western countries in their
introductory course offerings. Second, by following a common
approach in the analysis of individual political systems, it will
make it possible for teachers to compare these countries systematically and cumulatively. And third, it will contribute
toward reestablishing the classic relationship between comparative politics and political theory, a relationship which
has been neglected in recent decades. In brief, the series seeks
to be global in scope, genuinely introductory and comparative
in character, and concerned with broadening and deepening
our understanding of the nature and variety of political
systems.

The series has two parts: the Country Studies and the Analytic Studies. The Country Studies deal with a set of problems
and processes deriving from a functional, as against a purely
structural, approach to the study of political systems. We are
gratified that the participants, all of them mature scholars
with original insights of their own, were willing to organize
their discussions around a common set of functional topics in
the interest of furthering comparisons. At the same time, each
author has been urged to adapt the common framework to the
special problems of the country he is discussing and to express
his own theoretical point of view.

In this volume, Gabriel A. Almond and G. Bingham Powell,

Jr. provide a theoretical introduction to the Country Studies and make a contribution to the Analytic Studies. Some of the topics treated briefly in this volume are dealt with more comprehensively in *Aspects of Political Development* by Lucian W. Pye, *Political Communication* by Richard Fagen, and projected volumes dealing with such themes as political socialization, political culture, political structure, political economy, and the comparative analysis of interest groups and political parties.

Gabriel A. Almond
James S. Coleman
Lucian W. Pye

Acknowledgments

THE AUTHORS of this book have many debts to acknowledge. Their most important debt is owed to the political and social theorists, past and contemporary, upon whom they have drawn so heavily. Surely these debts go far beyond the ones specifically acknowledged in footnotes in the text. We have benefited greatly from critical readings of the manuscript by Lucian W. Pye, James S. Coleman, Robert Packenham, David Abernethy, Arnold Heidenheimer, Merle Kling, Henry Ehrmann, Lewis Edinger, and Norman Nie. David L. Giele of Little, Brown fought a noble battle for improvement in organization and style. Joanne Rauch supervised the preparation and revision of the manuscript with imagination, patience, and accuracy, and shared the typing burden with Virginia Martino.

Gabriel A. Almond

G. Bingham Powell, Jr.

July, 1966

Table of Contents

COMPARATIVE
POLITICS

CHAPTER I

Introduction

DURING THE LAST DECADE an intellectual revolution has been taking place in the study of comparative government. While it is impossible at this time to foresee in detail how this field will be reconstituted, it is possible to point to the main directions of innovation,[1] and to the dissatisfactions and criticisms which contributed to these changes. These developments are not confined to the field of comparative government, nor are they peculiar to the discipline of political science. The study of

[1] See *inter al.* Roy C. Macridis and Richard Cox, "Research in Comparative Politics," *American Political Science Review*, September, 1953; Pendleton Herring, "On the Study of Government," *American Political Science Review*, December, 1953; George McT. Kahin, Guy J. Pauker, and Lucian Pye, "Comparative Politics of Non-Western Countries," *American Political Science Review*, December, 1955; Gabriel A. Almond, Taylor Cole, and Roy C. Macridis, "A Suggested Research Strategy in Western European Government and Politics," *American Political Science Review*, December, 1955; Roy C. Macridis, *The Study of Comparative Government* (Garden City: Doubleday & Company, Inc., 1955); Gabriel A. Almond, "Comparative Political Systems," *Journal of Politics*, August, 1956; Gunnar Heckscher, *The Study of Comparative Government and Politics* (New York: The Macmillan Company, 1957); Sigmund Neumann, "Comparative Politics: A Half-Century Appraisal," *Journal of Politics*, August, 1957; Dankwart A. Rustow, "New Horizons for Comparative Politics," *World Politics*, July, 1957; David Apter, "A Comparative Method for the Study of Politics," *American Journal of Sociology*, November, 1958. For an excellent review of this polemic, see Harry Eckstein, "A Perspective on Comparative Politics, Past and Present," in Harry Eckstein and David Apter (eds.), *Comparative Politics* (New York: The Free Press of Glencoe, 1963).

1

foreign political systems has been greatly influenced by an earlier revolution in the study of American politics; and this in turn was the consequence of the penetration of American political studies by sociological, anthropological, and psychological methods and theories. Now the study of comparative politics holds out the promise of repaying its debt to those fields from which it has borrowed by providing a wider sample of man's experience with political institutions and processes, thus making its contribution to the common search for more adequate theories of politics.

Three themes dominated the criticism of the approach to comparative government characteristic of the period prior to World War II.[2] The first of these was concerned with its *parochialism.* As a coherent discipline, comparative government was largely confined to the European area — Britain (and the old Commonwealth), France, Germany, Italy, and Russia. Studies of the political systems of Asia, Africa, and Latin America were carried on by a small group of generally isolated individual scholars, or in the context of "area studies" rather than in the context of a general discipline of comparative government. Clearly the dominant core of the field consisted of the European "great powers," and whatever there was of general theorizing about forms of government and patterns of politics was based upon this small, though salient, sample of political systems.

Secondly, the dominant approach to the study of foreign governments was *configurative.* It was concerned with illuminating the peculiar characteristics of individual political systems. With the exceptions of Friedrich's *Constitutional Government and Democracy* and Finer's *Theory and Practice of Modern Government,* there was little systematic comparative analysis.[3] Even Friedrich's and Finer's works were confined to European political systems, and comparative analysis was often little more than the juxtaposition of specific institutional pat-

[2] For a summary of the critical point of view, see Macridis, *Comparative Government, op. cit.*

[3] Carl J. Friedrich, *Constitutional Government and Democracy* (New York: Harper and Brothers, 1937); Herman J. Finer, *Theory and Practice of Modern Government* (New York: Henry Holt & Company, Inc., 1949).

terns, rather than a way of introducing controls in the investigation of relations and causal sequences among political and social phenomena.

The third criticism was directed at the *formalism* of the discipline. The focus tended to be on institutions (primarily governmental ones) and their legal norms, rules, and regulations, or on political ideas and ideologies, rather than on performance, interaction, and behavior. It is a striking indication of the lack of coherence and communication in the discipline of political science that this formalism in the study of comparative government could persist in the same decades during which the study of American politics was bursting with innovation and iconoclasm. But the flowering of American political science which began in the 1920's and produced in rapid succession the searching and experimental works of such men as Merriam, Lasswell, Herring, Schattschneider, and Odegard [4] represented a response to stimuli and opportunities peculiar to the American setting. The rapid industrialization and urbanization of America, the challenges of great power status dramatized by participation in World War I, the shocks and dislocations of the depression, and the corresponding changes in the structure and process of the American political system, drew the energies of the growing cadre of American political scientists into self-study and self-appraisal. The absorbing themes of political science research during these decades were the pathologies and shortcomings of American democracy — the "boss" and the "machine," pressure groups and the lobby, the power of and control over the media of mass communication, judicial conservatism, and problems of politico-administrative leadership in the era of big government.

[4] Charles E. Merriam, "New Aspects of Politics," in Heinz Eulau *et al.* (eds.), *Political Behavior* (New York: The Free Press of Glencoe, 1956), pp. 24 ff.; Harold D. Lasswell, *Psychopathology and Politics* (Chicago: University of Chicago Press, 1930), and his *Politics: Who Gets What, When, How* (New York: McGraw-Hill, 1936); E. P. Herring, *Group Representation Before Congress* (New York: McGraw-Hill, 1929), and his *Public Administration and the Public Interest* (New York: McGraw-Hill, 1936); Elmer Schattschneider, *Politics, Pressures, and the Tariff* (Englewood Cliffs: Prentice-Hall, Inc., 1937); Peter Odegard, *Pressure Politics: The Story of the Anti-Saloon League* (New York: Columbia University Press, 1928).

The growth of political science in America has had a discontinuous as well as an incremental aspect. During the period prior to World War II, the bewildering variety of interrelated issues and problems of rapid internal social and political change focused attention on the domestic scene, and drew the more adventurous spirits into methodological experimentation and studies in depth of the relations between social structure and process, personality formation, and political process and behavior. Intellectual innovations such as psychoanalytic theory and the politico-sociological theories of Weber, Durkheim, Pareto, Toennies, and others, found greater receptivity in some academic communities in America than they did in their countries of origin.

The study of foreign governments during these decades continued largely along formalistic lines. Perhaps it would be more accurate to say that there was some real intellectual deterioration in this field of study. For historically, comparative government and political theory had been closely connected. The theme of the qualities and attributes of the various forms of polity was a central concern of political theory from the Greeks on through the nineteenth century. But in the early decades of the twentieth century the two fields separated, with political theory becoming an essentially historical subject matter, and comparative or foreign government becoming a formal and descriptive study of the great powers of western Europe.

Paradoxically, this separation in American political science of political theory and comparative government on the one hand, and the burgeoning of American political studies on the other, may have been the consequence of the Enlightenment itself. This mother of modern science, and of the skeptical secular outlook in which it flourishes, had its faith in the inevitable triumph of reason, which was assumed to bring along with it free social and political institutions. The liberal and populist currents in America were the most optimistic products of the Enlightenment faith, and it was from these sources that the growing profession of political science in America in the first decades of the twentieth century drew much of its inspiration. If democracy was to be the inevitable political form of the future, then the investigation and exposition of the nature of democracy and of its institutional and ethical properties could become the central theme of political science. Nondemocratic systems or unstable democratic systems could be examined in terms of their deviation from democratic ideological norms, or by comparison with the two historic versions of stable democracy — British parliamentarism and the American separation-of-powers system.

This optimistic faith in the inevitability of democracy, especially strong in America, dampened curiosity and interest in nondemocratic forms of politics. They had a purely temporary or exotic significance. This view continued in the period between the two wars, when even communism and fascism were viewed as temporary disorders or political pathologies; teaching in the field of comparative government was carried on under the rubric of "Democracy and Dictatorship," with dictatorship representing error and political pathology, and democracy representing truth and political health.

This naive conception of democratic progress, and the intellectual structure of the discipline of comparative government which it had produced and supported, became untenable in the period after World War II. Three developments were primarily responsible:

1. the national explosion in the Middle East, Africa, and Asia; the emergence into statehood of a multitude of nations with a bewildering variety of cultures, social institutions, and political characteristics;
2. the loss of dominance of the nations of the Atlantic Community; the diffusion of international power and influence into the former colonial and semicolonial areas;
3. the emergence of communism as a powerful competitor in the struggle to shape the structure of national polities and of the international political system.

The new situation, with all its uncertainty and threat, its confusion of political forms, its bewildering instabilities, has created a mood of doubt, of skepticism, in place of the naive optimism of the earlier political science tradition in America. Out of it has come a trend toward intellectual innovation, efforts to master the new complexities, and an attempt to create a new intellectual order. These efforts at innovation may be summarized under four headings: (1) the search for more comprehensive scope; (2) the search for realism; (3) the search for precision; and (4) the search for theoretical order.

(1) *The search for more comprehensive scope.* This is the effort to break out of parochialism and ethnocentrism. In not much more than a decade the pattern of publication in the field of comparative government has changed. Studies of non-Western governments and political processes have appeared in larger numbers than those dealing with the European area. It may also be that these non-Western studies have more frequently broken new ground in a theoretical and methodological sense than have European studies.[5] Furthermore, non-Western specialists no longer work in isolation from the discipline of political science and comparative government. The dominance in the political science profession by Americanists and Europeanists has given way to a more balanced representation of area specialists in the discipline. The modern non-Western-area specialist views himself as a political theorist carrying on research in his particular area on aspects of politics which have significance for the general theory of political systems. More recently the impulse toward sampling more completely the universe of man's experience with politics has led to the study of political systems of the past, based on available historical and ethnographic studies or on original historical research.[6]

[5] See *inter al.* David Apter, *The Gold Coast* (Princeton: Princeton University Press, 1956), and his *The Political Kingdom in Uganda* (Princeton: Princeton University Press, 1961); Leonard Binder, *Iran: Political Development in a Changing Society* (Berkeley: University of California Press, 1962); Lucian W. Pye, *Politics, Personality, and Nation Building* (New Haven: Yale University Press, 1962); Myron Weiner, *The Politics of Scarcity* (Chicago: University of Chicago Press, 1962).

[6] See, for example, S. N. Eisenstadt, *The Political Systems of Empires* (New York: The Free Press of Glencoe, 1962); S. M. Lipset, *The First New Nation* (New York: Basic Books, Inc., 1963); Reinhard Bendix, *Nation-Building and Citizenship* (New York: John Wiley & Sons, Inc., 1964).

(2) *The search for realism.* If by "the search for more comprehensive scope" we mean the escape from parochialism and
ethnocentrism, then by "the search for realism" we refer to
the escape from formalism, and from the dominant concern
with law, ideology, and governmental institutions, into an
examination of all the structures and processes involved in
politics and policy making. There is now a growing library
of studies of governmental processes, political parties, interest
groups, electoral processes, political communication, and political socialization processes dealing with the European and
non-Western areas.[7] The attainment of depth and realism in
the study of political systems enables us to locate the dynamic
forces of politics wherever they may exist — in social class, in
culture, in economic and social change, in the political elites,
or in the international environment. The slogan under which
this realistic-empirical tendency goes is "the behavioral approach." What it means, very simply, is the study of the actual
behavior of the incumbents of political roles, rather than of
the content of legal rules or ideological patterns. It does not
mean a disregard of legal norms, ideologies, and formal institutions, but rather a concern with them insofar as they reflect
or influence political action.

(3) *The search for precision.* This is a response in political
studies to the general diffusion of the scientific and technological attitude in Western societies. This tendency has influenced psychology and economics for some time, and has already

[7] Some of the recent monographic studies of interest groups in for-
eign countries are Henry Ehrmann (ed.), *Interest Groups on Four Continents*
(Pittsburgh: University of Pittsburgh Press, 1958); Harry Eckstein, *Pres-
sure Group Politics* (Stanford: Stanford University Press, 1960); S. E. Finer,
Anonymous Empire (London: The Pall Mall Press, 1958); Allen Potter,
Organized Groups in British National Politics (London: Faber & Faber,
Ltd., 1961); Henry W. Ehrmann, *Organized Business in France* (Princeton:
Princeton University Press, 1957); Jean Meynaud, *Les Groupes de Pression
en France* (Paris: Librairie Armand Colin, 1958); Hans Speier and W. Phil-
lips Davison (eds.), *West German Leadership and Foreign Policy* (New
York: Harper & Row, Publishers, 1957); Rupert Breitling, *Die Verbande in
der Bundesrepublik* (Miesenheim am Glan: Anton Hain, 1955); Joseph
LaPalombara, *Interest Groups in Italian Politics* (Princeton: Princeton
University Press, 1964); Weiner, *op. cit.*; James Payne, *Labor and Politics in
Peru* (New Haven: Yale University Press, 1965).

penetrated sociology and anthropology. The search for precision has affected all the fields of political science and has
produced studies of electoral trends based on voting statistics;
studies of factors affecting voters' choices based on sample
surveys; studies correlating quantitative social data and the
characteristics of political systems; studies of political culture
and socialization based on sample surveys, clinical case studies,
and anthropological field observation; quantitative studies of
political elite recruitment; quantitative content analyses of
political communications; observational studies of experimental or natural small-group processes; quantitative studies of
judicial decisions; and the development of mathematical
models for the analysis of political processes. These methods
have been, or soon will be, applied in American political
studies wherever precise measurement and controlled observation are possible, and they are spreading into European and
non-Western political studies.

(4) *The search for intellectual order.* The first three tendencies — the search for comprehensiveness, for realism, and
for precision — have strained our theoretical frameworks and
conceptual vocabularies beyond their capacity to codify and
assimilate the new insights and findings of political science research. Concepts such as the state, the constitution, representation, and the rights and duties of citizens cannot effectively
codify the activities of political parties, pressure groups, the
media of mass communication, and child-rearing and educational practices. Theoretical experimentation, relying primarily on sociological, psychological, and anthropological
concepts and frameworks, has become common; and new concepts such as political culture, political role, and political
socialization have already acquired currency in the field.
Among the chief influences in the development of theoretical
experimentation have been the works of Max Weber, Talcott
Parsons, and Harold Lasswell.

What we have described are different aspects of a great fer-
ment within the study of politics. It is premature to try to anticipate the structure of the discipline ten years from now, but
one point should be stressed. These new developments have

implications not only for the subdiscipline of comparative politics, but for the discipline of political science as a whole. Carried through to their logical conclusions, these trends point in the direction of a unified theory of politics. Thus, the classic relationship between comparative government and political theory is in process of being re-established. The world community of national political systems is now being viewed as a political system in itself, and the same theoretical categories are being applied in studying it and in comparing it with national political systems. Furthermore, as the role of the international political system in shaping the structures and processes of domestic politics is becoming more widely appreciated, the artificial separation between comparative government and international politics is being removed.[8] Similarly, there is now some systematic study of the effects of the characteristics of national political systems upon the functioning of the international political system. Finally, the structural subdisciplines of political science — the study of bureaucracies, legislatures, political parties, interest groups, public opinion, and the like — are becoming broadly comparative and, as a partial consequence, more theoretically sophisticated.

What we have described above are to be viewed as long-run trends and not as completed accomplishments. The most important work, both empirical and theoretical, is still to be done.

The publications program to which this book is an introduction represents a contribution in this broad stream of intellectual activity. It is a response, within the limits of available knowledge, to the challenges of comprehensiveness, realism, precision, and intellectual order. In its selection of countries to be included, it seeks to represent the variety of political systems which are of significance in the contemporary world and which will be helpful in studying and constructing theories of the political system. The approach to be followed in the country studies and stressed in the analytical series is realistic. That

[8] James Rosenau, *Theories and Pre-Theories of International Politics*, unpublished manuscript, 1964; Richard N. Rosecrance, *Action and Reaction in World Politics* (Boston: Little, Brown and Company, 1963).

is, we are concerned with the interrelationships between social structure and process, and political structure and process, and we will stress attitude and performance rather than ideology and norms. Wherever quantitative and precise information is available, we will use it; and where it is lacking, we will point to these significant research areas and qualify our inferences accordingly. Finally, this introductory volume spells out a conceptual framework which is employed in our country studies but which we hope will be elaborated and refined in our analytic series and eventually replaced.

The approach followed in this book has come to be called "the functional approach to comparative politics." It is only one among a number of innovative tendencies in the study of comparative politics. Its intellectual origins are of interest and deserve a brief treatment. This particular version of functionalism grows directly out of the classic tradition of political theory; in particular, out of that part which has been concerned with analyzing the political process, and with distinguishing the subprocesses or phases of political decision and action. In the seventeenth and eighteenth centuries this concern led to the formulation of the theory of *separation of powers,* the doctrine that political action involved the distinguishable processes of legislation, administration, and adjudication. Those political systems which provided for specialized institutions to handle these particular functions, or powers, were said to be more likely to protect liberty, property, and justice. And those political systems which provided for the effective representation of the major social and economic strata within such separation-of-powers systems were more likely to be stable and libertarian.[9]

The political theory of the *Federalist Papers* is pre-eminently a functional theory. Among its central concerns are the nature of legislative, executive, and judicial power; the question of

[9] See *inter al.* Aristotle, *Politics,* Rackham translation (London: Wm. Heinemann, Ltd., 1932), pp. 345 ff.; Chârles de Montesquieu, *The Spirit of the Laws,* Nugent translation (New York: The Colonial Press, 1899), Vol. I, pp. 151 ff.; John Locke, *Of Civil Government* (London: J. M. Dent, 1926), pp. 191 ff.; *The Federalist,* Beloff Edition (Oxford: Blackwell, 1948), Nos. 9 and 47–51, pp. 48 ff., 245 ff.

how best to maintain their separateness; the values resulting from such separation; and the problem of how best to mesh these separate institutions of government with the structure of society. The authors of the *Federalist Papers* were systems theorists as well for they dealt with the interaction and equilibrium of the other social systems with the political system, and with the interaction of the subsystems of the polity one with the other. That they were in some measure self-conscious systems theorists is reflected in the influence of Newtonian mechanics on their model of a stable libertarian polity: their primary concern was to provide for an equilibrated system of interaction among the three principal institutions of executive, legislature, and judiciary. To maintain this equilibrium they provided for a regulated system of "multifunctionality" (checks and balances), a mixture of functions which, by preventing the aggrandizement of any institution at the expense of the others, maintained the balance of power.

The tripartite approach to political function seemed to be an adequate theory for purposes of political analysis and institution building at a time when the politically active class was limited and socially homogeneous. However, much has happened since the eighteenth century. The development of universal suffrage, the emergence of mass political parties intended to mobilize the electorate, the rise of organized interest groups intended to express the interests of the component parts of a complex society and influence the course of political decision, and the development of the media of mass communication, have sensitized us to political functions which were not fully appreciated in the eighteenth and nineteenth centuries. Thus, we argue in this book that we need to complicate the separation-of-powers model (legislation, administration, adjudication) by adding three other functions which enable us to compare and describe the distinctive processes which precede or impinge on the original three. We speak of these as *interest articulation, interest aggregation,* and *communication,* and refer to what is now a sixfold classification of functions as the *conversion processes* of the political system — the processes which transform the flow of *demands* and *supports* into the political system into a flow of *extraction, regulation, distribution,* and the like, out of the political system into the society or international environment.[10]

In this study we go considerably beyond the systems theory of the *Federalist Papers* in other ways than simply in the number of functions. Our concept of "system" is more explicit. Here we have been influenced by recent sociological, anthropological, and communications theories which stress the concept of the social system. The advantages of thinking of politics as a system are elaborated in the chapters which follow. Here we need only say that much of the criticism of the applications of systems theory to politics has real merit. Those of us who have worked along these lines have been too much under the influence of mechanical and biological analogies, and surely this book does not escape from such analogistic thinking.[11]

Among the principal criticisms of functional-systems theories are the arguments that they imply an equilibrium or harmony of parts and that they have a static or conservative bias. The conception of "political system" which we follow in this book is one of interdependence, but not one of harmony. Perhaps we might speak of it as *probabilistic* functionalism. In other

10 The approach followed in this book differs from the "systems" approach followed in David Easton, *A Systems Analysis of Political Life* (New York: John Wiley & Sons, Inc., 1965), and Karl W. Deutsch, *The Nerves of Government* (New York: The Free Press of Glencoe, 1963), in that it grows directly out of separation-of-powers theory and the stream of empirical research critical of that theory; from this base it treats the functions of the political institutions which emerged after the broadening of the suffrage and industrialization — political parties, pressure groups, and the mass media. Both Easton and Deutsch — but particularly Deutsch — apply a communication, or cybernetic, model to politics. The approach followed here grows out of the tradition of political theory and reaches into sociological and communication theory for useful conceptual tools. The approaches in Easton and Deutsch grow out of sociological and communications theory and move toward the theory and data of politics. Both emphases have their uses and will no doubt converge in later theoretical work.

11 See, for example, Karl W. Deutsch, *op. cit.,* Chap. 1, and Alvin W. Gouldner, "Reciprocity and Autonomy in Functional Theory," in Llewellyn Gross (ed.), *Symposium on Sociological Theory* (New York: Harper & Row, Publishers, 1959), pp. 241–271.

words, if trade unions develop in a political system, there is a high probability that political parties, the electoral process, the legislature, and bureaucracy will be affected by these trade unions. The system of interaction which ensues may be anything but harmonic and stable, but it *will be* interdependent. And it is the task of political science research to ascertain how change in any one of the parts of a political system affects other parts and the whole.

The second criticism — that of the static and conservative implications of systems theory — has greater cogency and has produced substantial modification in our approach to the political system and its functions. Our earlier formulation [12] was suitable mainly for the analysis of political systems in a given cross section of time. It did not permit us to explore developmental patterns, to explain how political systems change and why they change. This static cross-sectional bias of the earlier formulations of the functional approach and, indeed, of much of the grand tradition of political theory and of contemporary political science research, raises some intriguing questions.

Political science as an empirical discipline has tended to concern itself with the problems of power and process, with the *who* and *how* of politics — who makes decisions and how they are made. The *what* of politics, the content and direction of public policy, has generally been treated in terms of what political systems ought and ought not to do, or has been inferred from structure and process. Nowhere is this approach to the outputs of the political system, or the identification of output with structure and process, more clearly formulated than in Aristotle's *Politics,* where the *what* of public policy is inferred from the number, the identity, and the virtue of the political rulers — whether they be one, few, or many; and whether they are concerned with the collective interest of the polity or with their own self-interest.

We need to take a major analytical step if we are to build political development more explicitly into our approach to the study of political systems. We need to look at political systems

[12] See Gabriel A. Almond and James S. Coleman (eds.), *The Politics of the Developing Areas* (Princeton: Princeton University Press, 1960).

as whole entities shaping and being shaped by their environments. For example, the development of a specialized bureaucracy and a professional army in a political system may be the consequence of the interaction of one political system with other nations in its environment. The rulers of the first nation may develop expansive ambitions, or they may be forced into developing its military capabilities by threats or actual invasions from its environment. Or the rulers of a political system may respond to changes which are initiated within their own societies: the growth of commerce, the accumulation of wealth, or famine or similar disasters. Such internal developments may increase the pressure on the political system, forcing it to develop if it is to survive. Unless our conception of the political system enables us to deal with the interaction of the political system with its domestic and international environments, we cannot come to grips with the processes of political development.

What we do in this book is to consider the activities, or *functions,* of political systems from three points of view. The first of these we have already referred to — the *conversion functions* of interest articulation, interest aggregation, political communication, rule making, rule application, and rule adjudication. The second consideration is the operation of the political system as an "individual" in its environments. We refer to this aspect of the functioning of a political system as its *capabilities.* Finally, we will need to consider the way in which political systems maintain or adapt themselves to pressures for change over the long run. We speak here of *system maintenance and adaptation functions — political recruitment* and *political socialization.*

The various terms and concepts which we have briefly introduced above are dealt with in detail in the chapters which follow. In Chapter II we provide an overview of our theoretical framework. In Chapter III we discuss the system maintenance and adaptation functions of political recruitment and socialization. Chapters IV through VII deal in some detail with the conversion functions of interest articulation, interest aggregation, political communication, rule making, rule application, and rule adjudication. Chapter VIII considers the interaction of political systems with their environments — their capabilities. In Chapters IX and X we use this theoretical framework in presenting a developmental classification of political systems, giving examples of some of the principal varieties. And in Chapter XI we conclude with some thoughts on the question of *levels of political development,* and the problem of *investment* in *political growth.*

CHAPTER II

An Overview

IT MAY BE USEFUL at the outset to introduce the principal concepts and terms we use in this book. They will be elaborated and illustrated in later chapters. But here they are presented in compact form and in a logical order so that they may serve as a guide to what follows, as a way of relating the various chapters one to the other. The principal concept that we use is that of "system."

THE POLITICAL SYSTEM

The term "political system" has become increasingly common in the titles of texts and monographs in the field of comparative politics. The older texts used such terms as "government," "nation," or "state" to describe what we call a political system. Something more is involved here than mere style of nomenclature. This new terminology reflects a new way of looking at political phenomena. It includes some new names for old things, and some new terms to refer to activities and processes which were not formerly recognized as being parts or aspects of politics.

The older terms — state, government, nation — are limited by legal and institutional meanings. They direct attention to a particular set of institutions usually found in modern Western societies. If one accepts the idea that the study of such

16

institutions is the proper and sole concern of political science, many problems are thereby avoided, including the thorny question of limiting the subject matter of the discipline. However, the costs of such a decision are very high. The role played by formal governmental institutions such as legislatures and courts in different societies varies greatly; in many societies, particularly in those outside the Western world, their role may not be so important as that of other institutions and processes. In all societies the role of formal governmental institutions is shaped and limited by informal groups, political attitudes, and a multitude of interpersonal relationships. If political science is to be effective in dealing with political phenomena in all kinds of societies, regardless of culture, degree of modernization, and size, we need a more comprehensive framework of analysis.

The concept of "political system" has acquired wide currency because it directs attention to the entire scope of political activities within a society, regardless of where in the society such activities may be located. What is the political system? How do we define its boundaries? What gives the political system its special identity? Many political scientists have dealt with these questions; while the precise language of their definitions varies considerably, there is some consensus. Common to most of these definitions is the association of the political system with the use of legitimate physical coercion in societies. Easton speaks of *authoritative allocation of values;* Lasswell and Kaplan, of *severe deprivations;* Dahl, of *power, rule, and authority.*[1] All these definitions imply legitimate, heavy sanctions; the rightful power to punish, to enforce, to compel. We agree with Max Weber [2] that legitimate force is the thread that runs through the action of the political system, giving it

[1] David Easton, *The Political System* (New York: Alfred A. Knopf, Inc., 1953), pp. 130 ff., and his *A Framework for Political Analysis* (Englewood Cliffs: Prentice-Hall, Inc., 1965), pp. 50 ff.; Harold D. Lasswell and Abraham Kaplan, *Power and Society* (New Haven: Yale University Press, 1950); Robert A. Dahl, *Modern Political Analysis* (Englewood Cliffs: Prentice-Hall, Inc., 1963), pp. 5 ff.

[2] See Max Weber, "Politics as a Vocation," in his *From Max Weber: Essays in Sociology,* ed. Hans H. Gerth and C. Wright Mills (New York: Oxford University Press, 1946), pp. 77–78.

its special quality and importance, and its coherence as a system. The political authorities, and only they, have some generally accepted right to utilize coercion and command obedience based upon it. (Force is "legitimate" where this belief in the justifiable nature of its use exists.) The inputs which enter the political system are all in some way related to legitimate physical compulsion, whether these are demands for war or for recreational facilities. The outputs of the political system are also all in some way related to legitimate physical compulsion, however remote the relationship may be. Thus, public recreation facilities are usually supported by taxation, and any violation of the regulations governing their use is a legal offense. When we speak of the political system, we include all the interactions which affect the use or threat of use of legitimate physical coercion. The political system includes not only governmental institutions such as legislatures, courts, and administrative agencies, but *all structures in their political aspects*. Among these are traditional structures such as kinship ties and caste groupings; and anomic phenomena such as assassinations, riots, and demonstrations; as well as formal organizations like parties, interest groups, and media of communication.

We are not, then, saying that the political system is concerned solely with force, violence, or compulsion; rather, that its relation to coercion is its distinctive quality. Political elites are usually concerned with goals such as national expansion or security, social welfare, the aggrandizement of their power over other groups, increased popular participation in politics, and the like; but their concern with these values as politicians is related to compulsory actions such as law making and law enforcement, foreign and defense policy, and taxation. The political system is not the only system that makes rules and enforces them, but its rules and enforcements go all the way to compelling obedience or performance.

There are societies in which the accepted power to use physical compulsion is widely diffused, shared by family, by clan, by religious bodies, or other kinds of groups, or taken up privately, as in the feud or the duel. But we consider even these as political systems of a particular kind, and still comparable with those polities in which there is something approaching a monopoly of legitimate physical coercion.

If what we have said above defines the "political" half of our concept, what do we mean by "system"? A system implies the interdependence of parts, and a boundary of some kind between it and its environment. By "interdependence" we mean that when the properties of one component in a system change, all the other components and the system as a whole are affected. Thus, if the rings of an automobile erode, the car "burns oil"; the functioning of other aspects of the system deteriorates, and the power of the car declines. Or, as another example, there are points in the growth of organisms when some change in the endocrine system affects the over-all pattern of growth, the functioning of all the parts, and the general behavior of the organism. In political systems the emergence of mass parties, or of media of mass communication, changes the performance of all the other structures of the system and affects the general capabilities of the system in its domestic and foreign environments. In other words, when one variable in a system changes in magnitude or in quality, the others are subjected to strains and are transformed; the system changes its pattern of performance, or the unruly component is disciplined by regulatory mechanisms.

A second aspect of the concept of "system" is the notion of boundary. A system starts somewhere and stops somewhere. In considering an organism or an automobile, it is relatively easy to locate its boundary and to specify the interactions between it and its environment. The gas goes into the tank, the motor converts it into revolutions of the crankshaft and the driving wheels, and the car moves on the highway. In dealing with social systems, of which political systems are a class, the problem of boundary is not that easy. Social systems are made up not of individuals, but of roles. A family, for example, consists of the roles of mother and father, husband and wife, sibling and sibling. The family is only one set of interacting roles for its members, who also may have roles outside the family in schools, business firms, and churches. In the same sense a political system is made up of the interacting roles of nationals, subjects, voters, as the case may be, with legislators, bureaucrats, and judges. The same individuals who perform roles in the political system perform roles in other social systems such as the economy, the religious community, the family, and voluntary associations. As individuals expose themselves to political communication, form interest groups, vote, or pay taxes, they shift from nonpolitical to political roles. One might say that on election day as citizens leave their farms, plants, and offices to go to the polling places, they are crossing the boundary from the economy to the polity.

Another example of a shift in the boundary of the political system might occur when inflation reduces the real income of certain groups in the population. When such a change in the economic situation of particular groups gets converted into demands for public policy or for changes in political personnel, there is an interaction between the economy and the polity. Certain psychic states resulting from changes in the economic situation are converted into demands on the political system. Demands are made on trade-union or other pressure-group leaders to lobby for particular actions by the legislature or by executive agencies. Somewhere in this process a boundary is crossed from one system to another — from the economic system to the political system.

The boundaries of political systems are subject to relatively large fluctuations. During wartime the boundaries become greatly extended as large numbers of men are recruited into military service, as business firms are subjected to regulations, and as internal security measures are taken. In an election the boundaries again are greatly extended as voters become politicians for a day. With the return to more normal conditions, the boundaries of the political system contract.

The problem of boundaries takes on special significance because systems theory usually divides interaction processes into three phases — input, conversion, output. Any set of interacting parts — any system — which is affected by factors in its environment may be viewed in this fashion. The inputs and outputs, which involve the political system with other social systems, are transactions between the system and its environment; the conversion processes are internal to the political system. When we talk about the sources of inputs, their number, content, and intensity, and how they enter the political system, and of the number and content of outputs and how they leave the political system and affect other social systems, we shall in effect be talking about the boundaries of the political system.

STRUCTURE AND CULTURE

The terms "structure" and "culture" are also of central importance in our analytical scheme. By "structure" we mean the observable activities which make up the political system. To refer to these activities as having a structure simply implies that there is a certain regularity to them. Thus, in a court one can speak of the interactions between the judge, the jury, the prosecuting and defense attorneys, witnesses, the defendant, and the plaintiff. This example should make clear that when we speak of political activity, we are not referring to the total activities of the individual who may be involved in it, but just to that part of his activities which is involved in the political process. Judges, lawyers, witnesses, defendants, and plaintiffs are all men who have a variety of other spheres of activity. That particular part of the activity of individuals which is involved in political processes we refer to as the role. The units which make up all social systems, including political systems, are *roles*. The individual members of a society usually perform roles in a variety of social systems other than the political system — for example, in families, business firms, churches, social clubs.

One of the basic units of political systems, then, is the political role. We refer to particular sets of roles which are related to one another as *structures*. Thus, judgeship is a role; a court is a structure of roles. The reason we use the terms "role" and "structure" rather than "office" and "institution" is that we wish to emphasize the actual behavior of the individuals who are involved in politics, and the actual performance of the particular institution with which we may be concerned. Both "office" and "institution" may refer to formal rules, such as those presumed to govern the behavior of judges and juries, or to some ideal mode of behavior toward which we might wish them to aspire. "Role" and "structure" refer to the observable behavior of individuals. Legal rules and ideal norms may affect that behavior, but they rarely describe it fully.

Beginning with the concept of role as one of the basic units of a political system, we may speak of a subsystem (for example, a legislative body) as consisting of related and interacting roles; and of the political system as a set of interacting subsystems (for example, legislatures, electorates, pressure groups, and courts).

We need to introduce two other concepts before we leave this discussion of role and structure. If this book is to have a developmental emphasis, we have to deal with those processes which maintain or change political systems over time. The incumbents of political roles are superseded or die. New sets of political roles are established, and old ones may be abolished or may atrophy. Every political system is continually involved in *recruiting* individuals into political roles. We speak, then, of the *recruitment function,* which must be performed in all political systems if its roles are to be manned and if its structures are to function. A principal aspect of the development or transformation of the political system is what we call *role differentiation,* or *structural differentiation.* By "differentiation" we refer to the processes whereby roles change and become more specialized or more autonomous or whereby new types of roles are established or new structures and subsystems emerge or are created. When we speak of role differentiation and structural differentiation, we refer not only to the development of new types of roles and the transformation of older ones; we refer also to changes which may take place in the relationship between roles, between structures, or between subsystems. Thus, for example, courts were established as separate structures long before they acquired independence or autonomy from the other structures of the political system. In speaking of the *developmental aspect* of role and structure then, we are interested not only in the emergence of new types of roles or the atrophy of old ones, but also in the changing patterns of interaction among roles, structures, and subsystems.

There is another principal dimension which runs throughout this book, the concept of political culture. We all know that there is more to a man than what shows on the surface. In the same sense, there is more to a political system than may be clearly manifested over a given period of time. For example, Italy under Fascism appeared to be a quite formidable and powerful political system. It repressed opposition, held massive and impressive parades, and defeated the Ethiopians. But then it had great difficulty coping with the Greeks, and it began to collapse in Africa when whole army divisions retreated and surrendered without much of a fight. A simple observational study of Italian politics during this period would not have helped us predict the capacity of the Italian political system to carry out its policies. Had we known more of the mood and the attitude of the Italian population, more of the morale and the commitment of its soldiers, more of the resoluteness of its officers and of the capacity for policymaking of its political elites, we might have been able to predict the viability of this political system when confronted with unusual pressure and opposition.

In studying any political system, therefore, we need to know its underlying propensities as well as its actual performance over a given period of time. We refer to these propensities, or this psychological dimension of the political system, as the *political culture*. It consists of attitudes, beliefs, values, and skills which are current in an entire population, as well as those special propensities and patterns which may be found within separate parts of that population. Thus, regional groups or ethnic groups or social classes which make up the population of a political system may have special propensities or tendencies. We refer to these special propensities located in particular groups as *subcultures*. Similarly, there may be traditions and attitudes current in the different roles, structures, and subsystems of the political system. Thus, French military officers or bureaucratic officials may have a special culture which differentiates them from French politicians, for example.

Thus, the analysis of the political system must consist not only of observation of the actual patterns of behavior and interaction over a period of time, but also of those subjective propensities located in the political system as a whole and in its various parts. As we learn about the *structure* and *culture* of a political system, our capacity to characterize its properties, and to predict and explain its performance, is improved.

We need also to speak of two concepts that are related to political culture. The propensities, attitudes, beliefs, and values to which we have referred are the consequence of *political socialization*. This is the process whereby political attitudes and values are inculcated as children become adults and as adults are recruited into roles. Finally, we need a concept to deal with the developmental aspect of political culture, a concept comparable to that of differentiation in the dimension of political structure. The term commonly used here is *secularization*. Secularization is the process whereby men become increasingly rational, analytical, and empirical in their political action. We may illustrate this concept by comparing a political leader in a modern democracy with a political leader in a traditional or primitive African political system. A modern democratic political leader when running for office, for instance, will gather substantial amounts of information about the constituency which he hopes will elect him and the issues of public policy with which that constituency may be concerned. He has to make estimates of the distribution and intensity of demands of one kind or another; he needs to use creative imagination in order to identify a possible combination of demands which may lead to his receiving a majority of the votes in his constituency. A village chief in a tribal society operates largely with a given set of goals and a given set of means of attaining those goals which have grown up and been hallowed by custom. The secularization of culture is the processes whereby traditional orientations and attitudes give way to more dynamic decision-making processes involving the gathering of information, the evaluation of information, the laying out of alternative courses of action, the selection of a course of action from among these possible courses, and the means whereby one tests whether or not a given course of action is producing the consequences which were intended.

When we use the developmental concepts "structural differentiation" and "cultural secularization," we do not imply that there is any inevitable trend in these directions in the development of political systems.[3] If we examine the histories of political systems, it becomes quite clear that regressions, or reversals, occur commonly in the development of political systems. Thus, the Roman Empire reached a very high level of structural differentiation and cultural secularization, and then fell apart into a large number of less differentiated and less secularized political systems. Whatever the direction may be in a given period of time and in a given political system, we may still speak of development in terms of the degree of differentiation and secularization.

INPUTS AND OUTPUTS

We have described the political system as consisting of interacting roles, structures, and subsystems, and of underlying psychological propensities which affect these interactions. Such a process may be viewed as consisting of inputs from the environment or from within the political system itself, the conversion of these inputs within the system, and the production of outputs into the environment. Outputs may produce changes in the environment, which in turn may affect the political system (feedback).

David Easton, the first political scientist to analyze politics in explicit system terms, distinguishes two types of inputs into the political system: *demands* and *supports*.[4] Demands may be subclassified in many ways. The following classification illustrates the range and the variety of demands made upon the political system: (1) demands for allocations of goods and services, such as demands for wage and hour laws, educational op-

[3] See S. P. Huntington, "Political Development and Political Decay," *World Politics*, April, 1965.

[4] David Easton, "An Approach to the Analysis of Political Systems," *World Politics*, April, 1957, pp. 383–408. For a full elaboration of Easton's approach, see his *A Systems Analysis of Political Life* (New York: John Wiley & Sons, Inc., 1965).

portunities, recreational facilities, roads, and transportation;
(2) demands for the regulation of behavior, such as provisions
for public safety, controls over markets, and rules pertaining
to marriage, health, and sanitation; (3) demands for participation in the political system — for the right to vote, to hold
office, to petition government bodies and officials, and to organize political associations; (4) demands for communication and
information, such as demands for the affirmation of norms, the
communication of policy intent from policy elites, or the display of majesty and power of the political system in periods of
threat or on ceremonial occasions. A political system may face
these sorts of demands in many combinations, forms, and degrees of intensity.

A second type of input is supports.

> Inputs of demands are not enough to keep a political system
> operating. They are only the raw material out of which finished
> products called decisions are manufactured. Energy in the form
> of actions or orientations promoting and resisting a political
> system, the demands arising in it, and the decisions issuing from
> it must also be put into the system to keep it running.[5]

Examples of support classifications are: (1) material supports,
such as the payment of taxes or other levies, and the provision
of services such as labor on public works or military service;
(2) obedience to law and regulations; (3) participatory supports, such as voting, political discussion, and other forms of
political activity; (4) attention paid to governmental communication, and the manifestation of deference or respect to public
authority, symbols, and ceremonials. If the political system and
the elites acting in its roles are to process demands effectively,
supports must be received from other social systems and from
individuals acting in the political system. Generally speaking,
demands affect the policies or goals of the system, while supports such as goods and services, obedience, and deference, provide the resources which enable a political system to extract,
regulate, and distribute — in other words, to carry out its goals.

We do not wish to leave the impression, of course, that in-

[5] Easton, *World Politics, op. cit.,* p. 390.

puts necessarily come only from the society of which the political system is a part. It is typical of political systems that inputs are generated internally by political elites — kings, presidents, ministers, legislators, and judges. Similarly, inputs may come from the international system in the form of threats, invasions, controls, and assistance from foreign political systems. The flow of inputs and outputs includes transactions between the political system and the components of its domestic and foreign environments, and inputs may come from any one of these three sources — the domestic society, the political elites, and the international environment.

On the output side of the process we may speak of four classes of transactions initiated by the political system. These usually correspond closely to the supports we have listed; they may or may not be responsive to demands, depending on the kind of political system which is involved. These are: (1) extractions, which may take the form of tribute, booty, taxes, or personal services; (2) regulations of behavior, which may take a variety of forms and affect the whole gamut of human behavior and relations; (3) allocations or distribution of goods and services, opportunities, honors, statuses, and the like; (4) symbolic outputs, including affirmations of values, displays of political symbols, statements of policies and intents.

THE FUNCTIONAL ASPECTS OF POLITICAL SYSTEMS

This discussion of flows of inputs and outputs leads logically to a consideration of the *functions* of political systems. We have already suggested that *functionalism* is an old theme in political theory. In its modern form, the stress on functionalism is derived from anthropological and sociological theory. The chief social theorists associated with functionalism are the anthropologists Malinowski and Radcliffe-Brown and the sociologists Parsons, Merton, and Marion Levy.[6] Although these

---

[6] Bronislaw Malinowski, *Magic, Science and Religion and Other Essays* (Garden City: Doubleday & Company, Inc., 1954); A. R. Radcliffe-Brown, *Structure and Function in Primitive Society* (New York: The Free Press of Glencoe, 1957); Talcott Parsons, *Essays in Sociological Theory Pure and Applied* (New York: The Free Press of Glencoe, 1959) and *The Social Sys-*

men differ substantially in their concepts of system and function, essentially they have said that the ability to explain and
predict in the social sciences is enhanced when we think of
social structures and institutions as performing functions in
systems. By comparing the performance of structures and the
regulatory role of political culture as they fulfill common
functions in all systems, we may analyze systems which appear
very different from one another.

The functioning of any system may be viewed on different
levels. One level of functioning is the system's *capabilities,* that
is, the way it performs as a unit in its environment. Animals
move while plants do not. Some machines process data; others
produce power. An economy produces and distributes physical
goods and services. Families produce children and socialize
them into adult roles and disciplines. At this level we are focusing on the behavior of the system as a unit in its relations to
other social systems and to the environment.

When we speak of the capabilities of a political system, we
are looking for an orderly way to describe its over-all performance in its environment. The categories of capability which
we use grow directly out of our analysis of types of inputs and
outputs. Some political systems are primarily *regulative* and
extractive in character. Totalitarian systems suppress demands
coming from their societies and are unresponsive to demands
coming from the international environment. At the same time,
they regulate and coerce behavior in their societies, and seek to
draw maximum resources from their populations. Communist
totalitarianism differs from fascist totalitarianism in having a
strong *distributive* capability as well. This means that the political system itself actively shifts resources from some groups
in the population to other groups. In democracies outputs of
regulation, extraction, and distribution are more affected by
inputs of demands from groups in the society. Thus we may

tem (New York: The Free Press of Glencoe, 1951); Talcott Parsons and
Edward Shils (eds.), *Toward a General Theory of Action* (Cambridge: Har-
vard University Press, 1951); Robert K. Merton, *Social Theory and Social
Structure* (New York: The Free Press of Glencoe, 1957); Marion Levy, *The
Structure of Society* (Princeton: Princeton University Press, 1952).

speak of democracies as having a higher *responsive* capability. These concepts of *regulative, extractive, distributive,* and *responsive* capability are simply ways of talking about the flows of activity into and out of the political system. They tell us how a system is performing in its environment, how it is shaping this environment, and how it is being shaped by it.

The second level of functioning is internal to the system. Here we refer to *conversion processes.* Physiological examples would be the digestion of foods, the elimination of waste, the circulation of the blood, and the transmission of impulses through the nervous system. The conversion processes, or functions, are the ways systems transform inputs into outputs. In the political system this involves the ways in which demands and supports are transformed into authoritative decisions and are implemented. Obviously the capabilities and the conversion processes of a system are related. In order for an animal to be able to move, hunt, and dig, energy must be created in the organism, and the use of the energy must be controlled and directed.

The conversion processes of one political system may be analyzed and compared with those of other systems according to a sixfold functional scheme. We need to look at the ways in which (1) demands are formulated (interest articulation); (2) demands are combined in the form of alternative courses of action (interest aggregation); (3) authoritative rules are formulated (rule making); (4) these rules are applied and enforced (rule application); (5) these applications of rules are adjudicated in individual cases (rule adjudication); and (6) these various activities are communicated both within the political system, and between the political system and its environment (communication).

Finally, we shall speak of *system maintenance and adaptation functions.* For an automobile to perform efficiently on the road, parts must be lubricated, repaired, and replaced. New parts may perform stiffly; they must be broken in. In a political system the incumbents of the various roles (diplomats, military officers, tax officials) must be recruited to these roles and learn how to perform in them. New roles are created and new personnel "broken in." These functions (in machines, maintenance and replacement of parts; in political systems, *socialization* and *recruitment* of people) were discussed earlier in this chapter. They do not directly enter into the conversion processes of the system, but they affect the internal efficiency and propensities of the system, and hence condition its performance.

THE COMPARISON OF POLITICAL SYSTEMS

When we compare classes of political systems with one another, or individual political systems with one another, we need to compare *capabilities, conversion functions,* and *system maintenance and adaptation functions,* and the interrelations among these three kinds, or levels, of functions. When we talk about political development, it will also be in these same terms. A change in capability will be associated with changes in the performance of the conversion functions, and these changes in turn will be related to changes in political socialization and recruitment.

While the individual categories of functions which we use may turn out to be inappropriate when fully tested in empirical cases, this threefold classification of functions is important for political analysis; we believe it will hold up under testing and examination. The theory of the political system will consist of the discovery of the relations between these different levels of functioning — capabilities, conversion functions, and system-maintenance and adaptation functions — and of the relation of the functions at each level.

In our series of country studies we deal with a wide variety of political systems. If we extend our perspective to include the whole of man's experience with politics, we are overwhelmed by the variety of forms, the differences in size and structural pattern, and in kinds of public policy and performance. It may be useful to suggest several common dimensions and characteristics so that we can begin to think about how we can compare, classify, and characterize these systems.

The first common characteristic can be stated concisely: All political systems can be compared in terms of the relationship between functions and structures. That is, in a particular political system at a particular interval of time, there is a given probability that function *A* will be performed by structure *X* (*e.g.,* that political demands will be made by associational interest groups). This proposition assumes that all the political functions can, *in some sense,* be found in all political systems, and that all political systems, including the simplest ones, have political structure.

There is no such thing as a society which maintains internal and external order without a political structure of some kind. In very simple political systems the interactions, or the structures, may be occasional or intermittent. They may not be clearly visible, but to say there are no structures would be to argue that the performance of the political functions is random. We may find that in some systems one or a very few structures perform all political functions. The leader of a primitive band may occupy such a dominant position. At the other extreme, in a highly differentiated system, such as that of the United States, political functions may be performed by a very large number of highly specialized structures: communication is dominated by the mass media; political recruitment, by the electoral and party structures; interest articulation, by a large variety of interest groups. However, the great differences between the United States and the primitive band merely represent extreme cases of the range of differentiation of structures. Both systems possess political structures performing political functions, and may be compared in such terms.

Any particular structure may perform more than one function. Just as we must be aware of the presence of political structures in relatively undifferentiated societies, we must also be cautious about assuming that a structure will perform only those functions which the formal rules lead us to expect. Political structures, in short, tend to be *multifunctional,* although the degrees of multifunctionality depends on many factors.

A simple example of multifunctionality can help to illustrate the problem. Typically, public schools are viewed in relation to the political system in terms of their effect on the formation of attitudes and the development of skills among the young. This is, unquestionably, a major impact which the educational structures may have upon the political system. However, schools also affect the recruitment of political elites by expanding or limiting the society's reservoir of skilled manpower. Schools give rise to informal, inter-elite communication patterns through the formation of "old school ties," and play a key role in communications processes in general, especially in nations with no powerful and independent mass media. Finally, they play important "input" roles in the political system by giving rise to special communities of interest and laying the basis for interest-group organization. Teachers' unions are an example. Student riots, which have played such an important role in such countries as Turkey, Indonesia, and Korea, illustrate the impact of another school or university-based group.

One can infer from this example that in a nation with relatively few formal and differentiated structures, such organized structures as do appear are likely to be quite multifunctional. While multifunctionality is more obvious in simple, less differentiated societies, it is a universal phenomenon, and is a characteristic of modern bureaucracies and courts as well as of kingships and chieftainships in primitive and traditional societies.

In the discussion of cultural patterns, too sharp a line is often drawn between societies characterized by traditional cultures and those characterized by modern cultures. The modern societies have been presented as secular and rational. Their cultures have been represented as embodying attitude patterns which treat individuals in universalistic fashion, according to their formal and relevant roles rather than according to personal relationships and attributes. The bureaucrat looks with equal favor upon all applicants for services; he does not favor his brother or his cousin. Traditional societies, on the other hand, have been viewed in terms of ascription of particular statuses, and diffuse and particularistic relationships. That is, individuals attain position according to criteria other than their merit (such as status of parents), and personal relationships and informal communication patterns permeate the political process.

However, modern social science research has demonstrated the continuing significance of primary groups (*e.g.*, families, peer groups) and informal organizations in the social processes of Western societies. The first attitude-survey studies of voting provide a classic example.[7] The researchers expected to find that political voting attitudes in modern America were shaped by the modern media of mass communication and by the opinions of those with expertise in relevant areas. Such would be the expected rational pattern. But these studies showed how exaggerated and oversimplified our conception of modern political culture was. We now know that face-to-face communication channels have a continuing vital role in opinion formation, in spite of the presence of the mass media. The typical opinion leader, moreover, is not an expert in a relevant field, but a trusted individual whose political influence is often a diffuse consequence of other roles. (For example, the opinion of a wealthy member of the leading social circle is likely to have great weight with individuals in certain strata, quite apart from any qualifications of special knowledge or even proven judgment.)

Thus, while one cannot question the fact that important differences do exist in the cultural characteristics of traditional and modern systems, any analysis of modern political systems must take account of the continuing importance of the informal and traditional relationships which shape the attitudes and actions of individuals. Therefore, our second major characteristic is: All political systems have mixed political cultures. The most primitive societies have threads of instrumental rationality in their structure and culture. The most modern are permeated by ascriptive, particularistic, and informal relationships and attitudes. They differ in the relative dominance of one against the other and in the pattern of mixture of these components. Secularization is a matter of degree and of the distribution of these "rational" aspects.

[7] See Paul F. Lazarsfeld, Bernard Bereleson, and Hazel Gaudet, *The People's Choice* (New York: Duell, Sloan & Pearce, Inc., 1944).

THE DEVELOPMENT OF POLITICAL SYSTEMS

The events which lead to political development come from the international environment, from the domestic society, or from political elites within the political system itself. A political system may be threatened by a rival nation, or be invaded by it. In confronting this challenge it may find that it needs more resources and more effective ways of organizing and deploying its resources — a standing army, for example, or an officialdom to collect taxes. It may have to adapt itself structurally, that is, develop new roles, if it is to survive. If the international threat continues over a long period of time, it may have to adapt itself culturally, inculcating attitudes of militance and acquiring the skills and values associated with warfare.

The challenge may come from internal change in the society of which the political system is a part. Thriving commerce and manufactures may create a middle class which demands that it be heard in the making and implementation of public policy. The political elites themselves may confront the political system with a challenge as they seek to increase the resources available to them for the purpose of constructing impressive buildings or monuments, or for creating a military force capable of conquering neighboring political systems.

The impulses for political development consequently involve some significant change in the magnitude and content of the flow of inputs into the political system. *Development* results when the existing structure and culture of the political system is unable to cope with the problem or challenge which confronts it without further structural differentiation and cultural secularization. It should also be pointed out that a decline in the magnitude or a significant change in the content of the flow of inputs may result in "development" in the negative or regressive sense. The capabilities of the political system may decline or be overloaded; roles and structures may atrophy; the culture may regress to a more traditional pattern of orientation. History is full of cases of the decline of empires and their breakup into less differentiated and less secularized components.[8] Transitional and developed societies also may exhibit the collapse of differentiated modern structures and the dominance of irrational appeals and attitudes when the strains become too great.

We need some way of talking about these challenges which may lead to political development, these changes in the magnitude and content of the flow of inputs which put the existing culture and structure under strain. As a beginning we may suggest four types of problems for or challenges to a political system. The first of these is the problem of penetration and integration; we refer to this as the problem of *state building*. The second type of system-development problem is that of loyalty and commitment, which we refer to as *nation building*. The third problem is that of *participation*, the pressure from groups in the society for having a part in the decision making of the system. And the fourth is the problem of *distribution*, or welfare, the pressure from the domestic society to employ the coercive power of the political system to redistribute income, wealth, opportunity, and honor.

The problem of state building may arise out of a threat to the survival of the political system from the international environment. It may also arise out of a threat to the political system from the society in the form of revolutionary pressure challenging the stability or the survival of the political system. Or, it may result from the development among the political elite of new goals, such as national expansion or the creation of an extravagant court life. State building occurs when the political elite creates new structures and organizations designed to "penetrate" the society in order to regulate behavior in it and draw a larger volume of resources from it. State building is commonly associated with significant increases in the regulative and extractive capabilities of the political system, with the development of a centralized and penetrative bureaucracy related to the increase in these capabilities, and with the development of attitudes of obedience and compliance in the popu-

---

[8] Samuel P. Huntington, "Political Development and Political Decay," *World Politics,* April, 1965; S. N. Eisenstadt, *The Political Systems of Empires* (New York: The Free Press of Glencoe, 1962).

lation which are associated with the emergence of such a bureaucracy.

While it is an oversimplification to put it this way, we might view the problem of state building and its successful confrontation by a political system as essentially a structural problem. That is to say, what is involved is primarily a matter of the differentiation of new roles, structures, and subsystems which penetrate the countryside. Nation building, on the other hand, emphasizes the cultural aspects of political development. It refers to the process whereby people transfer their commitment and loyalty from smaller tribes, villages, or petty principalities to the larger central political system. While these two processes of state and nation building are related, it is important to view them separately. There are many cases in which centralized and penetrative bureaucracies have been created, while a homogeneous pattern of loyalty and commitment to the central political institutions has never emerged. The Austro-Hungarian Empire and even modern Italy represent cases in point. In fact, there are examples, particularly among the great empires such as Imperial Rome, in which the elite never sought to create a common national culture of loyalty and commitment, but were content to develop a centralized and penetrative bureaucracy, while at the same time permitting culturally distinct component units to survive and retain some autonomy.

The problem, or challenge, of participation commonly has to do with rapid increases in the volume and intensity of demands for a share in the decision making of the political system by various groups and strata in the domestic society. Such increases in demands for participation are usually associated with, or have the consequence of producing, some form of political infrastructure — political groups, cliques, and factions, and representative legislative assemblies. Demands for participation may also challenge a political system to develop political competence and the attitudes associated with it among groups in the society, and responsive attitudes and bargaining skills among the elite.

Finally, the problem of distribution, or welfare, occurs when there is a rapid increase in the volume and intensity of demands that the political system control or affect the distribution of resources or values (for example, opportunity) among different elements of the population. A positive response to such a challenge by the political elite may produce fundamental changes in bureaucratic organization, and in the political attitudes of both the political elite and the general population.

We have listed these problems of system development in the sequence in which they have occurred in the emergence of the political systems of Western Europe. By and large, state and nation building occurred before the nations of Western Europe had to confront the problems of participation and welfare. But our purpose is to develop an analytical scheme which will enable us to explain the characteristics of any political system. In our efforts to account for the peculiar patterns of performance of political systems, we must examine the ways in which they have encountered these system-development problems in the past or are encountering them in the present. Relating system challenges to system responses is the way to explanation and prediction in the field of political development. In the broader sense, it opens up for us the whole of man's history of experimentation and innovation in politics as a source for the creation of a useful theory of political change. If we can relate the structural and cultural characteristics of political systems to the ways in which they have confronted and coped with these common system-development problems, we have taken the first steps in the direction of a theory of political growth which, for example, can help us explain why French and British politics differ in particular ways. Such a theory may also be helpful to people who are concerned with the question of how to influence political development — our own governmental officials and the elites of the new nations.

We will discuss these questions in detail at various points in later chapters. Here we need only stress a number of general points. First, the way in which a political system responds to the four types of challenges, or problems, has to be described in terms of the three functional levels to which we have already referred. Thus, the confrontation of a system-development problem may be related to the changing patterns of political-system capabilities — *i.e.*, growth or decline in *regulative, extractive, distributive, symbolic,* and *responsive* capabilities. The manner in which a system responds to these problems must also be described in terms of the consequences for the performance of the conversion functions of the political system. Thus, when we say that Britain was confronted with the challenge of participation in the course of the eighteenth and nineteenth centuries, we must describe her response to this challenge in terms of what happened to the conversion functions and to interest groups, political parties, media of communication, Parliament, and Cabinet which performed these conversion functions. Finally, the response of the political system to a challenge must also be described in terms of the system-adaptation processes of role differentiation and secularization.

If a political system centralizes and nationalizes — in other words, if it successfully confronts the challenges of state and nation building — how is this reflected in the development of new political roles and structures and in its recruitment processes to these roles and structures; and how does it create the attitudes and propensities appropriate to the new pattern of operations of the political system? As we examine the interaction between challenges to the system and the cultural and structural and performance responses to these challenges, we may begin to develop a theory which will tell us how a particular pattern of challenge-and-response at a certain stage in the development of a political system affects and conditions the future capacity of that system to respond to other challenges and problems. A good illustration of this is the experience of Prussia and Germany with the problem of state building. The degree of bureaucratization, centralization, and militarization which entered into the response of the Prussian elite in the eighteenth century is said to have created a cultural and structural pattern which prevented the German political system from responding effectively in the nineteenth and twentieth centuries to demands for increased participation. In general this kind of analysis will direct our attention to the question of how the solution to one problem affects the capacity of the system to solve other problems of development.

There are at least five major factors which must be considered in the analysis of political development. First, there is no doubt that the stability of a system is heavily dependent upon the types of problems it faces. Much of the stability and success of the gradual development of the political systems of the United States and of Great Britain may be attributed to their relative isolation during long periods of their formative history. In comparing the British experience with the Italian and German, one can hardly avoid noting how in the latter cases the systems were subjected to many diverse and intense pressures simultaneously. Demands for unification, participation, and welfare appeared suddenly. The effect was cumulative and reinforcing. It is generally recognized that a major problem in the new nations today is the cumulative revolutions they must face. People demand participation, national unity, economic betterment, law and order — simultaneously and immediately.

A second factor is the resources the system can draw upon under various circumstances. Support as well as demand can fluctuate, and may descend to critical levels. For example, the French Fourth Republic collapsed in 1958. Although a cumulation of demands, from the Algerians, the army, and various internal groups, was the immediate cause, the Republic fell so quickly and so easily because few people bothered to try to save it. The rate of tax evasion and of general civil disobedience, as well as popular statements and the findings of opinion polls, had long hinted at the low support level; the change in the system was no surprise to most observers.

Developments in other social systems constitute a third factor which may affect political development. The extent to which the political system is loaded or overloaded will vary with the capabilities of other social systems in the domestic society and the international system. When an economy develops new capabilities — new systems of production and distribution — the loading of the political system with demands for welfare may be significantly reduced, thereby affecting political development. Or a religious system may develop regulative capabilities, reducing the flow of innovative demands on the political system. Or the international political system may develop a regulative or distributive capability which reduces the pressure on the domestic political systems. A case in point is the international military or technical assistance units of the United Nations, which may reduce the pressure for the development of extractive and regulative capabilities in some of the new nations. Thus, the existence or the development of capabilities in other social systems may affect the magnitude of the challenges confronting political systems, keep the flow at an incremental and low-intensity level, and, perhaps, help avoid some of the disruptive consequences of cumulative pressures. On the other hand, a breakdown in family, religious, or economic systems may create discontent, disorder, and new demands which load and perhaps overload the polity.

A fourth factor to consider is the functioning pattern of the system itself. Some kinds of political systems can withstand demand and support fluctuations better than others. In general terms we may note that a system with a developed and differentiated bureaucracy can accommodate demands for new regulations and services much more readily than can a less differentiated system. Law and order can be maintained much more easily if an organized army or police force is available. And a system geared to a high level of responsiveness to inputs from many sources can cope with demands from new groups and with loss of support from some old ones. Some systems are geared for change and adaptation; others are not.

A final factor is the response of the political elites to political-system challenges. Such responses cannot be predicted, at least not entirely, from the system's cultural patterns. In a given system some sorts of responses may lead to accommodation of new demands without changes of the political system or with a minor level of such change, while other responses may lead to disaster. Elites may misjudge the seriousness and intensity of input fluctuations, and either radically modify the system or fail to respond until it is too late. The arguments about how important such responses are have long occupied the attention of historians. What sort of responses by Louis XV and Louis XVI could have averted the French Revolution? At what point had the demands become so intense that no response would have resulted in peaceful accommodation?

Political change is one of the most pervasive and fundamental concerns of our analysis. We shall return to it, by different routes, in every chapter. The world of politics has never waited for the observer to finish his quiet contemplation. In the present century political development seems to be proceeding at an ever-accelerating rate, overwhelming our comparative "snapshots" by making them obsolete before we finish our books and articles. It is increasingly obvious that the study of politics must be a dynamic system-and-process analysis, and not a static and structural one.

CHAPTER III

Political Structure and Culture

THE THEMES OF POLITICAL STRUCTURE AND CULTURE run throughout this book, in our treatment of the conversion functions and capabilities, in our classification of political systems, and in our theory of political development. We need to discuss political structure and culture in terms of their most significant attributes, and to examine the processes by which they are perpetuated and changed.

POLITICAL STRUCTURE

Let us look at political structure first. There are at least two important respects in which the structures of political systems may differ: (1) the degree to which there is differentiation or specialization of political roles, structures, and subsystems; and (2) the autonomy or subordination of these roles, structures, or subsystems to each other. An illustration may help make these dimensions clear.

The political system of the Eskimo is among the simplest known to man. The Eskimos are scattered from the Bering Straits to Greenland in small communities, each numbering around one hundred inhabitants, most of the members of each community related by blood or marriage. There are only two specialized roles that are politically significant, those of the headman and the shaman, and these are both mixed roles. The shaman is the religious leader, but he also may punish those who violate taboos. In the extreme case he may order an offender exiled, which in the Arctic may mean death. The headman is a task leader, making decisions about hunting or the selection of places for settlement. In matters related to political order he is an influential leader rather than a leader with power to coerce.

Violations of order are handled mostly through such means as fist fights and "song duels," or in extreme cases through family feuds. An individual who threatens the community by repeated acts of violence, murder, or theft may be dealt with by an executioner, who is given the task by the community or assumes the responsibility for the execution with the approval of the community.

We speak of this kind of polity as an *intermittent* political system. It has no set of roles, no structure, which is specialized for political purposes. Some of the activities of the shaman and of the headman may be viewed as political or governmental activities. Some social processes such as duels and blood feuds may be viewed as Eskimo ways of adjudicating disputes. Other community activities may perform the functions of communicating information, articulating different points of view, and making political decisions that have the effect of law.

An intermittent political system is one in which there are no differentiated political roles and no specialized political structure. For comparative purposes we may say, as political analysts, that at certain times in relation to certain problems an Eskimo community is performing political functions, as, for example, when two men quarreling over a woman engage in a butting duel while the rest of the community sits around enforcing the rules. The boundaries that separate an intermittent political system from the religious or the economic system are diffuse. The Eskimos do not draw these boundaries, but we may draw them for analytical purposes. The roles themselves are combined, as are the attitudes and orientations to the roles in the mind of the individual Eskimo.

The intermittent political system, of which the Eskimos' political system is an example, is the extreme case of a relatively

undifferentiated political system. There are others like it, such
as the primitive hunting and gathering bands of Africa. Intermittent political systems are not of great importance today, but
intermittent structures and roles are to be found in all political
systems, even in the most specialized and modern. The citizen
of the modern democracy is an intermittent politician or, as
Max Weber might have put it, an "occasional politician." And
the family in modern society, as it communicates about politics
or as it forms political attitudes and skills in children, is an
intermittent political structure.

The classic typology of traditional political systems is that
of the German sociologist Max Weber.[1] He distinguishes three
main types of traditional authority: patriarchal, patrimonial,
and feudal. A *patriarchal* system of authority is one in which
membership is based on kinship and in which authority is exercised by the oldest male. It is characterized by the complete
absence of an administrative staff. A *patrimonial* system is one
in which there is an administrative staff, specialized roles, and
offices of one kind or another which are directly controlled by
the ruler. *Feudalism* is defined by Weber as a system of relations of purely personal loyalty between a lord and his vassals.
Both lord and vassals are patrimonial rulers; they are loosely
articulated one with the other by bonds of mutual obligation.
In Weber's threefold classification of traditional authority, the
significant dimensions of variation are structural differentiation and the autonomy of parts. The feudal and patrimonial
systems are more structurally differentiated than the patriarchal, and the feudal system is more loosely articulated than the
patrimonial.

Suppose we consider the whole range of political systems in
their structural aspect, from the simplest and most primitive
ones to the most complex and modern ones: We have already
spoken of the patriarchal type of political system as having an
intermittent political structure. The patrimonial political sys-

[1] Max Weber, *Theory of Social and Economic Organization* (New York:
Oxford University Press, 1947), pp. 341 ff.; Reinhard Bendix, *Max Weber:
An Intellectual Portrait* (Garden City: Doubleday & Company, Inc., 1960),
pp. 329 ff.

tem is different from the patriarchal system in that it has a *specialized officialdom*. This means that roles having to do with the implementation of policies and decisions are specialized. It is no longer a case of a patriarch ordering a servant, a son, or a wife to do a particular task; the patrimonial king or chief orders officials to collect taxes, to lead a military force, or to punish an offender. Patrimonial systems can be quite complicated, involving several levels of authority and a variety of types of administrative officials.

S. Eisenstadt in a recent book [2] refers to another class of political systems, which he places between the traditional political systems and the modern ones. He refers to this class as the *historical bureaucratic empires*. He includes in this class the bureaucratic empires of the Egyptians, the Persians, the Romans, and the Byzantines, as well as the absolutist kingdoms of Europe of the seventeenth and eighteenth centuries.

One difference between the patrimonial kingdoms described by Max Weber and the bureaucratic empires described by Eisenstadt is the extent of structural differentiation and structural autonomy in these two political systems. A patrimonial kingdom has a relatively undifferentiated officialdom. It may even lack a standing army. This means that the capacity of the patrimonial ruler to penetrate his society, to regulate behavior in it, to draw resources from it, and to use these resources for his own purposes, whether within the society or in relation to other nations, is quite limited. In the historical bureaucratic empire, on the other hand, a more differentiated and larger administrative staff with a standing army creates a more autonomous political system, one that is better able to extract resources from and regulate behavior in its own society, to expand its territory, to increase its own resources, and to pursue autonomously other political goals.

If we think of the great political "inventions" in history, certainly the specialized officialdom of patrimonialism is among the very significant ones. The jump from this relatively limited officialdom to the more elaborated and more effective admin-

[2] S. N. Eisenstadt, *The Political Systems of Empires* (New York: The Free Press of Glencoe, 1963), Chap. 1.

istrative apparatus of the great empires represents a second significant advance.

Another difference between the patrimonial kingdom and the bureaucratic empire is the extent of political role differentiation. In the patrimonial kingdom, administrative officials tend to be immediate subordinates of the ruler, personal confidants and "table companions." The titles of their offices (*e.g.*, chamberlain, cupbearer, keeper of the purse) often reflect their origins in the patriarchal households. In the historic empires the officialdom is larger, specialized into a greater variety of functional units, and the relations of these units to one another and to the ruler tend to be more impersonal. In modern political systems these tendencies are more pronounced. Roles and subsystems are more specialized in their functions, and their relations to one another and to the ruler are more impersonal. But it is an interesting and important point that even as administrative roles and subsystems become more specialized, the primordial institution of personal confidants, cronies, and table companions persists as a device to make more direct and effective the relations between presidents, prime ministers, dictators, and department heads, bureau chiefs, division directors, and section heads, one with the other. Nothing seems to be lost in the evolution of political systems.

Eisenstadt also tells us that as bureaucratic empires increase in size, conquer other political systems, and assimilate other ethnic groups, as social and occupational strata become differentiated, and as churches and religious sects emerge, a more or less open and legitimate process of struggle over political goals develops. Thus the bureaucratic empires tend to be transitional between patrimonial kingdoms and feudal systems on the one hand, and modern democratic or authoritarian systems on the other.

A third major step in the development of political systems is the emergence of a specialized political infrastructure, the development of subsystems such as political parties, pressure groups, and the media of mass communication, to process political demands and proposals. Here we are dealing with both role differentiation and autonomy, since in the democratic system the components of the infrastructure tend to be not only specialized but also relatively independent of the governmental elite and bureaucracy.

If we were to compare modern democratic systems with totalitarian systems from the point of view of the emergence of these specialized institutions to handle political inputs, we would have to rely on the dimension of underlying autonomy to make the meaningful distinction. For, as we know, totalitarian as well as democratic systems have specialized media of communication, institutions which at least in the formal sense look like our interest groups, and one or more political parties. But if we examine the actual functioning of the two political systems, it becomes quite clear that in democratic systems this political infrastructure consists of relatively autonomous institutions, while in totalitarian systems the media of mass communication, interest groups of various kinds, and political parties are all closely, hierarchically articulated with the ruling elite and the bureaucracy. They are subordinated to the government rather than being relatively independent of it and able to transmit impulses, demands, and proposals from the society.[3]

Political Recruitment. We use the term "differentiation" to refer to those processes of political development in which new types of roles and structures are created and articulated with the old. We use the term "political recruitment" to refer to the function by means of which the roles of political systems are filled. Recruitment into political roles may be based on universalistic or general criteria on the one hand, or particularistic criteria on the other. The selection of office holders by lot, by election, or by some proof of ability or performance, such as an examination, are illustrations of recruitment on the basis of universalistic criteria. On the other hand, recruitment from a particular tribe or ethnic group is illustrative of particularistic criteria of recruitment. Selection by examination

[3] In Chapters IX and X we shall utilize these concepts of differentiation and autonomy to suggest a developmental typology of political systems. Readers may wish to refer to the opening comments and detailed examples in those chapters to further clarify their understanding of these concepts and their uses.

would be a good example of selection according to criteria of performance; selection from royal or aristocratic families illustrates recruitment by ascription or status.

Although it is generally true that primitive and traditional political systems tend to recruit into political roles on the basis of particularistic and ascriptive criteria, it is probably never true that a political system recruits purely on the basis of such criteria. In most if not all political systems, ability and performance somehow get taken into account in recruitment. Similarly, in modern systems particularistic and ascriptive criteria enter into the recruitment process even though to a lesser extent than is true in primitive and traditional systems. Thus, family relationships, social status and class, school ties, and friendship enter into political recruitment in all modern political systems.

A study of the historical sociology of recruitment practices would produce many fascinating examples of how different criteria of selection are combined. For example, in patrimonial kingdoms the rulers have sought to select administrative staffs upon whom they could rely. Officials have been required to hold loyalty to their ruler above loyalty to family, clan, or status groups. The variety of ways in which patrimonial rulers have sought to insure the dependability of their administrative staffs includes the use of slaves, mercenaries, eunuchs, special families and lineage groups solely dedicated to service to the ruler, a celibate clergy, and professional men such as lawyers and clerks who are drawn from outside the aristocratic class.

The recruitment function cannot be fully separated from the socialization function. Recruitment from particular aristocratic strata, from nonaristocratic strata, from slaves, and from foreign populations brings into political roles people with different propensities, interests, values, and attitudes. The background of those who are recruited into political roles is bound to have some impact on their performance of these roles, no matter how thoroughly they are socialized into new values, attitudes, and skills once they have taken over their offices.

Structural Differentiation, Autonomy, and Capabilities. The extent to which a political system is structurally differentiated and the relative autonomy of its roles and subsystems will affect the performance, or capability patterns, of the political system. Thus, a political system which has specialized roles for the extraction of resources will be able to extract resources more efficiently than one which lacks these specialized roles. The ways in which individuals are recruited into political roles similarly will affect the capabilities of political systems. Administrative officials chosen on the basis of performance criteria tend to be more effective in the performance of these specialized functions.

When we examine the role differentiation of a political system, we should be concerned not only with the number of roles, but also with the kinds of roles which have been specialized, and with the relationship between these types of specialized roles and the capabilities of the political system. Higher levels of extraction, more extensive and penetrative regulation, and more thorough distribution of the social product are associated with the differentiation of sets of roles which are related to these specific kinds of capability. On the other hand, the development of a responsive capability is connected with an autonomous political infrastructure, one which enables demands from the society to be brought to bear effectively on the governmental and administrative structures. Thus, when we are studying political structure from the point of view of specialization and autonomy, we are basically concerned with the ways in which structural characteristics are associated with the performance characteristics of the political system in its domestic and international environments.[4] Similarly, in our consideration of political culture, we shall be interested in the ways in which cultural characteristics affect the conversion and performance characteristics of political systems.

[4] Two discussions of the relationship between differentiation, capability, and development which consider various aspects of the problem in more detail than is here possible — though making the same general argument — are: S. N. Eisenstadt, "Social Change, Differentiation, and Evolution," pp. 375–387, and Talcott Parsons, "Evolutionary Universals in Society," pp. 339–357; both in *American Sociological Review*, June, 1964.

POLITICAL CULTURE

Political culture is the pattern of individual attitudes and orientations toward politics among the members of a political system. It is the subjective realm which underlies and gives meaning to political actions. Such individual orientations involve several components, including (a) *cognitive orientations,* knowledge, accurate or otherwise, of political objects and beliefs; (b) *affective orientations,* feelings of attachment, involvement, rejection, and the like, about political objects; and (c) *evaluative orientations,* judgments and opinions about political objects, which usually involve applying value standards to political objects and events.[5]

Individual orientations toward any political object may be viewed in terms of these three dimensions. Thus an individual may have a relatively high degree of accurate knowledge about how his whole political system works, who the leading figures are, and what the current problems of policy are. This would be the cognitive dimension of orientation toward the system as a whole. He might, however, have feelings of alienation or rejection toward the system; perhaps his family and friends have long harbored such attitudes. He would be unlikely to respond favorably to demands upon him by the system. This is the affective dimension. Finally, he may have some moral evaluation of the system. Perhaps his democratic norms lead him to evaluate the system as not sufficiently responsive to political demands, or his ethical norms lead him to condemn the level of corruption and nepotism.

These three dimensions are interrelated and may be combined in a variety of ways, even within the same individual as he considers various aspects of the political system. The kinds of orientations which exist in a population will have a significant influence on the ways in which the political system works. The demands made upon the system, the responses to laws and to appeals for support, and the conduct of individuals in their political roles, will all be shaped and conditioned by the com-

[5] For the origin of these particular categories, see Talcott Parsons and Edward A. Shils (eds.), *Toward a General Theory of Action* (Cambridge: Harvard University Press, 1951), pp. 58 ff.

mon orientation patterns. They constitute the latent political tendencies, the propensities for political behavior, to which we have referred, and as such they are of great importance in explaining and predicting political action. However, a careful analysis of a political culture still provides no sure guide, perhaps at best a probabilistic one, for the prediction of individual behavior in a given case. Individual actions can at times have great impact on the performance of the political system, but it is unlikely that any analysis of the political culture of the United States could have predicted the behavior of a Lee Harvey Oswald. Nor can a consideration of the political culture of Ghana fully explain the actions of Nkrumah.

Political culture is not a residual explanatory category. It involves a set of phenomena which can be identified and to some degree measured. Public-opinion and attitude surveys are the primary tools with which this can be attempted with large groups. Depth interviewing and psychological techniques can provide data on individual cases. Public statements, speeches and writings, and myths and legends can also provide clues to the nature of political culture patterns. Finally, behavior itself gives obvious clues to the sort of orientations with which it is associated. Needless to say, inferences about political culture from attitude surveys, public statements, and political behavior all contain hazards in analysis. Individuals slant their responses in many ways; problems in communication and interpretation are numerous. So many factors operate on behavior that it is difficult to isolate them. Nonetheless, political culture is of such importance in regulating the performance of a political system that it is worth a substantial effort to get relatively reliable information about it.

Political culture may provide us with a valuable conceptual tool by means of which we can bridge the "micro-macro" gap in political theory. How does one make the transition from the study of the individual in his political context to the study of the political system as a whole? How does one relate individual interviews and responses, and case studies of individual actions, to the aggregate statistics and group behavior patterns which reflect the course of a system's total behavior? Political culture by revealing the patterns of distribution of orientations to political action helps us connect individual tendencies to system characteristics.

Objects of Political Orientations. Objects of political orientation include the political system as a whole, particular political roles or structures, individual or group incumbents of such roles, and specific public policies and issues. They also include other political actors and the self as a political actor.

The question of orientations to the national political system as a whole constitutes one of the most serious developmental problems in the political culture of the new nations. In many cases, particularly in Africa, these nations have been constructed from a great variety of ethnic, political, and geographic subnational units which have no common political bonds and whose members by and large have little information and loyalty beyond their local unit. The process of nation building involves in some respect the dissemination of information about and the commitment to the national unit. At some point in the history of any new nation, as loyalty to the traditional subnational units conflicts with national loyalties and goals, the issues of national identity are likely to become paramount.

This problem of national identity is not limited to the new nations. In recent years the school segregation question has raised the problem of national identity for many Southerners in the United States. While for the most part the answer has been clear — most Virginians, for example, are Americans first and Virginians second — there have been many exceptions, as the resistance to federal authority in Mississippi has emphasized. The problems are intensified in a nation without a long tradition of national involvement.

Achieving a resolution in commitment may be a difficult and complex task. The local tribe may accurately perceive that its whole social and religious structure is threatened by the creation of schools, by the induction of young men into the national army, or by the building of a neighborhood industry. This is not to say that accommodation is impossible. An extreme form of resolution of conflicts of loyalty may be intense nationalism focused around a charismatic political figure such as Nasser in Egypt. More moderate solutions are illustrated by systems such as Mexico, where a high degree of general system support, a dominant party, and well-accepted revolutionary symbols create a measure of cohesion among a diversity of groups and points of view. India, working from a much more diversified base, has attempted to do roughly the same thing — but only time can tell whether it will succeed in establishing a national identity of sufficient depth and intensity to prevent subnational loyalties from tearing the system apart.

The concept of orientation to the political system as a whole may be refined in many directions. One way of characterizing political cultures is in terms of the distribution of general attitudes toward the political system and the input and output processes. We may thus describe a political culture in terms of the awareness of these political objects and of their significance in individual activities. In these general terms we can classify as *parochials* those people who manifest little or no awareness of the national political systems. Such individuals are to be found in any society, but in modern Western societies they are relatively rare. In some transitional societies large regional groups of parochials may be found in certain areas not yet affected by the national polity.

Among those citizens who are aware of the national system we may distinguish two important general classifications. *Subjects* are those individuals who are oriented to the political system and the impact which its outputs, such as welfare benefits, laws, etc., may have upon their lives, but who are not oriented to participation in the input structures. *Participants* are those individuals who are oriented to the input structures and processes, and engage in, or view themselves as potentially engaging in, the articulation of demands and the making of decisions.[6]

We may classify political cultures according to the combination of parochials, subjects, and participants. One may go far

[6] These terms were developed in Gabriel A. Almond and Sidney Verba, *The Civic Culture* (Princeton: Princeton University Press, 1963), pp. 17–21 ff.

toward a theory of democratic politics based on these simple characterizations, and the differences which political systems exhibit in this regard provide an insight into at least one important dimension of the political culture. Robert Scott, for example, has discussed the changes in Mexican political culture between 1910 and 1960 in this fashion. He estimates that in 1910 some 90 per cent of Mexican citizens were parochials, 9 per cent were subjects, and 1 per cent were participants. For 1960 he draws upon attitude studies to arrive at the figures of 25 per cent parochials, 65 per cent subjects, and perhaps 10 per cent participants.[7] Scott's characterization of changes in the Mexican system illustrates the utility of considering these orientations to input and output structures — they reflect far-reaching system changes.

In part the maintenance of law and order in a society centers around positive orientations toward governmental agencies. Often the citizens of the new nations are oriented only to the benefits of governmental outputs and, perhaps, to the channels through which demands can be made. They have not acquired a positive and supportive subject orientation — that is, they have not learned to obey the laws. Consequently, the political order has little support to draw upon in time of internal crisis. This problem, dramatically illustrated in the Congo, has been encountered in some degree in most of the new nations.

Orientations to politics include the individual's notions of himself as a political actor. Even if an individual has a reasonably accurate knowledge of the workings of the political system, he may still have a range of personal attitudes toward the appropriateness of his personal actions vis-à-vis politics. We may particularly note the significance of attitudes of personal political *competence*. Individuals who are oriented toward the input structures and who possess such attitudes of political competence may be expected to attempt to influence political action when it is in their interest to do so. Beyond this, how-

[7] Robert E. Scott, "Mexico: The Established Revolution," in Lucian W. Pye and Sidney Verba (eds.), *Political Culture and Political Development* (Princeton: Princeton University Press, 1965), pp. 335, 345 ff.

ever, the individual's particular recognition of what channels of action may be open to him becomes paramount.

In a comparative study of attitudes in five nations, the difference between attitudes in the United States and in the other nations illustrates this dimension.[8] Only in the United States did a very large proportion of the respondents say that when faced with a local political problem they would form a local political group and seek legitimate means of rectifying their grievances. Such expressions of competence and willingness to work actively through legitimate input channels were striking. All too often, as in Italy, the individual feels that he can have little influence as an individual on government actions. At best, this leads to passive acceptance where dissatisfactions are not overwhelming. At worst, resentments and frustrations will be submerged until the pressure is too great, and then will erupt in violence. Even in societies where interest groups and political parties have begun to develop, the emergence of an appropriate set of individual orientations to them is essential before they can be effectively employed.

It is also important to ascertain the general level of political trust in a society. Are political competitors and opponents viewed with suspicion? Does political interaction and discussion take place on a relatively free and easy basis, or are the channels of communication regarding political matters constricted? In societies such as Italy and Germany the traumatic political experiences of the past half century have made politics a subject to avoid in personal interaction. This affects the cohesion of political groups and their willingness to interact with each other.

Closely related to this question of trust is the basic conception of politics as either a harmonious or a discordant process. In a nation such as Great Britain, the general presumption seems to be that those engaged in politics are undertaking legitimate representations of interest.[9] The tradition of consultation and negotiation with all interested parties in the

---

[8] Almond and Verba, *op. cit.*, pp. 191 ff.

[9] See Samuel Beer, "Pressure Groups and Parties in Britain," *American Political Science Review*, March, 1956, pp. 6 ff.

process of lawmaking reflects this conception of the political process as a way of aggregating legitimate needs and demands. Sharply contrasted to this view is the conception of politics as a continuing struggle for supremacy. The classic Marxist view perhaps expresses this perspective most clearly — all political actions represent attempts by the dominant class to maintain its mastery over the subordinate classes, or efforts of the oppressed to throw off their chains. The distinction between these contrasting views of the political process is important in the political culture of both elites and masses. Indeed, Rolf Dahrendorf has shown how it pervades even the highly abstract views of sociologists and political theorists.[10]

In considering attitudes toward interpersonal relationships, we may also take note of the level of civility in political interaction — that is, the degree to which more or less formal norms of courtesy tend to dampen the harshness of political disagreement. The formal and informal customs of legislative bodies in Britain and the United States reflect such tendencies. It is perhaps doubly difficult for democratic politics to function in many of the new nations because they lack such moderating norms.

We have devoted considerable attention to the problem of interpersonal relationships because these constitute a crucial problem area in the political culture of the new nations. An ultimate test of a responsive and democratic system is its ability to transfer the power of government from one set of leaders to another. This may occur either between parties or within a single party. But if the level of personal trust is low, if the political process is viewed as a life-and-death conflict, and if little political courtesy mitigates the raw conflict, it will be very difficult for the incumbent elites to relinquish their roles in the political process and step aside for a new group of political actors. The stakes will seem too high; the opposition will seem too dangerous.

This problem of the "stakes" of politics, the goals of political activity, brings us to a consideration of policies as objects

[10] Rolf Dahrendorf, *Class and Class Conflict in Industrial Society* (Stanford: Stanford University Press, 1959), pp. 157 ff.

of political orientations. We do not mean to get into a consideration of individual day-to-day political and governmental decisions; the population at large is usually unaware of most of these decisions and problems. But the political culture is likely to support certain general political goals and procedures and to reject others. Here we are concerned with the relation between political culture and the capabilities of the political system.

Perhaps most fundamental is the question of the proper role of the political system itself in the society. Is the political system viewed as a vehicle for the maintenance and regulation of existing patterns of economic and social behavior, or is it viewed as an instrument for change? Are the capabilities of the political system to be increased, or is the political system viewed — as it often is in the United States — with distrust, to be kept in check where possible? Is foreign policy to be aggressive and expansionistic, or accommodative? Is the state to engage in extensive public welfare programs, or to support a free-enterprise economic system? These questions are often not brought out in public policy debate — more often the political culture sets certain limits, and the debate is carried out in terms of whether or not a specific policy flaunts or expresses these underlying premises.

Secularization of Political Culture. Writings about American politics have often emphasized the marketplace attitude which permeates the conduct of politics. Politics is seen by the participants as a set of give-and-take interactions, in which each side bargains for a set of more or less limited objectives. Jean Grossholtz, in her analysis of the political culture of the Philippines, also emphasizes the bargaining nature of the conduct of politics.[11] She writes of the "manipulative attitude toward human interaction and a perception of politics as an extension of the set of human relationships created for dealing with strangers," and notes the reciprocity of pragmatic bargaining for votes and benefits which arises between politicians

[11] Jean Grossholtz, *Politics in the Philippines* (Boston: Little, Brown and Company, 1964), Chap. 7.

and their constituents.¹² This is not to imply that the Philip-
pine political culture is identical with that of the United
States. But there is a striking contrast between the pragmatic
bargaining styles of these two systems and the relatively rigid
ideological styles of politics which typify elite political culture in France and Italy.

The emergence of a pragmatic, empirical orientation is one
component of the secularization process. A second attribute of
the process of cultural secularization is a movement from
diffuseness to specificity of orientations. In a traditional or
primitive political culture, the roles of the polity are not differentiated from other societal roles. Anthropologists and
political scientists studying Eskimo society may analytically
distinguish certain sets of actions on the part of a shaman or
a hunting chief as being political in character. There is, however, no such distinction in the mind of the Eskimo. Both the
attitudes and the roles themselves are diffuse. Political cultures
characterized by diffuseness correspond to what we called
"parochial cultures" in our analysis of the objects of orientation. Parochial individuals in a political system are those who
manifest highly diffuse social orientations, having little or no
awareness of the political system as a distinct and specialized
entity. Such individuals may be found in systems which have
elaborate governmental structures, but the tribesman in the
backwoods remains a parochial because he has no specific
notion of these structures. For him the political system remains, at most, on the border line of awareness.

An individual may become aware of a variety of governmental roles, such as those of tax collectors and military
officers. Such an individual may, however, have no specific
knowledge of the ways in which they can influence the political
system, no understanding of the input structure of the society.
By the same token, their image of themselves as initiators of
demands remains diffuse and undeveloped, perhaps limited to
some vague notions of seeing the local chief or family head if
problems arise. We have referred to such individuals as political subjects.

The political participant develops a set of specific attitudes

¹² *Ibid.*, p. 159.

toward the political input structures, such as parties and interest groups, and toward the role he can play in these structures. In such a case the individual has reached a level of cultural secularization (or specificity) with which we are familiar in democratic systems. Of course, in even the most modern and secularized political systems, there remain individuals who never reach this level of orientation. However, in nations such as Britain, the Scandinavian countries, the United States, and Switzerland, a very large proportion of the population does reach this level. As literacy spreads, an increasing specificity of orientation is likely to spread also.

However, it should be remembered that in some political systems the input structures are themselves highly diffuse, or have become differentiated without being autonomous. In totalitarian and authoritarian states, a single party may dominate the political system and so limit the autonomy of the substructures that they hardly constitute input channels except under certain quite carefully specified conditions. In such a case the average citizen may develop what we might call a "subject-participant orientation." He knows that he must be active, be a participant, but the party and other groups afford little opportunity for sharing in decisions.

In the discussion of political structures we spoke of the structural "inventions": the officialdom of the patrimonial system, the efficient bureaucracy which succeeded it, and the emergence of specialized political agencies such as political parties. We must recognize that these aspects of political development tend to be accompanied by or preceded by crucial developments in political culture. In general, we suggest that a political culture must become increasingly secularized if the new, differentiated structures are to operate effectively.

It is very difficult for a specialized bureaucracy, for example, to operate effectively in a traditional society. In such a society the conduct of politics is governed by custom. Individuals are treated according to ascribed statuses, not according to particular merits and needs relevant to a special political domain. If the rules of a bureaucracy are imposed on such a culture, they will soon be undermined by the persisting traditional rules. Universalistic treatment of individuals according to the spe-

cifically political rules will eventually be distorted by the considerations arising from diffuse societal relationships such as
tribe, caste, or family ties. The bureaucracy will also find it
difficult to penetrate and overcome the traditional rules of the
society, no matter how rational new regulations may seem.
Men will resist bitterly any efforts to make them shave their
beards or abandon traditional ways of dress. They may subject
bureaucratic officials to intense pressure to avoid the formal
universalistic rules, and demand special treatment for relatives
and friends. Such problems have troubled not only patrimonial
officialdoms, but also the westernized bureaucracies inherited
by transitional nations such as Nigeria. The inefficiencies resulting from the diffuse and closed nature of such traditional
orientations toward politics and political objects are problems
widely discussed in the literature dealing with these nations.

It is through the secularization of political culture that these
rigid, ascribed, and diffuse customs of social interaction come
to be overridden by a set of codified, specifically political, and
universalistic rules. By the same token, it is in the secularization process that bargaining and accommodative political
action become a common feature of the society, and that the
development of special structures such as interest groups and
parties becomes meaningful. It is true, of course, that both
secular and nonsecular elements are present in all political
cultures. Accommodation and behavior in accordance with
specific and universalistic rules may be found in traditional
societies, and diffuse, ascriptive favoritism and rigidified interaction patterns may be found in modern political systems. But
the general process of secularization involves a shift from one
predominant pattern to another. In a modern political culture the specific roles and structures, and the pattern of open,
accommodative relationships may in some cases permeate even
the political aspects of family activity. In a traditional society,
the specific structures and manipulative interactions play a
secondary role.[13]

In developmental analysis we distinguish a number of stages

[13] This point is made with some force by Lucian W. Pye, *Politics, Personality, and Nation Building* (New Haven: Yale University Press, 1962).

and combinations which may exist along the continuum from traditional to secularized political culture. One of the most interesting of these is the ideological political culture. An ideological style emerges when the individual develops a *specific* set of political orientations, but fails to develop the open, bargaining attitudes associated with full secularization. Instead of the diffuse, ascribed statuses and rigid norms of conduct given by custom, there is an explicit — but equally rigid and closed — set of rules of conduct spelled out by the ideology. While accommodative interaction may be acceptable within the context of ideological bounds (it may be legitimate to manipulate the enemy for purposes of attaining the ideological goals, a pattern that is equivalent to the accommodative bounds set by custom in traditional society), it is never acceptable to step beyond those rigid rules. The ideology provides an inflexible image of political life, closed to conflicting information, and offers a specific explanation and code of political conduct for most situations.

In the modern world the various forms of communism and clericalism are the most common examples of ideological political cultures. Such cultures seem to emerge either from a traditional heritage, where the cultural style makes a direct transition from traditionalism to ideology, or from the politics of uncertainty and immobilism. Very often, elements of both heritage and circumstance are present. The patterns of political culture commonly found in the developing areas seem to be a product of a way of political life in which bargaining plays a limited role in the politics of tribe, clan, and caste, and also of the frustrations and uncertainties which accompany the experiences of colonialism, modernization, and associated culture conflict. In such times of trouble and fear, an ideology offers a means by which the individual can escape the freedom given him by an open, secularized culture and its structural concomitants. It is significant to note that communism itself had its origins in the frustrating, unresponsive political systems of nineteenth-century Germany and Russia, and that it often made a great impact on those very recently subjected to the trials of industrial and urban life. In unresponsive systems such as modern Italy and France, ideology remains of compelling importance. As such, it results from and contributes to the problems of these nations. The distinct set of ideologically bound parties and interest groups — Catholic, Communist, Socialist — often find it impossible to come to common working agreements, to form stable coalitions, even when it is in the compelling national interest to do so.

Before leaving the question of secularization of political culture, a final developmental problem must be noted. We have suggested that there is, in general, an association between structural differentiation, cultural secularization, and an expansion of the capabilities of the political system. These associated attributes are involved in the *development* of political systems, although, of course, such development is neither inevitable nor irreversible. But we must be aware that the relationship between these factors has many complex facets. It is clear, for example, that certain elements in traditional, nonsecular cultures may serve, at least temporarily, to support national leaders in efforts towards differentiation and increasing system capability, giving the system time to develop its capacity to satisfy the new demands and meet the strains of secularization. In Japan and in England, for example, certain attitudes of deference, obedience, and loyalty to superiors and to the centralized governmental structures seem to have helped ease the process of transition. Clearly, however, other types of traditional attitudes may hinder in this process.[14]

By the same token, under circumstances of tension and strain such as international threat, secularization of attitudes regarding goals and values among the people may weaken the support for the system. An implicit set of values, agreed upon and unquestioned, which supports the political institutions and general leadership policy, may be an invaluable basis for build-

[14] See, for example, the discussions of Japan and England by Robert E. Ward, "Japan: The Continuity of Modernization," pp. 27–82, and Richard Rose, "England: The Traditionally Modern Political Culture," pp. 82–129, both in Pye and Verba, *op. cit.* For an example of incompatibility of most elements in traditional political culture and political development, see David E. Apter, *Ghana in Transition* (New York: Atheneum Publishers, 1963).

ing the capability of the political system to meet a crisis. In this sense of political *goals,* it may be argued that the British and American political cultures have strong underlying nonsecular components which give these systems the ability to mobilize their capabilities in time of emergency, and which enhance stability and capability at all times. The rational, secular support based on good system performance is supplemented by a more implicit and diffuse sense of general support. It has been argued that transitional systems are often weakened by the very intensity with which *all* possible goals and ends become questioned and challenged in the secularization process. It may be that only underlying, nonrational agreement on some values and goals makes it possible to bargain and manipulate pragmatically in other areas.[15]

But these questions, though important, become too complex to explore in all their dimensions here. Much depends, obviously, on the nature and homogeneity of such traditional or tacit beliefs, and on the circumstances which challenge system capability. We are willing to stand behind the argument that in terms of the general *means* of political action, there is a strong relationship between specialized and pragmatic orientation — secularization — and the effective performance of modern, differentiated political structures.

Distribution of Political Attitudes: Political Subcultures. Thus far we have treated political culture as though it were the same throughout the entire population of a political system. In fact, the degree of homogeneity of political culture is a matter for empirical investigation. There may be a high degree of agreement in attitudes toward general classes of political objects. Or differences may emerge according to level of education, ethnic membership, geographic location, economic and social position, and religious faith.

When a particular set of political orientations is distinguishable from others in the system, we speak of a political subculture. What we do and do not define as a separate subculture depends largely on the nature of the concerns and problems in

15 See Sidney Verba, in Pye and Verba, *op. cit.,* pp. 544–550.

question. The observer of American politics may be concerned with the liberal and conservative wings of the Democratic party as policy subcultures, while a comparative analyst might dismiss them as being so firmly within the more general American political culture as to be unworthy of the separate designation.

However, there is no question of the importance of some of the subcultural differences which exist in certain nations. France is the classic case of a nation whose political culture, although manifesting a strong national identity in some respects, appears to be so fragmented as to make effective political performance almost impossible except in crisis, or under an authoritarian regime.

In many of the nations in the developing areas, this problem of political subculture is also crucial. In a nation such as India the differences of language, religion, class, and caste pose enormous problems for the political regime. Even after an effective national identity has been established, the resolution of these subcultural differences and the inculcation of some commonly accepted "rules of the game" is necessary. For any political system to operate effectively, there must be some level of agreement on the basic nature of politics, the general role of government in the society, and the legitimate goals of policy and participation.

The efforts of the new nations to create such common bases for action and to bridge the gap between subcultures have been of great interest to social scientists. This question of changing and adapting the political culture brings us, however, to the "system maintenance and adaptation" level of functions, and particularly to political socialization.

Political Socialization. Political socialization is the process by which political cultures are maintained and changed. Through the performance of this function individuals are inducted into the political culture; their orientations toward political objects are formed. Changes in the patterns of political culture also come about through political socialization. When the totalitarian state revises the account of history in school textbooks, or when the new nation expands the school system, political elites are attempting to shape and control this process of creating political orientations.

The study of political socialization seems to be one of the most promising approaches to understanding political stability and development. Its special significance in the modern world is a consequence of the great changes which are affecting so many contemporary societies. The emergence of the new nations, the ever-expanding network of communications linking old nations and new ones, and the impact of technological innovations on social, economic, and political affairs in even the most stable Western systems, mean that old methods of providing orientations to social action are no longer valid. The traditional socialization structures must compete with new ones and with new, immediate experiences.

As a basis for understanding the political socialization process, two points must be clarified. In the first place, the socialization process goes on continuously throughout the life of the individual. Attitudes are not established during infancy and untouched after the age of ten. They are always being adapted or reinforced as the individual goes through his social experiences. Early family experiences can create a favorable image of a political party, for example, but subsequent education, job experience, and the influence of friends may alter that early image to a hostile and unfriendly one.

Certain events and experiences may leave their mark on a whole society. A great war or a depression can constitute a severe political trauma for millions of individuals who may be involved. Or involvement in a mass movement for independence, such as the nationalist struggles which are prominent in the histories of many ex-colonial nations, can provide a learning experience which shapes the orientations of large segments of the population. Through participation in such movements, these groups acquire new conceptions of the role of politics in their lives and new goals for which they may strive.

Political socialization may take the form of either manifest or latent transmission. It is manifest when it involves the explicit communication of information, values, or feelings toward political objects. The civics courses in public high schools exemplify manifest political socialization. Latent political socialization is the transmission of nonpolitical attitudes which affect attitudes toward analogous roles and objects in the political system. Such latent political socialization may occur with particular force in early experiences. For example, the child acquires certain general attitudes of accommodation or of aggression toward other individuals. Such orientations will affect his attitudes toward political leaders and his fellow citizens. They will shape his view of politics as a process of struggle for dominance or as a means of attaining legitimate goals. Latent political socialization involves many of the most fundamental characteristics of the general culture, which may in turn have great effect on the political sphere.

The Agents of Political Socialization. The family unit is the first socialization structure encountered by the individual. The latent and manifest influences inculcated at the early stages in life have a powerful and lasting influence. Among the many important latent influences, perhaps the most distinctive is the shaping of attitudes toward authority. The family must make collective decisions, and for the child these decisions are authoritative. They are backed with potential sanctions. An early experience with participation in decision making can increase the child's sense of political competence, provide him with skills for political interaction, and thus enhance the probability of his active participation in the political system when he becomes an adult.[16] By the same token, the child's pattern of obedience to decisions can help to predispose his future performance as a political subject.

Manifest political socialization by the family can also have important effects. General attitudes toward the political system can make a great impression on children. Wylie's study of a small French town illustrates how a general attitude of contempt for the political system can dominate children's attitudes, even when the official school texts present another picture.[17] Studies of the intergenerational continuity of party

16 Almond and Verba, *op. cit.*, pp. 346–352.
17 Laurence Wylie, *Village in the Vaucluse* (Cambridge: Harvard University Press, 1957).

identification in the United States show how children may be disposed to consider themselves Republicans or Democrats according to their parents' loyalties.[18] The early exposure to the image of the President, and the identification of him with the father, apparently facilitates an early and continuing affiliation with the political system in the United States,[19] and provides an example of an interesting manifest and latent socialization process.

The school structure is a second powerful influence in political socialization. The five-nation study found without exception that educated persons were more aware of the impact of government on their lives, paid more attention to politics, had more information about political processes, and manifested a higher degree of political competence.[20] This is presumably the effect both of manifest transmission of political knowledge, and of the development of general awareness of one's social environment and of experience participating in it.

Schools can also play an important role in shaping attitudes about the unwritten "rules of the political game," as the traditional British public schools inculcate the values of public duty, informal political relations, and political rectitude. They can bring an awareness of other values and circumstances, providing a basis for new political aspirations. They can reinforce affection for the political system, and can provide common symbols for the expressive response to the system. The emphasis on the flag and the Pledge of Allegiance attempts to do this in American schools, and the introduction of African cultural history attempts to do it in the new African nations.

We must add a word about the latent socializing influence of the educational structures as well as their manifest role. As in the case of the family, the school contains a particular pattern of authoritative decision making to which all students are exposed. Participation in decision making at school can do something to make up for a lack of it at home — or can rein-

---

[18] V. O. Key, Jr., *Public Opinion and American Democracy* (New York: Alfred A. Knopf, Inc., 1961), p. 298.

[19] Robert D. Hess and David Easton, "The Child's Changing Image of the President," *Public Opinion Quarterly*, Winter, 1960, pp. 632–644.

[20] Almond and Verba, *op. cit.*, pp. 380–381 ff.

force the previous patterns. This problem of participation and authority patterns is important at the adult as well as the primary level of education. Myron Weiner gives a dramatic example in his account of the socialization of university students in India:

> We have tried to suggest that indiscipline within the universities or colleges reflects a breakdown in communication between the university or college authority and the students. . . . The result may be—and thus far has been—not only to widen the breach between students and authorities, but, more seriously, to widen the gap between politics and public policy in students' minds—the former being thought of as a futile but exciting outlet for personal protest, the latter as the edicts and actions issuing from an aloof and nonresponsive goverment or university. The concrete demands by organized student groups against university and nonuniversity authorities, while often irresponsible in their initial appearance, are often potentially negotiable and manageable. If university authorities are able to develop procedures by which students may present their grievances, universities and colleges will do more than eliminate indiscipline. They will educate students to recognize the relationship between politics and public policy, and thereby strengthen the capacity of students to function as adults within a democratic society.[21]

While the school and the family are the agencies most obviously engaged in the socialization process, there are several other important sources of attitude formation. Peer groups or reference groups, for example, play an important role in shaping values and orientations. Particularly where family ties are loosened in an industrial society, or where family training seems incongruous with the youth's social environment, we may expect the formal and informal peer groups to have considerable impact on individual views of politics. Since orientations to other political actors constitute a particularly important area of political culture, the ways in which peer-group contacts affect these orientations has a bearing on future

[21] Myron Weiner, *The Politics of Scarcity* (Chicago: University of Chicago Press, 1962), p. 185. A more familiar illustration would be the Free Speech Movement among students at the University of California.

political behavior. Such relationships may build or break down attitudes of hostility and aggression. They may develop skills in human interaction and participation in group decision making.

Experiences in employment may also shape political orientations. The job and the formal and informal organizations built around it — the union, the social club, and the like — may be channels for the explicit communication of political information and beliefs. Participation in the process of collective bargaining or involvement with a strike can be a powerful socializing experience for worker and employer alike. The striking laborer not only learns that he can shape the authoritative decisions being made about his future, but he gains knowledge of specific action skills, such as demonstrating and picketing, which may be used in political participation.

The role of the mass media in political socialization must not be overlooked. In addition to providing information about specific and immediate political events, the mass media act over the long run to shape the individual's basic "cognitive map." Certain facts are emphasized; other facts are not. Certain symbols are conveyed in an emotive context, and the events juxtaposed with them take on the affective color. A controlled system of mass media can be a powerful force in shaping political beliefs, and can provide bases of support as important to a totalitarian state as its police forces.

Finally, a word must be added about the influence of direct contacts with the political system. No matter how positive the view of the political system which has been inculcated by family and school, when a citizen is ignored by his party, cheated by his police, starved in the bread line, and finally conscripted into the army, his views of the political realm are likely to be altered. Direct formal and informal relationships with specific elites in the political system are inevitably a powerful force in shaping orientations of individuals to the system. In Chapter V we shall discuss in some detail the role of political parties in socialization.

Continuity and Discontinuity in Socialization. In a stable political system the socialization process is usually homogeneous and consistent. The family authority pattern, the teacher-pupil relationship in the schools, the interaction of employer and employee, and direct contacts with the political system tend to establish and maintain a given type of political orientation. This may be deferential and passive, or aggressive and participatory. But in a homogeneous socialization process the elements influencing the individual do not seriously conflict either with each other or with his adult political activities and expectations.

In many societies, however, the socialization process may be highly discontinuous. Such discontinuity creates an important potential for dissatisfaction and conflict, and a high potential for system change. We cannot fully explore this complicated problem, but perhaps an example of discontinuous socialization and its effects will illustrate the concept.[22]

Students of the Weimar Republic have long been aware of the dichotomy between the hierarchical authority patterns which pervaded Germany's nonpolitical social institutions, and the needs and expectations of the democratic system. Family training stressed obedience. Primary, secondary, and university education drew a sharp line between the learning activities of the student and his unquestioning obedience to the moral and intellectual authority of his teacher. German political experience before 1918 was characterized by obedience and support, but not by active participation in decision making. Even the socialist political parties, as Michels pointed out, were characterized by an authoritarian structure and culture.[23]

This discontinuity between latent and manifest exposure to authority patterns and the new participation expectations of the Weimar Republic helped to limit popular acceptance of and engagement in the new political structures. When the economic and international events failed to provide a positive socialization experience, but rather acted to create new dissatisfactions and pressures, the existing discontinuity could not be bridged, and the political system ultimately broke down.

[22] For a more complete treatment, see Sidney Verba, "Conclusion," in Pye and Verba, *op. cit.*, pp. 553 ff; Harry Eckstein, *A Theory of Stable Democracy* (Princeton: Center of International Studies, 1961); and Pye, *Politics, Personality, and Nation Building, op. cit.*

[23] Roberto Michels, *Political Parties* (London: Jarrold and Sons, 1915).

Subcultures are perpetuated through time by the action of socializing agencies. They are broken down either through the impact of new agencies of socialization, as when schools are introduced into a backward area, or by a change in the operation of the existing socialization agencies. In either case the problem of breaking down local subcultures is a long and slow process. No citizen fully overcomes the effects of his latent primary socialization, which means that the problem of time lag in changing political cultures is a serious one. Furthermore, it is difficult to change the functioning of many of the agencies of socialization, particularly that of the family. Even the schools are difficult to re-orient in this respect. Where teachers themselves remain tied to subcultural values, these values can only be broken down with difficulty. Where the gap between school and everyday life is too great, the content of schooling is relegated to abstract memorization with little effect even on cognitive political orientations.

However, since the schools are the socialization agency most easily controlled by the political system, many nations have attempted to use the public schools to bridge the gap between subcultures and the national political culture. Such efforts have been markedly successful in the United States, where generation after generation of the children of immigrants have been socialized with considerable effectiveness into the mainstream of American life. In the Philippines the public schools have been the vehicle for providing a common language and a relatively homogeneous political culture for the people of the islands, but subcultural elites often bitterly resist the efforts to change their attitudes and ways of life. India's language riots suggest the depth of this kind of problem. If the political system yields to the demands of the local subcultures for autonomy in their socialization processes, it perpetuates the differences in orientations which threaten to tear the nation apart. But the attempt to control and shape that socialization process may itself be the cause of resistance which significantly damages the capability of the political system long before any beneficial results can make themselves felt. The bitter conflict between public and parochial schools in France is another example of this dilemma.

One of the most marked cultural divisions occurs between traditional and modern subcultures. This phenomenon is evident in many of the newer nations, where a small elite has been modernized — has been socialized in the specific, universalistic, and pragmatic orientations which typify "modern" culture — while the vast majority remains tied to the rigid, diffuse, and ascriptive patterns of tradition. But, as we have noted, these distinctions are oversimplified. Modern political science has demonstrated the continuing prevalence of traditional elements in modern societies. The nature of individual socialization makes this duality of cultural style almost inevitable. Regardless of the type of society, the earliest stages of political socialization involve a diffuse, ascriptive, and latent process which affects the child before he learns to use reason. A baby is not a pragmatic, bargaining creature; rather, he has powerful primary needs and develops diffuse and rigidly dependent relationships with those who satisfy them. Political socialization in primitive societies usually stops at this primary level; it is developed only to a very limited degree into specific adult roles through later socialization. The adult roles are rather diffuse societal roles, without specifically political components, and the primitive adult enters into them on the basis of his father's status, or perhaps through his physical prowess.

In modern societies the family, the school, and other socialization structures expose the child and youth to new and specifically political roles, and to an achievement-oriented and universalistic style. To a greater or lesser degree the citizen of such a society is socialized into the secularized political culture. Yet, no citizen of any political system ever fully overcomes the effects of those primary socialization experiences, or outgrows the needs which he feels for the security and support which the intimate ties of the primary group provide. These limitations and needs suggest not only the reasons for the continuing cultural dualism of modern systems, but also for the desperate need for the support of a familiar ideology, a political party, or a charismatic leader, which the most secularized citizen may feel in those moments of crisis when the social, economic, and political structures of a society seem to be crumbling.

CHAPTER IV

Interest Articulation

EVERY POLITICAL SYSTEM has some way of processing demands. Political decisions involve advantage or disadvantage for various individuals and groups in the society, including the political elites themselves. Some sorts of demands, even if only individual goals or desires, or even if stemming predominantly from the elites themselves must be brought to the attention of the decision makers to form the basis for political choice. The process by which individuals and groups make demands upon the political decision makers we call interest articulation. It is the first functional step in the political conversion process.

Interest articulation may be performed by many different structures in many different ways: An angry mob of shouting and gesticulating students converges on the Korean, or Turkish, or Vietnamese capitol to protest government regulations; an American trade union conference releases a statement calling for an increased minimum wage; a Soviet military officer suggests to a member of the Politburo that further arms reduction may endanger Soviet security. These diverse events illustrate the variety of ways interest articulation is performed in political systems.

Interest articulation is particularly important because it marks the boundary between the society and the political system. If groups within the society do not find open channels through which to express their interests and needs, these demands are likely to remain unsatisfied. The resultant dissatisfactions may erupt in violence, or may require suppression by the elites. It is through interest articulation, whether from elites or from the masses, that the conflicts inherent in the political culture and the social structure become evident. The manner of expression can serve either to intensify the conflict, or to reconcile and mitigate it.

The forms which interest articulation take, the degree to which interest articulation structures are specialized and autonomous, and the style of interest articulation constitute distinguishing features of different types of political systems. This chapter deals with four aspects of interest articulation: (1) the kinds of structures which perform the interest articulation function; (2) the variety of channels through which demands are articulated; (3) the styles of interest articulation; and (4) the effects of modernization on articulation. The examples and illustrations used are taken primarily from modern systems. Illustrations of interest articulation in primitive, traditional, and authoritarian systems are to be found in Chapters IX and X.

INTEREST ARTICULATION STRUCTURES:
INTEREST "GROUPS"

A variety of structures, from an undisciplined mob to a businessmen's conference, may be involved in interest articulation. Such structures may be classified according to two major components: the type of *group* initiating the articulation, and the type of *access channel* through which it passes the message. It would be convenient, of course, if we could construct a typology which includes both of these features. We could speak of the associational groups as always articulating interests through regular and legal channels, and of the regional and kinship groups as always working through informal and intermittent channels. But in fact, associational groups, such as trade unions, may organize riots and strikes. All groups may and do utilize the channels of intermittent and informal personal contact. By the same token, speakers for unorganized, but important, language and ethnic groups may address party conventions.

Thus, although particular types of groups may be drawn by their organizational and representational nature to certain kinds of access channels, the general rule is that the interests will be articulated through those channels which are most available and which seem most likely to bring the demands to the attention of the relevant decision makers.

The term "interest group" has become the object of considerable dispute among political scientists. We do not wish to engage in the polemic or to insist upon our own definition as of particular merit. By "interest group" we mean a group of individuals who are linked by particular bonds of concern or advantage, and who have some awareness of these bonds. The structure of the interest group may be organized to include continuing role performance by all members of the group, or it may reflect only occasional and intermittent awareness of the group interest on the part of individuals. In subsequent discussion we shall attempt to identify some of the most important groups which may initiate interest articulation.

Perhaps we should begin by drawing attention to the importance of individuals as articulators of their own interests. Such individual self-representation, commonly cast in the guise of the articulation of more general societal or group interests, is a common feature of political systems. It may take the form of seeking to influence political decisions for financial or professional gain, or it may involve the articulation of interests perceived as more noble in scope.

In a society with group controls over individual elite behavior, such individual interest articulation is checked and ordered. But in societies where a small elite makes all the political decisions, where the articulation takes place from person to person or within a small group, it is a powerful factor in explaining the course of political decisions. Such interest articulation has been a common feature, for example, in the history of strongman dictatorships.

Somewhat akin to individual self-representation are the structures called *anomic interest groups,* the more or less spontaneous penetrations into the political system from the society, such as riots, demonstrations, assassinations, and the like. Of course, much of what passes for anomic behavior is really the use of unconventional or violent means by organized groups. But, particularly in cases where explicitly organized groups are not present, or where they have failed to obtain adequate representation of their interests in the political system, latent discontent may be sparked by an incident, or by the emergence of a leader, and may suddenly impinge upon the political system in unpredictable and uncontrollable ways.[1] Political systems may be marked by a high frequency of such violent and spontaneous group formation (as in France of the Fourth Republic, Italy, and the Arab nations), or notable for its absence. The peasant roadblocks in the French Fourth Republic, the Italian protests over the disposal of Trieste, and the British rural unrest and "rick burning" in the period before the Reform Act of 1832 provide us with a few examples of anomic behavior.

Self-representation and anomic groups are marked by limited organization and a lack of constant activity on behalf of the group. To them we must add what we call *nonassociational interest groups*. By nonassociational interest groups we refer to kinship and lineage groups, and ethnic, regional, status, and class groups which articulate their interests intermittently through individuals, cliques, family and religious heads, and the like. Examples might include the complaint of an informal delegation from a linguistic group regarding language instruction in the schools, a request made by several landowners to a bureaucrat in a social club regarding the tariff on grains, or the appeals by kinsmen to a government tax collector for preferred treatment for the family business.

The distinguishing characteristics of such interest groups are the intermittent pattern of articulation, the absence of an organized procedure for establishing the nature and means of

[1] An analysis of the necessary prerequisites to anomic violence (and other types of mass action), and of the sequence of steps which lead to it, may be found in Neil J. Smelzer, *Theory of Collective Behavior* (London: Routledge and Kegan Paul, 1962). See also E. J. Hobsbaum, *Primitive Rebels: Studies in Archaic Forms of Social Movements in the 19th and 20th Centuries* (New York: W. W. Norton & Company, Inc., 1959).

articulation, and the lack of continuity in internal structure. In highly differentiated modern societies, the influence of such groups is limited for two reasons. First, interest-group studies have shown that organization is highly advantageous for successful interest articulation. In modern societies competition from numerous organized groups is too great to permit a high degree of successful articulation by nonassociational groups. Second, important nonassociational groups with continuing interests soon develop organized structures, and hence fall into one of the two following classes of interest groups.[2]

Institutional interest groups are found within such organizations as political parties, legislatures, armies, bureaucracies, and churches. These are formal organizations, composed of professionally employed personnel, with designated political or social functions other than interest articulation. But, either as corporate bodies or as smaller groups within these bodies (such as legislative blocs, officer cliques, higher or lower clergy or religious orders, departments, skill groups, and ideological cliques in bureaucracies), these groups may articulate their own interests or represent the interests of other groups in the society.

We should note here that political parties may constitute the bases for institutional interest groups. In making such a statement we distinguish between the function of the party in representing and aggregating interests of its members, and the behavior of cliques within the party utilizing their institutional position to articulate particular interests. Conservative business interests have operated effectively within conservative parties, as have trade unions in Social Democratic parties.

Institutional interest groups may occupy particularly powerful positions in the society because of the strength provided by their organizational base. The prominent part played by military cliques, bureaucratic groups, and party leaders in articulating interests in underdeveloped areas, where associa-

[2] LaPalombara finds this to be the case in Italy. Joseph LaPalombara, *Interest Groups in Italian Politics* (Princeton: Princeton University Press, 1964), pp. 81–82. It also seems to be happening in the case of caste and language groups in India.

tional interest groups are limited in number or ineffective in action, is obvious. Even in a society such as the United States, with its thousands of associational interest groups, one cannot ignore the role of the institutional military-industrial complex in articulating the numerous interests connected with defense industry.

The *associational interest groups* are the specialized structures for interest articulation — trade unions, organizations of businessmen or industrialists, ethnic associations, associations organized by religious denominations, and civic groups. Their particular characteristics are explicit representation of the interests of a particular group, a full-time professional staff, and orderly procedures for the formulation of interests and demands. As the importance of associational interest groups in interest articulation has been recognized,[3] they have been the object of many studies in the more developed societies. Where these groups are present and are allowed to flourish, they tend to regulate the development of the other types of interest groups. Their organizational base gives them an advantage over nonassociational groups; their tactics and goals are often recognized as legitimate in the society; and by representing a broad range of groups and interests they may limit the influence of real or potential institutional interest groups and of self-representation.

Some knowledge of the internal dynamics of interest-group behavior is useful in understanding the way certain groups perform their interest articulation functions. A group's ability to mobilize the support, energy, and resources of its members will surely influence its effectiveness. A loose, voluntary group may find it hard to mobilize support and resources. A tightly organized interest group may be very effective, but may represent its leaders' interests and not the interests of the group membership.[4]

[3] See footnote 7 in Chapter I for a brief bibliography of recent interest-group studies.

[4] A much more inclusive analysis of these dynamics, an analysis beyond the scope of this discussion, may be found in Peter M. Blau, *Exchange and Power in Social Life* (New York: John Wiley & Sons, Inc., 1964), especially in pp. 238–246 and in Chap. 10. Among other significant analyses

One other characteristic of the interest-articulating groups should be stressed: the degree of differentiation and of autonomy among the groups. Of particular importance is the extent to which associational interest groups articulate autonomous goals of their leaders or members, or are subordinate to other groups and institutions. In France and Italy, for example, many associational interest groups, such as trade unions and peasant organizations, are controlled by the Communist Party or the Catholic Church. These associational groups may not articulate the needs felt and perceived by their members, but may serve only as instruments to mobilize support for the political parties or social institutions which dominate them. This lack of autonomy can have serious consequences for the political process. The denial of independent articulation to interests may lead to anomic outbreaks. Furthermore, the subordination of interest groups by political parties may limit the mobility of the political process, create monopolies in the "political market," and even stalemate the political system.

Of course, the extreme case of lack of autonomy and differentiation in interest groups is to be found in totalitarian societies, where the dominating elite organizations penetrate all levels of the society and exercise close control over such interest groups as are permitted to exist. In systems such as those of Soviet Russia and Communist China, there is an effort to penetrate the entire society by the central party elite. Interest articulation takes the form of very low-level suggestions within specific bounds, or receives only latent expression. Important, overt interest articulation is limited to members of the elite, who can utilize their position in the various political institutions as a base from which to express their demands. The degree to which control is exercised over general interest articulation and over the processes of communication in a society provides an interesting way of classifying political systems, and one to which we shall return in our discussion of political parties.

---

is the "rational self-interest" problem raised by Mancur Olson, *The Logic of Collective Action* (Cambridge: Harvard University Press, 1965), Chap. 1.

INTEREST ARTICULATION STRUCTURES:
CHANNELS AND MEANS OF ACCESS

The structures performing the function of interest articulation in a political system are not fully identified by designating the various kinds of interest groups. Such groups may express, formally or informally, the interests of their members and yet fail to penetrate the political decision-making structure. In order to analyze interest articulation structures, one must consider also the degree to which groups have access to political elites engaged in making relevant decisions.

The question of channels and means of access is, of course, largely a question of political communication. In Chapter VIII we shall consider political communication in detail. However, communication pervades the entire political process, and we cannot adequately consider the interest articulation structures without noting the specific communication structures available for the expression of political demands.

In communicating political demands the individuals representing interest groups or themselves are usually concerned with doing more than merely conveying information. They wish to articulate their interests to those elites engaged in making decisions relevant to their interests, and they wish to articulate their interests in the fashion most likely to gain a favorable response. Only the most prominent and powerful groups and those operating in an open society can afford to cast their demands upon the public airways and trust that the appropriate response will be forthcoming. A nationally known figure like Martin Luther King or a powerful group like the AFL-CIO can perhaps utilize mass media effectively, but the messages of most groups would be lost among the innumerable demands and bits of information pouring in upon decision makers.

Consequently, interest groups attempt to find special channels for articulation of their demands and special means for convincing the decision makers that the demands are deserving of attention and response. Interest articulators need not be students of formal decision making and communication theory to realize that the impact of a message will vary according to many factors. One of these is the relation between the information the message carries and the perceptions and knowledge of the recipient. Control over information is always a powerful tool for an interest group. But the impact also depends upon the attitudes of the decision makers — feelings of hostility or sympathy toward the interest group or individual, belief in the legitimacy of the claim, or a general attitude regarding group participation. Of particular importance is the decision maker's perception of the consequence of his rejection or his response to the demand. On the one hand, he may consider the impact of the decision upon the society; on the other, he has to weigh the group's reaction to his decision and its possible consequences for the political situation and his own political future.

The nature of the access channels for interest articulation in a given society are of great importance in determining the range and effectiveness of group demands. As was the case in our discussion of the interest groups themselves, we can only touch on the most important general classes of access channels, and suggest some of the reasons for their prominence and some of the consequences of their availability.

One obvious means of articulating demands is through *physical demonstrations and violence*. Such behavior is, of course, characteristic of anomic interest groups spontaneously articulating deeply felt interests. However, the use of riots, assassinations and demonstrations by other interest groups is not an uncommon phenomenon. For this reason it is important to distinguish between (a) spontaneous violence by anomic interest *groups*, and (b) violence and demonstrations as a *means* of access, which any group may use. Nor should the use of violence be associated in all cases with general alienation and blind frustration, on one hand, or with deliberate efforts to overthrow the political system itself, on the other. James L. Payne has argued forcefully that in Peru, for example, demonstrations and the threat of mass violence are an integral part of the system itself, the means by which labor groups bring pressure to bear upon the centralized executive. Utilized in a rational and calculating fashion in the particular circumstances of Peruvian politics, mass violence becomes almost the equivalent of free elections in other political systems — the regularized means by which incumbent elites are threatened with loss of office if they do not accede to expressed demands of important groups in the populace. Rather than constituting a threat to the system's usual performance, mass violence has become a part of the regularized pattern of performance, a structured channel of access into the political system.[5]

However, even when used deliberately, violence always has the possibility of passing beyond the control of its promoters. It has serious liabilities as a form of access, not the least of which is real danger to life and property for those who use it. Characteristically violence has been employed by those groups in the political system which feel that they have least to lose from chaotic upheaval, and which face an enormous gap between possessions and expectations. The culture of a society can also serve to promote or inhibit the incidence of violence. But due to its obvious liabilities, the violence is usually less frequent where other channels for the articulation of demands are open to a wide range of groups in the society. Payne notes that among the factors shaping the development of "structured violence" in Peru were the nonrepresentative conditions of the electoral system, the exclusion of the opposition from formal decision making, the centralization of decision making in the executive, the levels of uncertainty in the bargaining process, and the absence of adequate channels of communication between workers, management, and government.[6] Groups which have access to established nonviolent channels of the type to be discussed below are less likely to have to resort to violent behavior to transmit their demands.

Personal connection constitutes a second important means

5 James L. Payne, *Labor and Politics in Peru* (New Haven: Yale University Press, 1965). This work may prove a landmark in the reassessment of the more ethnocentric views of possible roles of violence long held by Western political scientists.

6 *Ibid.*, Chaps. 13 and 14 in particular. Smelzer, *op. cit.*, also discusses the availability of other channels and means of action as a factor in the structural preconditions for various types of collective behavior, including revolutionary movements as well as anomic outbursts.

of access to political elites. By personal connection channels we mean the use of family, school, local, and social ties as intermediaries. An excellent example of such channels would be the informal communication network within the British elite, a network based on "old school ties." Similarly, in the United States, Japan, and other countries, the contacts and friendships among alumni of a particular university have proved to be important channels of access for the articulation of many interests. The Herrenklub of Weimar Germany, the Jockey Club of Argentina, and similar social and recreational groups in other countries have served as channels to governing elites.

While personal connection channels are commonly utilized by nonassociational groups such as those representing family or regional interests, they are important to all sorts of groups. This is true in all polities, perhaps largely because messages conveyed through such channels can have particular impact upon the receiver. Studies of opinion formation have clearly demonstrated that face-to-face contact is one of the most effective means of shaping attitudes. Where the contact occurs in an atmosphere of cordiality and friendship, the likelihood of a favorable response is improved. Demands articulated by a friend, a relative, or a neighbor are much more effective than a formal approach to a total stranger. Thus, even in very modern political systems we are likely to find personal connections being cultivated with care. Indeed, in Washington there is something approximating a profession with personal contacts in government to advise interested groups and individuals on access problems.

Elite representation on the behalf of an interest group constitutes a channel of access which can be utilized with great effect by some interests. It may take the form of the presence of a group member in the rule-making structure, or of sympathetic representation by an independent elite figure. Rather than having to use personal connection or formal channels to gain access, the group that has elite representation can rely on direct and continued articulation of its interests by an involved member of the decision-making structure. For ex-

ample, representation of interests on a continuing day-to-day
basis on legislative committees is an advantage enjoyed by
Italian labor unions, and a fact lamented by the industrial
giants of the Confindustria organization.[7] Although in the
United States the presence of associational interest-group members in Congress or the executive is frowned upon (though
hardly absent), the legislatures of Great Britain, France, Germany, and other nations include many interest-group representatives in their ranks.

Legislatures are not, of course, the only bodies engaged in
decision making. Indeed, in many nations their role is only a
formal one, if they are present at all. Governmental institutional interest groups have particular influence, since their
members often find themselves in daily contact with the active
decision-making elites, and usually constitute part of the elite
structure directly concerned with relevant interests.

Elite representation may also serve as a channel for interest
groups which have no other means of articulation. In the
1830's and 1840's in Great Britain certain aristocratic and
middle-class members of Parliament took it upon themselves
to articulate the interests of the working class. They were not
responding to channeled pressures and demands from below
as much as they were acting as independent, self-appointed
guardians of these neglected and suppressed interests. Their
work on Committees of Inquiry and the like did much to promote the passage of factory and mines legislation. Such elite
members may read latent cues of group needs and desires, and
serve to communicate these interests into the decision-making
structure. This channel of access often comes into play today
in the developing areas where the infrastructure of a modern
political system, an effective associational group and party
system, has yet to appear or fails to reach a majority of citizens.
Representation on the basis of cue reading, however, is an un-
reliable form of access, and articulation through it may result
in miscalculations on the part of the elite.

Finally, we must consider the numerous *formal and institutional* channels of access which exist in a modern political sys-

[7] LaPalombara, *op. cit.,* pp. 25–251.

tem. The mass media constitute one such access channel, although, as we have noted, the "static" created by the number of messages and by their lack of specific direction limits their effectiveness for many less important groups. Where the mass media are controlled by the political elites and messages are subject to censorship, the media are to some degree eliminated as a useful channel of access, or reserved only for favored groups. However, in an open society the use of the mass media to convey political demands is a major approach to the political decision makers.

Political parties constitute a second important institutional access channel. A number of factors condition their usefulness. A highly ideological party with a hierarchical organizational structure, such as the Communist party, is more likely to control affiliated interest groups than to communicate demands which those interest groups generate. Decentralized party organizations like those in the United States, whether inside or outside the legislative organization, may be less receptive to demands than individual legislators or blocs. In a nation such as Britain, on the other hand, the various components of the party organization, particularly parliamentary committees such as the Conservative "1922 Committee," serve as channels of continuing importance. They are significant channels for articulating demands with some prospect of impact upon the Cabinet and the party in power. In nations such as Mexico and India, where a single-party structure dominates the political system, the party becomes a vital channel for the articulation of many interests.[8]

Legislatures, bureaucracies, and cabinets also constitute

[8] There is debate among specialists on Mexico over the extent to which the dominant party (P.R.I.) controls the political input process. It seems clear that at least some very important business and financial interests rely on continuing access to the president, and have little use to make of the P.R.I. In effect, these interests rely mostly on elite representation: their leaders — major businessmen and financiers — constitute part of the decision-making elite. For the two major positions on the role of the party in Mexico see Robert E. Scott, *Mexican Government in Transition* (Urbana: University of Illinois Press, 1959) and Frank Brandenburg, *The Making of Modern Mexico* (Englewood Cliffs: Prentice-Hall, Inc., 1964). Also see our discussion of Mexico in Chapter X.

common channels of access. Standard lobbying tactics include representation before legislative committees, provision of information to individual legislators, and similar activities. Contacts with the bureaucracy at various levels and in different functional departments may be particularly important where a considerable decision-making authority has been delegated to the agencies of the bureaucracy, or where the group is more interested in shaping specific implementation than basic policy goals. The different sorts of relationships between interest groups and bureaucracies constitute a topic which has been subjected to considerable research. The appearance of regular mechanisms for consultation and negotiation with interest groups, such as the committees, conferences, and informal communications found in the British system, constitutes an unusually explicit form of interest-group access through the bureaucracy.[9] But a multitude of less formalized relationships have been analyzed in the United States, France, Italy, Germany, and such nations in the developing areas as Egypt, Thailand, and the Philippines.[10]

STYLES OF INTEREST ARTICULATION

The performance of the interest articulation function may be manifest or latent, specific or diffuse, general or particular, instrumental or affective in style. These pairs of characterizations refer to mode of expression of the demands by various interest groups. A manifest interest articulation is an explicit formulation of a claim or demand; a latent articulation takes the form of behavioral or mood cues which may be read and transmitted into the political system. This is the contrast existing between explicit statements of demands made by a business

9 See Eckstein, *op. cit.*, for an account of these mechanisms in action.

10 See, for example, Francis E. Rourke (ed.), *Bureaucratic Power in National Politics* (Boston: Little, Brown and Company, 1965), especially section II; Henry W. Ehrmann, *Organized Business in France* (Princeton: Princeton University Press, 1957); Gerard Braunthal, *The Federation of German Industry in Politics* (Ithaca: Cornell University Press, 1965), Chaps. 9 and 10; LaPalombara, *op. cit.*, especially Chaps. 8–10; Morroe Berger, *Bureaucracy and Society in Modern Egypt* (Princeton: Princeton University Press, 1957), Chap. 6; and F. W. Riggs, *The Ecology of Public Administration* (New Delhi: Indian Institute of Public Administration, 1961).

leader or an N.A.A.C.P. official, and such behavior as work slowdowns, minor civil disobedience, and vague grumbling, which may be observed by individuals and groups outside the disgruntled group, and then articulated into the political system by these individuals. When much of the articulation in the society is latent, it is quite difficult for the elites accurately to gauge and to respond to the demands.

A second important style characteristic is the degree of specificity of demands. Such diffuse statements as "We need change," "Politics is too corrupt," and "Wipe out Communism" may be manifest; but they seldom provide accurate cues for decision-making policy. They indicate dissatisfaction, but not the desired means of correction. Specific requests for legislation, such as for a two-dollar minimum wage, represent the other extreme and are more simply handled.

Demands may also be either general or particular. General demands are couched in class or associational-group terms, as in demands that the rich be taxed more heavily, or that the large estates be divided. Particular demands are couched in individual or family terms. Examples of these would be a request for an exception to immigration laws, for individual legislation to let a person now in the United States stay here (the United States Congress receives many such requests each year), or an offer of a bribe in exchange for a political favor.

Finally, the articulation of interests may be instrumental or affective. An affective articulation takes the form of a simple expression of gratitude, anger, disappointment, or hope. An instrumental articulation takes the form of a bargain with the consequences realistically spelled out. The instrumental style is common in American politics, where associational interest groups often threaten to make their future financial or voting support directly contingent upon a legislator's support of a certain bill.

Style characteristics are also distinguishable in the continuing nature of demands. This style reflects, of course, the political culture of the articulating group. The distinction between a pragmatic, instrumental style and an ideological one is particularly important in interest articulation. If a group is unwilling to settle for anything less than total capitulation to a demand that all of society be reorganized, the political elites can hardly respond satisfactorily. This problem is, of course, intensified where competing ideologies are articulated by a large number of controlled — not autonomous — interest groups. The Catholic and Communist groups in France and Italy provide an example of the strain placed upon the political system by continuing ideological demands from nonautonomous interest groups.

CONSEQUENCES OF PATTERNS OF
INTEREST ARTICULATION

The complexity of political systems and the interdependence of their parts make formidable the task of analyzing a single political function in isolation from other functions. It is even more difficult to suggest consequences of different performance patterns. Certain interest articulation structures and styles are more consistent with some aggregating and decision-making structures than others. It will be possible to examine this in more detail when all the functions have been discussed. The nature of the political culture in which the system must operate also helps to determine the effectiveness of a particular pattern of functional performance.

What are some of the consequences of the way the interest articulation function is performed? In the first place, it determines which groups do *not* influence the decision-making process in the society. Mere achievement of articulation and of access is no guarantee of successful influence, but *to fail to gain articulation* even through sympathetic elite members is to forego any chance of shaping political decisions. Thus it was that a decade or so ago the American Negro lacked the effective means, the political knowledge, and the awareness to engage in influential interest articulation. Since World War II a wide variety of types of interest groups have succeeded in making the Negro's needs and demands a living force in American politics. Where certain groups in a society are denied the right to form political groups and to engage in interest articulation, as is the case of the Bantu in South Africa and of the

Negro in many areas of the United States, the responsiveness of the system is limited and discontent can easily arise.

The style of interest articulation also shapes the relative effectiveness of the groups which succeed in making themselves heard. If elites are to respond effectively to group demands, those demands must be communicated in a clear and unambiguous fashion, and must accurately reflect the needs which generate them. The more latent and diffuse the style of interest articulation, the more difficult it is to aggregate interests and translate them into a public policy which will alleviate sources of discontent. This is, in fact, another liability of anomic group violence; the very complex dynamics which lead to such outbursts are not easily interpreted by decision makers. For example, while the demands articulated by Negro civil rights groups are often pragmatic and specific, it may be difficult, even for a sympathetic national leadership, to interpret the meaning of the tragic riots which struck Los Angeles in 1965. Varying explanations, such as the presence of "outside agitators," may be urged upon the elites, and may serve to obscure the complex basic sources of unrest. The political decision makers cannot easily recognize the bases of the spontaneous group violence.

Rigid ideological perspectives, highly particularistic demands, and emotionally charged expressions of desires also make reconciliation of diverse interests more difficult than when the style of these interests is more pragmatic and instrumental. For example, the ideological gap between socialism and Catholicism in the late nineteenth century in Germany prevented unity, or even close association, of these two elements in the trade union movement; the articulation of the demands and needs of these strata of the population suffered accordingly.[11]

The access structure can also hinder effective responsiveness. If only one major legitimate access channel is available, as in a political system dominated by a single, comprehensive party, it is difficult for all groups to achieve adequate articulation.

[11] Philip Taft, "Germany," in Walter Galensen (ed.), *Comparative Labor Movements* (Englewood Cliffs: Prentice-Hall, Inc., 1952), pp. 256–257.

Access may easily be closed, and entrenched interests may dominate whatever access exists. Demands which do receive articulation through these channels may be distorted and shaped by the interests of the dominant groups. Under these conditions the leadership is hampered in efforts to maintain a continual awareness of the specific needs and demands of important groups in the society. Where the associational groups are directly tied to the hierarchical party structure, autonomous goal formation is limited and the problem is intensified. Over the long run this situation can easily lead to miscalculations on the part of the leadership and to unrest on the part of the groups. In his study of Mexico, Scott notes the internal conflicts which continually threaten to spill over and split the party's labor and agricultural organizations in spite of the president's efforts to balance the various groups and subgroups.[12] The centralized African one-party states seem to have encountered the same problem. For example, Guinean students rioted in 1961 in protest to the arrest and trial of five prominent intellectuals. The inability of students and intellectuals to make themselves heard through the narrow channels of a one-party state, clogged by entrenched interests of the older and more established groups would seem to be a major factor in the dissatisfaction. That student restiveness came as a surprise to most people in the system would seem to confirm the point.[13]

In addition to affecting the clarity with which decision makers perceive group demands, the performance of interest articulation can mitigate or intensify the problem of resolving conflicts between groups in the society. In a society marked by a fragmented political culture and an inequitable distribution of resources, the conflict between groups can be a dangerous threat to continued responsiveness and stability. The structure of interest articulation as well as its style can help either to mitigate conflict by forcing a degree of reconciliation at various levels in the input process or to intensify it by articulating raw

12 Scott, *op. cit.*, p. 171.
13 Victor D. Du Bois, "Guinea," in James S. Coleman and Carl G. Rosberg (eds.), *Political Parties and National Integration in Tropical Africa* (Berkeley: University of California Press, 1964), p. 210.

and unaggregated demands directly to the decision makers. When the articulation of interests into the political system is orderly and controlled by channels allowing the political aggregation function to be performed gradually (we shall expand upon this point in the next chapter), the task of the top-level decision makers is simplified.

A high incidence of direct institutional interest-group articulation is particularly indicative of poor boundary maintenance. Institutional groups relying upon the party, the bureaucracy, the army, or the legislature as bases for interest articulation are in a position to impose *direct* and powerful demands upon the decision makers. Their conflicting demands may be difficult to process effectively, yet impossible to ignore. Where numerous and autonomous associational groups, with access to political agencies through a variety of legitimate channels, are present the institutional interests can be checked and combined with other interests.

MODERNIZATION AND INTEREST ARTICULATION

Something should be said about the environmental factors which shape the channels and means of access for interest articulation, and how their modernization affects this political function. Most directly, perhaps, the channels of access are dependent upon the structures of *political communication* available in the society. As the number of newspapers and radios in the society increases, so does the potential for use of the mass media to articulate interests. If elaborate nonassociational ties, such as an extended family system or castes, are prevalent in the society, these traditional structures are more likely to emerge as important channels of interest articulation. Emerging associational groups are likely to seize upon all the channels of access which have been discussed, pressing them into service for the articulation of interests.

A second important and related factor is the *political culture* of the society. Attitudes towards violence, for example, will affect the extent to which riots and demonstrations are a pervasive form of behavior. Special subcultures formed by common socialization experiences, such as the influential group of

Japanese leaders who are alumni of the University of Tokyo, may provide bonds which can be utilized as access channels. Ideological beliefs may also create sympathetic attitudes which may affect access; they may also reflect and intensify irreconcilable demands which become self-defeating through their inacceptability to elites. The degree to which open relationships between interest groups and elite members are sanctioned by the political culture will also significantly shape the avenues of articulation. Traditionally, American politicians and administrators have been much more suspicious of regularized consultation between bureaucratic agencies and interest groups than have their British counterparts. For this reason, perhaps, the establishment of continuing committees and conferences for negotiation and consultation on the implementation of legislation has been limited in the American political system. The degree of alienation and hostility in the political culture will also govern the extent to which potentially available channels will be utilized by various interest groups. Suspicious attitudes toward government, such as that which recent survey data have found in Italy,[14] almost certainly inhibit group articulation through legal channels. Finally, levels of education and awareness, the whole set of characteristics associated with the "participant" attitude in the political culture as suggested in Chapter III, will increase citizen activity and group formation and participation.

A third basic factor is the *distribution of resources* in the society. The representation of interests on a continuing basis is an expensive procedure. Gathering information to influence opinions and maintaining a regular staff, to say nothing of bribery or more subtle lobbying techniques, require considerable financial resources. Only interests with substantial funds are likely to be able to use such techniques. Groups whose greatest resource is in numbers of supporters rather than in money may have to rely on parties and on the election process — and perhaps subsequently on direct representation in the

[14] Gabriel A. Almond and Sidney Verba, *The Civic Culture* (Princeton: Princeton University Press, 1963). See especially pp. 108–109, 117, and 185–186 for summaries of relevant data.

legislature — as channels for interest articulation. The distribution of resources within a society also influences the degree to which "radical" techniques of articulation, as well as radical policy goals, are adopted.[15] In poorer countries with a large gap between the "haves" and "have-nots," the poor are less likely to regard the risks and costs of violence as serious restraints in their efforts to make their demands effective.

We have set forth this analysis as if communication structures, political cultures, resources of the society, and other characteristics of the political system, were independent factors in shaping the performance of interest articulation. We know, of course, that this is not the case. All these factors are intertwined in a complex pattern.

But in describing and analyzing political systems, and particularly in considering *political development,* the very interdependence of these factors makes possible certain kinds of generalization and classification. As we noted in Chapter II, there are many possible sources of system change. But one of the most powerful and predictable of these is radical change in the socio-economic environment of the political system. If there is one element in "political development" upon which various observers seem to agree, it is that certain almost irreversible processes of social and economic change seem to drive political systems along certain very general but discernible paths of change in their own structure and culture.[16]

The most clear-cut of these forces of socio-economic change are related to the industrial, technological, and scientific revolutions. The past few centuries have witnessed remarkable

[15] Seymour M. Lipset, *Political Man* (Garden City: Doubleday & Company, Inc., 1960).

[16] See for example, James S. Coleman, "Conclusion," in Gabriel A. Almond and James S. Coleman (eds.), *The Politics of the Developing Areas* (Princeton: Princeton University Press, 1960), pp. 532–576; Karl W. Deutsch, "Social Mobilization and Political Development," in Harry Eckstein and David E. Apter (eds.), *Comparative Politics* (New York: The Free Press of Glencoe, 1963), pp. 582–603; Daniel Lerner, *The Passing of Traditional Society* (New York: The Free Press of Glencoe, 1958); Lipset, *ibid.,* Chaps. 2 and 3; Lucian W. Pye, *Aspects of Political Development* (Boston: Little, Brown and Company, 1966), especially Chap. 2; and Lucian W. Pye and Sidney Verba (eds.), *Political Culture and Political Development* (Princeton: Princeton University Press, 1965).

changes in man's way of life and thought which have been in large part associated with the economic advantages of the specialization of labor and of the adoption of new technologies to master the environment. Among the consequences of these changes has been an increasingly widespread belief that the conditions of life are not inevitably fixed, that they can be altered through human action. Associated secondarily with these changes have been the processes of urbanization and education, a radical growth in communication and in interdependence of thought and economic activity, and in most cases a real improvement in the physical conditions of life. The same socio-economic changes have also been associated, however, with a breakdown in traditional patterns of belief and in traditional forms of family and social life. Although the individual forms which these changes have taken have been varied, the general patterns have emerged with remarkable regularity in association with the spread of technology and communication.[17]

It is these changes which make it possible, as it has perhaps never been possible before, to speak of "modern" political systems. They are modern because they rest on the consequences of largely unique and irreversible socio-economic changes.[18] These changes affect political systems in many ways, of course. As noted before, they increase the capability of the political system to tap the resources of the society, both by increasing such resources and by creating a higher potential for effective operation of political administration. But more importantly they have the general effect of greatly *increasing* both (a) the need for coordinated social action in order to solve new problems, and (b) the likelihood of increased political participation and political demands from members of the society.

The needs for coordinated social action stem from many sources. Clearly the greater population densities of urban living create collective needs for increased regulation of behavior.

17 See Deutsch, *ibid.,* on this point.

18 In theory any pattern is reversible. But in practice the pervasive nature of the changes and the enormous incentives they offer to individual and society have made them unidirectional. It would seem that only a worldwide catastrophe, such as a nuclear war, could possibly reverse the process.

Sewage, water supplies, and traffic regulation become problems which can no longer be left to individual initiative. In a more general sense, the increasing interdependence of the economy makes individuals, and the society as a whole, more susceptible to fluctuations of inflation and depression; it is no longer possible to return to the land in such times. And the increasing specialization of labor and the technological complexity of everyday life create problems of educational training and socialization which can no longer be handled by the family. The simultaneous tendency of extended family structures to break down under the pressures of industrial employment and urban life compounds all these problems and raises new ones. Care of an increasing number of aged, no longer living in the extended family, is among the other problems likely to be thrust into the political system.

But the actual emergence of all these problems as political problems reflects something more than the changes in society; it reflects also the development of a set of attitudes which define these problems as problems which human beings *can* solve, which need no longer be left to fate. Examples of change in other societies and in other groups, contact with tools of manipulation and with control of physical environment, and experience with government intervention as a force in everyday life, can all create an awareness of the potential of responsive governmental action in creating a new and "better" life. It is the common emergence of such an awareness which has led Eisenstadt to suggest that the basic "legitimacy" of governments in all modern nations — in all nations which have experienced some of these socio-economic changes — rests on the claim of the rulers to act in the interests of the ruled. This is as true of communist as of democratic ideology.[19] It is partially in this sense, as well as in terms of specific and instrumental orientations, that we have spoken of the secularizing tendency of modern political culture.

The specific mechanisms by which attitudes become part of the political culture, and subsequently come to affect the struc-

[19] S. N. Eisenstadt, *The Political Systems of Empires* (New York: The Free Press of Glencoe, 1962), Chap. 1, p. 13.

tures and functioning of interest articulation, are the processes of socialization and recruitment. Processes of social and economic change can affect directly several components of political culture: the level of political information, the degree of political participation, feelings of political competence, and perception of the impact or potential impact of government on the life of the individual. These components of political culture are affected not through some mysterious transference process, but by the fact that social and economic development (a) greatly increases the flow of information and contact between parts of the society, and (b) increases the level of education, wealth, and status which the individual member of the society is likely to have. And a great deal of evidence exists to suggest that increases in educational level and socio-economic status are closely related to level of political awareness, participation, and feeling of political competence.[20]

Thus, the general trends in societies experiencing modernization are those which are closely related to the emergence of "participant" attitudes in the political culture. At the same time, the specialization of labor leads to the formation of a large number of special interests, which can be the basis for associational interest groups. The actual processes by which associational groups emerge and sustain themselves are complex.[21] However, the emergence of the mass media, of a more extended bureaucracy, and of other political structures provides additional channels through which emergent groups can act. The existence of such channels is in itself an incentive for group formation, as is the greater flow of political information.

Thus, it is possible to argue that as a society undergoes processes of economic and technological change, and acquires

[20] For data relating attitudes and education see Almond and Verba, *op. cit.*, Chap. 12. For a more extensive analysis, relating the Almond and Verba data to aggregate economic data and attempting to test some of these general hypotheses, see Prewitt and Nie, "Economic Development and Political Culture," unpublished mimeo, 1964. Also see the discussion of the factors influencing political participation in Lester W. Milbrath, *Political Participation* (Chicago: Rand McNally & Co., 1965). Also see Pye and Verba, *op. cit.*

[21] A more extended discussion of the process of group formation may be found in Olson, *op. cit.*

the social and attitudinal concomitants of these processes, both the orientations and the means of action which lead to higher levels of political interest articulation will emerge. The emergence of the problems of participation and distribution is an extremely likely consequence. The leaders may, of course, attempt to control this process, often at the same time as they stimulate it through their efforts to modernize and industrialize. This effort to control may involve subsuming special interest groups within a dominant party organization, control over the flow of information, and the suppression of demands and dissent. The development of complex and differentiated political infrastructures, either to accommodate or to control such new awareness and articulation, is typical of modern political systems, whether "authoritarian" or "democratic." The variety of forms is, however, very great.

CHAPTER V

Interest Aggregation and Political Parties

THE FUNCTION OF CONVERTING DEMANDS into general policy alternatives is called interest aggregation. A political party convention, as it receives the complaints and demands of labor unions and business organizations, and juggles, bargains, and compromises these conflicting interests into some form of policy statement, is engaging in interest aggregation. So is the legislature as a legislative committee listens to representatives of the military argue that an increase in manpower is vital for national defense, and then hears a treasury official argue that a tax increase or deficit financing will be necessary if such measures are to be put into effect.

In a nation such as the Soviet Union the process may take place in rather different fashion. A central group of party leaders may hear the demands of military officers, party subordinates, and administrative officials for and against shifting industrial production to manufacture more consumer goods. Information bearing on the problem may come from the levels of blackmarket activity and from the impending crisis levels on the foreign scene. In the course of these considerations various policy alternatives are formulated. They may emerge through a combination of ideological analysis and pragmatic balancing, or may appear as a clique makes a bid for power behind a leader committed to a "hard" or a "soft" line policy.

Interest aggregation can occur at many points in the political system, either through the explicit formulation of general policies or through the recruitment of political personnel more or less committed to a particular pattern of policy. The associational interest group continually aggregates the demands of its subgroups. A single individual may take into account a variety of claims and considerations before articulating his own demands. In this context, however, we reserve the term "interest aggregation" for the more inclusive levels of the combinatory process — the structuring of major policy alternatives — and also distinguish it from the final process of authoritative rule making.[1]

Although the performance of interest aggregation by specialized agencies has particularly interesting ramifications in certain types of open, democratic political systems (as we shall see below), interest aggregation occurs in all political systems. The functions of articulation, aggregation, and rule making may overlap, or may occur almost simultaneously within a single structure. Thus, in a tribal society the headman may hear the "murmurings in the tents," aggregate these in his own mind into policy alternatives, and then make a policy decision which has the force of law upon his followers. Or, a dominant totalitarian party may control interest articulation as well as shape policy and control the making of decisions. On the other hand, in a modern democracy associational interest groups may dominate interest articulation; a political party system may regulate interest aggregation through policy formation and recruitment; and a cabinet and parliament may engage in the final rule making choices. Whether or not this conversion process is carried out by differentiated and specialized

---

[1] For a discussion of decision making as a choice *between* a limited number of alternative projects, such as action and non-action as the smallest number of alternatives, see, for example, Richard C. Snyder, "A Decision-Making Approach to the Study of Political Phenomena," in Roland Young (ed.), *Approaches to the Study of Politics* (Evanston: Northwestern University Press, 1958), pp. 3–37.

structures, the function of interest aggregation can be located and analyzed in all political systems.

POLITICAL STRUCTURES AND INTEREST AGGREGATION

Interest aggregation may be performed within all the subsystems of the political system. Indeed, some degree of aggregation is almost inevitably carried out at all levels from individual interest articulation to the final decision-making. But the pertinent question for us is: what structures play the *major* role in aggregating the articulated interests into major policy alternatives? From these alternatives the authoritative policies for the political system are subsequently produced.

The nature of the articulated demands is a significant factor in determining which structures perform the interest aggregation function and what the consequences of that performance will be. In political systems where articulation is quite limited, as certain traditional systems in which the majority of the population is bound by custom and does not formulate autonomous goals, or where the articulation of demands is controlled from the center, as in totalitarian systems, the process of aggregating these demands may be managed successfully by a small elite. But in large and open systems, confronted by a wide range and variety of articulated interests, a more specialized and complex mode of aggregation is needed to prevent disruptions in system performance.

All the various types of structures performing interest articulation may also perform interest aggregation. In a traditional empire the king's favorite minister may hear many grievances and structure some of them into policy proposals. In more modern societies, large associational interest groups, such as the Federation of German Industries in West Germany, or the British Trades Union Congress, may represent a great variety of associated organizations and aggregate diverse and conflicting demands into policy alternatives to present before party and cabinet. And in all societies the decision-making structures themselves will do some aggregation as they formulate a law and decide upon its passage or rejection. In highly developed

political systems, however, specialized structures are differentiated which mediate between the great range of articulated
interests and the final making of authoritative rules.[2] The
political party and the governmental bureaucracy are the two
most likely candidates for this specialized mediating role. Both
types of structures provide direct links between large numbers
of interest groups and the decision makers, and yet are capable
of aggregating interests as well as articulating and transmitting
them. For this reason, we shall discuss these structures at
greater length.

The Bureaucracy. The governmental bureaucracy is the
group of formally organized offices and duties, linked in elaborate hierarchy, subordinate to the formal rule makers. Its
development is characterized by specialization of task, formal
responsibility for set duties, and formal and standardized rules
of procedure. Although established primarily for the implementation of the rules made by higher authorities, the various
bureaucratic agencies and informal groups within them also
engage in the performance of many other political functions.
The role of bureaucratic groups in interest articulation was
discussed in the last chapter, and other roles will be discussed
below in Chapter VI. In order for the bureaucracy to aggregate
effectively, a system with a strong and effective decision-making
center outside of the bureaucracy itself is generally necessary.
Without such a center the bureaucracy may not be able to
maintain its autonomy and coherence. Particular agencies can
become, in this case, "colonized" by the powerful interest
groups who are their clients. The bureaucracy may become incapable of reconciling and balancing these dominating groups,
whose demands then press directly upon decision makers.

Such loss of autonomy and coherence within the bureaucracy
has been characteristic of Italy and France, and to a lesser
degree of the United States, where Congress limits the unifying
central role of the President as a force independent of the
bureaucracy. The classic American example of this problem

[2] Such differentiation constitutes our definition of political development,
the reader may recall.

concerns the Corps of Army Engineers, an agency which has worked with relevant congressional committees to shape river and power project policy in direct defiance of the President's wishes.

Totalitarian and authoritarian systems also utilize the bureaucracy as an interest aggregator. Their rules, however, attempt to control carefully the sorts of demands and claims considered. A major problem for the rulers of such systems, both traditional and modern, is the maintenance of control over the bureaucracy and independence from it. They try to use the bureaucracy to filter out some demands and to aggregate and control others. The relative efficiency and degree of control possible in carrying out routine tasks makes the bureaucracy ideal for such regularized aggregative procedures. But need for independence and information has led rulers in systems like the Soviet Union to set up competing bureaucratic hierarchies, both within the administrative agencies and between these agencies and the party and secret police organizations.

The Political Party. The political party may be considered the specialized aggregation structure of modern societies. Political parties seem to emerge where the number and variety of interests being articulated becomes too great to receive satisfaction through informal interaction. In a competitive system, the party aggregates certain interests into a set of policy proposals, and then attempts to garner a victory at the polls to install decision makers who will use the previously aggregated policy structure as a basis for rule formation. In non-competitive systems the party may aggregate interests in a manner similar to that of a large bureaucracy, although its structure and activities may enable it to perform other functions more effectively than a bureaucracy. Needless to say, the party may or may not be a major interest aggregator in a given system. There may be parties which have little importance in interest aggregation.

It is also true that some party systems aggregate interests much more effectively than others. The number of parties is a factor of importance. Two-party systems which are responsible to a broad electorate are usually forced toward aggregative policies. The desire to seek widespread electoral support will require both parties to include in their policy "package" those demands which have very broad popular support and to attempt to avoid alienating the most prominent interest groups. Where the parties aggregate in terms of certain general considerations, the policy alternatives are likely to be more clear cut and consistent. But, in any case, where a chief objective is the election of partisan candidates, the two parties have a strong incentive toward aggregating at least the most prevalent patterns of demands.[3]

While such mediating aggregation is commonly associated with systems dominated by only two major parties, it may also be found in one-party or multi-party structures. In the Scandinavian nations, for example, considerable aggregation occurs at the intra-party and electoral levels, although the process continues within party *coalitions* at the parliamentary and cabinet levels. But, as has often been suggested, the presence of a large number of fairly small parties makes it increasingly likely that each party will merely transmit the interests of a special subculture or clientele with a minimum of aggregation. A highly ideological orientation in party subcultures increases the probability that this will occur. A single-party structure, such as Mexico's, may also perform a mediating role in aggregation, although a strong possibility that intra-party channels of access may be closed to various interests always is present, limiting system responsiveness or forcing the rejected groups to approach the bureaucracy or central executive directly.

British Health Service Legislation — Interaction between Party and Bureaucracy. As has been stressed, one structure seldom works alone in performing a particular function. It may be helpful, then, to examine a situation in which two structures — the party and the bureaucracy — interacted to perform the function of interest aggregation. The case in point is the initiation of the British health service legislation — an example from the British system which utilized both structures

---

[3] Anthony Downs, *An Economic Theory of Democracy* (New York: Harper & Row, Publishers, 1957), sets forth an interesting theoretical model of this bargaining process.

very effectively, although aggregation through the party predominates as a means for shaping basic lines of policy.

At the 1945 Labour Party Conference interests pressing for an active and positive National Health Service pushed through resolutions calling for a speedy implementation of earlier governmental proposals, and for "public control over voluntary hospitals, a single standard of services for all, local authority over Health Centres, abolition of the sale of practices, and liberalized medical education." [4] A health program was not solely the invention of Labour, however. The Conservative Party, too, had recognized the general demands for improvement in medical service, although its program was somewhat different. Thus, regardless of the winner, the Government would have been able to enact some form of Health Service policy after the election. Labour won the 1945 election, and it was clear that the Government would introduce new legislation for a Health Service.

The bureaucracy also functioned effectively as an interest aggregator. The new Minister of Health, Aneurin Bevin, announced that the Labour Government, following the election, had decided to institute a National Health Service. The initial bill was formulated almost entirely within the government. However, in setting up the organization, procedure, and the specific terms of the program, the bureaucracy was allowed to engage in detailed negotiations with the British Medical Association. The B.M.A. had opposed the idea of a health service initially, but its hostility was mitigated by its success in obtaining several important concessions for the program's implementation. [5] In the area of salaries, for example, the Ministry of Health beat a slow but total retreat. Such use of the bureaucracy for continued aggregation — through a limited delegation of authority — made it possible to incorporate the interests and win the acquiescence, if not the support, of an interest group whose cooperation was vital to the success of the program.

[4] Harry Eckstein, *The English Health Service* (Cambridge: Harvard University Press, 1958), pp. 156–157.
[5] Harry Eckstein, *Pressure Group Politics* (Stanford: Stanford University Press, 1960), pp. 89–112.

DIFFERENTIATION AND FUNCTIONAL
SPECIALIZATION OF STRUCTURES

Political development has been defined as the increased differentiation and specialization of political structures and the increased secularization of political culture. The significance of such development is, in general, to increase the effectiveness and efficiency of the performance of the political system: to increase its capabilities. In the case of interest aggregation the development of specialized structures for the aggregation of a wide range of interests into a limited number of policy alternatives tends to increase system capability in several ways. It becomes easier for decision-makers to take account of all elements in the society and to respond to them. It also means that a wide range of voices can be heard without overwhelming the decision-making structures by the sheer volume of demands and thus rendering them helpless to construct effective and consistent policy. The development of specialized interest aggregation structures thus creates a potential for greater system responsiveness and effectiveness. Without such structures an "immobilism" in meeting system problems may result, as well as a failure to consider systematically the full range of articulated demands. The heavy load of raw, unstructured demands may bring policy making to a halt.

We must avoid, of course, assuming too easily that this "immobilist" pattern, which seems to have characterized postwar Italy, Third and Fourth Republic France, and other systems, is a "bad" or clearly "ineffective" pattern for the system. Such immobilism favors the status quo in major policy matters, of course, and certain kinds of special interests with good access to the bureaucracy (through party or interest group), may be favored at the expense of those who would change the system or who have no access. The possibility must be kept in mind, however, that in systems with high levels of conflict and disagreement over policy directions, the maintenance of the status quo may be as satisfying to as many groups and individuals as any single possible pattern of change. Or, at least we must avoid assuming that some groups are more worthy of benefit

than others, and of imposing our own prejudices upon the
conflict. The problems of intense minority beliefs and the relative balances of policy gain are difficult both for the system and
for the normative theorist, and they should not be prejudged.
However, immobilism may be a salient characteristic of the system with significant consequences for its stability and survival.[6]

The performance of interest aggregation by specialized
mediating structures seems to be related to increased system
responsiveness for a third reason, in addition to the reduction
of the load on decision makers and the increased capability to
respond effectively to a large number of demands. When there
exist specialized structures to aggregate interests before they
reach the governmental decision-making structures, it is easier
to make demands for various kinds of change without threatening the central decision-making structures and the support for
the entire political system. In totalitarian systems, the autonomous expression of interests by any group is often looked upon
as a menace to the nation itself. By the same token, when a
political party declares that it is the primary instrument for
mobilizing the nation behind a single set of charismatic leaders and goals, it is difficult for other parties and groups to chal-

[6] The problem of finding a criterion of system "effectiveness" is no
simple matter, however. The reader should see, for example, Charles E.
Lindblom, *The Intelligence of Democracy* (New York: The Free Press of
Glencoe, 1965), for a discussion of the complexity of the problem and an
analysis suggesting circumstances under which decentralization and dis-
unified decision-making may be "desirable" for the system. It is all too easy
in examining a political system to believe that its decision-making processes
are ineffective because it does not respond to the demands of those groups
whom we personally favor. Or we may transpose our own cultural norms
to suggest that perhaps high levels of "corruption" indicate a "weakness"
in the system — ignoring the possibility that in fact such "corruption" may
be solidifying system support, building stable political parties, or performing some other function which might be desirable from certain points of
view. We can, as a solution, simply select any given criterion we please and
measure the system's performance against that standard. This is a perfectly
legitimate exercise; as long as the criteria are openly specified. Thus, when
we discuss the responsive capability of political systems, or the degree of
subsystem autonomy, we do not pretend that these are the only ways in
which systems can be described — and certainly not the only ways in which
they can be evaluated. They are interesting and significant characteristics
which are tied to a number of system relationships in which we are
interested.

lenge that party without appearing to threaten the support for the entire political system. Dominant parties in many under-developed nations, having led the struggle for independence, regard subsequent challenges to their rule as a threat to all that they have fought for and achieved. Opposition parties in these areas often receive little tolerance. The lack of differentiation between people, party, and government — between articulation, aggregation, and decision-making structures — is a partial explanation for this phenomenon.[7]

In the emergence of specialized structures for interest aggregation there is, we must recall, a two-fold differentiation. Aggregation structures must be differentiated from the central decision-making structures. They must also be differentiated from the major interest articulation structures. As has been suggested above, the competitive two-party system perhaps most easily secures and maintains this differentiation in an open and developed system, all other factors being equal, and presuming a genuine commitment to the electoral process on the part of the parties. Periodic competitive elections force each party to aggregate a wide range of interests within its ranks and prevent it from becoming too closely tied to any one group. The electoral majority of one party in the election means that the new decision makers will have considerable flexibility in their actions and be able to act to some degree autonomously of the party system. Other types of specialized aggregation structures are, of course, quite feasible, as the discussion of one-party and multi-party systems above has indicated. The problems of governing by party coalitions, in the case of multi-party systems, and the difficulty of remaining open to, but differentiated from, important groups in the case of one-party systems, are apt to make effective and responsive aggregation somewhat more difficult in these cases, however. Obviously, many factors complicate the applicability of any generalization. The internal cohesiveness of the parties themselves, and the centralization of the decision-making structure

---

[7] This point is developed in somewhat different form by Niel J. Smelzer, *Theory of Collective Behavior* (London: Routledge and Kegan Paul, 1962), pp. 278–281.

must be considered. And, as we have seen, even in the case of a cohesive and competitive two-party system like the British, performance of aggregation usually involves at least the bureaucracy as well as the party system, and often other structures as well.

THE STYLES OF INTEREST AGGREGATION

While considering the effect of different interest aggregation structures upon the political system, we need to bear in mind two other characteristics of aggregation performance: style and degree of fragmentation. By style, of course, we are referring to the way in which the structure performs the function: the general operating rules it manifests. There are at least three different styles of interest aggregation, corresponding roughly to increasingly secularized political subcultures of the interest aggregation structures. These three styles are pragmatic bargaining, absolute-value oriented, and traditionalistic.

The *pragmatic-bargaining* style characterizes aggregation in such systems as those of the United States, Great Britain, and the Philippines. In these countries a wide variety of interests are often combined into a limited number of alternative policies. This aggregation is sometimes guided by more general ideological perspectives, but the accommodation of diverse interests is its more notable characteristic. Compromise and the "atmosphere of the marketplace" dominate the aggregation process, whether the function is performed by party, legislature, or cabinet. The presence of this style greatly facilitates system responsiveness.

The *absolute-value oriented* style of aggregation refuses to compromise the principles of policy for the sake of accommodating diverse interests. This style may appear as a very rigid rationalism. The aggregator works out the "logical" solution to a problem and develops policy to correspond to it. Interests are aggregated in strict accordance with the theoretically perfect solution. Observers have sometimes characterized the public policies proposed by French intellectuals as cast in this absolute-value oriented mold.

However, perhaps even more commonly, the absolute-value

oriented style takes the form of a particular *Weltanschauung* or *ideology*. In this case a rigid framework is imposed upon the expression and aggregation of all group interests. It is usually a framework with special, particularistic appeal to certain needs or groups at the expense of others.[8] The ideology may, for example, blame certain groups such as "exploitative capitalists," or "imperialists," or members of a "Red menace," for all the problems of the nation. All policy formation is based on this basic rigid framework, even where some flexibility in tactics emerges in the application of the ideology to specific cases. Such a style often results in the systematic exclusion of the demands and interests of major groups in the population. Communist and Fascist ideologies in their "pure" form are typical of such styles, and ideological aggregation has compounded the aggregative problems of nations such as Weimar Germany, Fourth Republic France, and Italy. However, many other groups may manifest an ideological style under certain circumstances, particularly when they feel insecure and threatened.

Traditionalistic styles of aggregation rely upon the patterns of the past in suggesting policy alternatives for the future. They typically manifest both rigidity and diffuse societal role orientations. Such aggregation is typical of systems in which the resources and energies of most members of the society are committed by the social and economic patterns of the traditional culture to long-established and predetermined goals. Such demands as may be articulated apart from these traditional goals, either by specialized and differentiated groups such as a commercial class or by members of a progressive elite or by influences arising out of the international environment, are not easily assimilated by the traditional political elite. Such societies are, in Eisenstadt's terms, marked by limited resources available to the political system and limited autonomy in political goals on the part of the elite.[9]

[8] For a more extensive analysis of this point, see Peter M. Blau, *Exchange and Power in Social Life* (New York: John Wiley & Sons, Inc., 1964), especially pp. 236 ff.

[9] S. N. Eisenstadt, *The Political Systems of Empires* (New York: The Free Press of Glencoe, 1962), Chap. 1.

FRAGMENTATION IN AGGREGATION PATTERNS

After identifying the structures and styles of interest aggregation, the policy alternatives which may be produced by the
aggregation structures must still be considered. Where articulation, aggregation, and decision making are not differentiated
from one another, it is difficult to specify what degree of fragmentation is introduced or reduced at the aggregation stage.
Where some specialization and differentiation begin to emerge,
the level of conflict between the policy alternatives produced
in interest aggregation becomes a highly salient matter. One
can imagine a system in which interest articulation involves a
vast number of demands impinging upon the political system.
This system is headed by a small number of centralized decision
makers, separated from direct contact with the various interest
groups by some intervening structure, such as several political
parties. The parties might in such an instance act so as to face
the decision makers with many possible patterns of policy, so
many that interests can virtually be said to be transmitted, but
not aggregated. This would place a heavy load on the decision
makers; it would be impossible for them to handle all the demands responsively and consistently. At the other extreme the
parties might present the decision-making structure with only
two or three sets of coherent policy alternatives. In this latter
case the volume of demands no longer presents a problem.
But suppose the alternatives are completely contradictory,
rather than merely somewhat diverging. Suppose further that
each of the groups represented by the parties threatens to dis-
rupt the system if its demands are not followed and the demands of others are not ignored. This kind of conflict may
render the decision-makers helpless to make any kind of a positive choice. The system may become immobilized, not by the
volume of demands, but by the degree of fragmentation and
the conflict which directly confronts the decision-making elites.

A fragmented pattern of interest aggregation is generally associated with a fragmented political culture: a fundamental
division in the values and aspirations of different groups in the
society. However, the aggregation pattern is not determined

by the cultural pattern. Differences may rather be bridged and compromised through the actions of parties or other structures performing mediating aggregation, or at least some elements of the societal differences may be reconciled. Thus, the political cultures in Italy and Austria would seem to share much in common, being fragmented into three or four major divisions of a rural, agricultural, Catholic subculture; a modernizing, middle-class, technocratic one; and an anti-clerical, lower-class, urban subculture. In Italy the parties aggregate interests only within subsections of these major cultural fragments, creating a badly fragmented aggregation pattern. But in Austria there are only two major parties. One of these, the ÖVP, (*Öster-reichische Volks-partei*) subsumes within its ranks a considerable diversity of rural, Catholic, agricultural interests along with conservative middle-class industrial interests. In spite of a highly ideological style in inter-party competition, the need for all interests to be subsumed within only two parties has meant that considerable interest aggregation has taken place at the party level. The central decision-making structure (until recently a coalition of the leaders of the Catholic and Socialist parties) has thus been faced with a still fragmented set of policy alternatives, but one in which considerable aggregation of conflicting social and cultural elements has already taken place. This has served to reduce, it seems, the relative strain on the Austrian system.

Thus, while the emergence of fragmented policy alternatives in the aggregation process is "caused" by basic cultural and economic features of the society, it can be alleviated or exacerbated by the way in which mediating interest aggregation is performed. When the performance of the aggregation function fails to bridge such differences, and particularly when fragmented aggregation appears together with other sources of strain, such as an ideological style and low level of specialization, the political system begins to face very severe problems. Contemporary Italian politics is a good illustration of the reinforcing tendencies of these different aspects of aggregation. The fragmented multi-party system in Italy transmits conflicting and ideologically rigid demands into a fragmented legislature and a coalition Cabinet. Important institutional interest groups also articulate interests directly to the decision makers. Such aggregation as occurs is undertaken by the relatively weak and multi-centered decision-making structure. It is hampered by the ideological style of party activities and the fragmentation of policy supported by Communists, Socialists, Christian Democrats, and more rightist groups. This pattern has placed great strains upon the decision-making structure and the entire system. Immobilism and ineffectiveness in policy have tended to be the result.

INTEREST AGGREGATION AND POLITICAL DEVELOPMENT

Many of the considerations suggested in the discussion of environment and interest articulation apply to patterns of aggregation as well. Factors of communication, resource distribution, and political culture which intensify or ease the number and divisiveness of articulated interests, also affect the problem of aggregating those interests. Clearly, the tendency of social and economic modernization to expand communication levels, to increase inclinations toward participation, to widen the gap between rich and poor (at least in the short run in many cases), and generally to increase the number of autonomous demands arising from the society, places growing stress upon the aggregation structures. This burden is intensified in situations where — as is often the case in modernizing nations and particularly in those with socialist ideologies — the political system becomes involved in a vast number of societal institutions and activities.[10] Although central coordination may be necessary for the most efficient utilization of resources, it has the disadvantage that the demands relating to any of the societal institutions, from job to school, may become political demands. Protest over societal problems becomes political protest — in part because the government has involved itself directly in so many facets of social life. Where the political system is highly

10 Smelzer, *op. cit.*, p. 280, notes, however, that many other societies face this problem. Thus in medieval societies, where religious and political authority are fused, protests against specific laws and rules "inevitably tend to generalize into heresies" which threaten the regime itself.

centralized and the society is undergoing the strains which always accompany modernization, a large number of conflicting demands and incessant crises are to be anticipated. Thus, some political observers have urged decentralization of governmental activities where possible. Myron Weiner has suggested decentralization in education as one means of insulating India's regime from some of its aggregative burdens.[11]

But although limiting the responsibilities of the central government may be desirable, the need to aggregate — or control — a large and diverse number of articulated demands presents itself to any modernizing system. Efforts of modernizing systems to create a controlled form of participation and a hierarchical and unified aggregation represent the "authoritarian" stance towards the process of political development. Although Communist Chinese, Ghanaian, and the early Soviet efforts may represent more or less extreme examples of this approach to the means and effects of modernization, trends in this direction are notable in many new nations. In some cases, as in Mexico, the system may become more open and responsive, and may attempt to incorporate increasing diversity within a formally united one-party framework. An elaborate party and bureaucracy can be utilized to accommodate and aggregate the increasing number of demands. But there is ever the threat that the demands will overload this centralized system, and that they will either be blocked or will cause conflict-bound immobilism in policy making. Apparently the presence of a strong figure or institution — in Mexico, the presidency — behind the party can to some degree serve to balance conflicting interests and to shape coherent policy in response to national needs.[12] In such cases the one-party system takes on many of the aspects of a mediating two-party or multiparty system with a strong executive. Many of the leaders in the new nations profess aspiration to such a system, but the temptation to sup-

[11] Myron Weiner, *The Politics of Scarcity* (Chicago: University of Chicago Press, 1962), pp. 220 ff.

[12] At least Scott suggests that this solution to the possible immobilism — the "dilemma of Mexico's development," according to Raymond Vernon — is available. See Robert E. Scott, *Mexican Government in Transition* (Urbana: University of Illinois Press, Rev. 1964), pp. 309 ff.

press new demands is always present. It is clear that there is no simple solution to the problems of aggregation in meeting the challenges of participation and distribution. Even in cases of "authoritarian" solutions, the divisions and conflict often reappear in new form within the ruling party or the elite itself, as Ghana discovered. Aspirations often outstrip capabilities in the initiation of modernization, and a nearly intolerable burden is quite commonly placed upon the aggregative function.

POLITICAL PARTIES AND POLITICAL FUNCTIONS

Since we have shown political parties to be a major structure for performing the function of interest aggregation and have also discussed their role as institutional interest articulators, it is appropriate and useful here to discuss parties in light of some of the other functions they can perform. The discussion in this chapter and the last has concentrated on the performance of particular political functions by a wide range of political structures, and in a variety of fashions. The structural-functional approach may also be used to consider the way a particular structure performs a wide range of functions. For reasons we shall suggest below, the modern political party is an especially interesting structure to consider in terms of this possibility of multifunctional performance. Parties may and do perform many functions besides interest aggregation. On the other hand, of course, in some systems parties may not perform interest aggregation at all. Consideration of a single structure as it performs various functions clarifies our understanding of the complex patterns of political interaction in different political systems. In the following discussion, we shall analyze the way in which political parties may be involved in political recruitment, political socialization, and interest articulation and aggregation. As is becoming increasingly clear, in no political system is there simple identity of political structure and political function.

Parties and Developing Societies. The mass-based, "organized" political party is a relatively new institution in the realm of politics. Factions and competitive elites have always been a feature of human society. Military and bureaucratic organizations have ancient historical roots.[13] But the modern political party, an organized institution relating elites and masses in terms of political goals and concentrating at least manifestly on recruitment to elite offices, is less than two centuries old. Perhaps the mass-oriented parties of Jacksonian Democracy in the United States were the first real examples of this new political structure. But modern political parties, capable of tracing their ancestry to the Jacobin Clubs of the French Revolution, appeared in Europe about the same time. Unlike the demogogic movements and factions of ancient Greece or medieval Europe, all these organizations shared a continuing structure, and they all involved a far wider range of ties than did the elite factions of Whig England or the Roman Republic.

Yet, parties are now found almost universally around the world. Totalitarian or democratic, developed or modernizing, large or small, modern nations have turned to the political party as an essential institution of the political system. The empirical fact is beyond serious dispute; the interesting question is, "why?" Before undertaking a specific consideration of the role of parties in performing various functions in political systems, we may suggest a few reasons for the practical universality of this institution.

Political stability and achievement of political goals are dependent upon the ordered behavior of the masses of individuals composing the society. In primitive and traditional societies political behavior, like all behavior, is determined by traditional norms. These norms generally limit participation in politics to a select few, and even their activities are curtailed by tradition. Traditional systems often display a high degree of stability, as they did in ancient Egypt and China, but the attainment of elite goals is strictly limited by the very tradition which binds the obedience of the masses.

[13] Weber cites Egypt during the period of the New Empire as the earliest historical example of a bureaucracy, and notes as well the cases of ancient China and the Roman Principate. See Max Weber, *From Max Weber: Essays in Sociology,* ed. Hans H. Gerth and C. Wright Mills (New York: Oxford University Press, 1958), p. 204.

In a modernizing society the traditional norms of a culture are broken down by the shocks and abrasions of the transition. To a large degree the disintegration of these norms is a necessary and inevitable step for any society aspiring to technological and industrial strength. Individuals of the society must adopt patterns of behavior consistent with the dynamics of a modern, interdependent economy. They must also be willing to pay taxes, to obey laws, and to provide regularized economic activity in order to support a political system embarked on a program of development. Obedient participation can, of course, be obtained by force and coercion; but these may be costly and inefficient tools. If carried too far they may even defeat their purpose by disrupting those regularized social and economic interaction patterns which they were supposed to insure. Even a totalitarian system engaged in the most radical rebuilding process needs the active support of large numbers of people.[14]

Confronted by needs to mobilize widespread support for political activities, to create new, nontraditional bases of legitimacy, and to provide new sets of values to initiate and sustain economic modernization, the new nation often sees unified political parties as important investments. Parties, as we shall note, can engage the individual in new patterns of values, and subsequently reinforce these through continued contact and participation.

Eisenstadt has suggested that when traditional norms have broken down, only a promise of some sort of action in the interests of the people can rally voluntary support for the elites.[15] Whether or not one accepts this statement absolutely, one cannot fail to notice that even totalitarian regimes today claim to be acting on behalf of their citizens, and utilize parties and elections to arouse support and to put a stamp of legitimacy on their activities. In open and responsive political systems the elites must manifestly and positively incorporate the

[14] See Barrington Moore, Jr., *Terror and Progress USSR* (Cambridge: Harvard University Press, 1954), for an analysis of this need for legitimacy and support in the Soviet Union.

[15] Eisenstadt, *Political Systems, op. cit.,* Chap. 13.

interests of the major groups in the society. This aggregation process is often carried out most effectively, as we have pointed out above, within the political party system. Thus, all types of political systems rely heavily on the political party: totalitarian societies, as a means to mobilize support; democratic societies, as a channel to articulate and aggregate demands; and transitional societies, as an agency to create and structure new norms of behavior.

The key role of political parties may be graphically illustrated by examining a political system which does not have political parties and is attempting to initiate modernization without them. Ethiopia provides such an example. According to Hess and Loewenburg, Ethiopia has attempted to follow the examples of other African nations by creating new sources of legitimacy, by providing new sets of norms to initiate economic modernization, by allowing the expression of new interests, and by expanding education and communication. Rather than introducing party organizations, the emperor and an ascriptively recruited elite have monopolized these tasks. But they have been unwilling to press the direction of change very far for fear of undermining their own bases of authority. Attempts to inculcate the new values and to win mass acceptance of a new order have been confused, inconsistent, and apparently unsuccessful. Under these conditions it seems likely that the forces of change can only undermine present legitimacy and stability without providing an acceptable basis for sustained modernization. Ethiopia's problems suggest the difficulties of finding suitable agencies to substitute for political parties in the modernization process.[16]

We should not wish to extend this crude analysis of the necessary "requisites" of controlled change too far at this time. Nevertheless it may serve to introduce the complex and fascinating variety of levels and points of view which constitute the study of political parties. Intraparty structural organization, political subcultures of various ideological or pragmatic orientations, and relationships with other political structures —

[16] Robert L. Hess and Gerhard Loewenburg, "The Ethiopian No-Party State," *American Political Science Review,* Dec., 1964, pp. 947–950.

all these factors affect party performance and the political system. While the development of "tight" hypotheses in the study of parties has lagged, we can draw upon a rich and growing literature to illuminate some of the important aspects of party activities in different kinds of political systems.[17]

Parties and Political Recruitment. Participation, real or formal, in the recruitment of political elites is one of the defining characteristics of political parties. However, the first question to raise in examining the performance of any political function by a political structure is that of salience (that is, the relative importance of the *particular* structure in performance of *that* function in the system). To what degree in fact do the operations of political parties affect the recruitment of individuals into specific elite roles? One might contrast the salience of parties in a spoils systems, where the victorious party in an election fills a very large proportion of offices in the governmental structure, with the salience of parties in a system operating on a "merit" recruitment system. Certainly political parties are much less important in recruitment to positions in the United States bureaucracy today than they were in the nineteenth century. Or, it may also be that party candidates in elections are actually recruited by other political structures, and the choice is merely ratified by the party organization. In Mexico, for example, the new president is selected by the incumbent president in consultation with the top-level elite, and the selection is then ratified by party nomination and election. (At the same time, however, the salience of the P.R.I. party elite and membership is much greater in recruitment to lower level posts.) In spite of formal party participation in recruitment, it may be the military, the bureaucracy, or the ruling clique which dominates the performance of recruitment.

17 For example, James S. Coleman and Carl G. Rosberg (eds.), *Political Parties and National Integration in Tropical Africa* (Berkeley: University of California Press, 1964); Maurice Duverger, *Political Parties* (New York: John Wiley & Sons, Inc., 1954); Harry Eckstein, "Political Parties," in *The Encyclopedia of the Social Sciences,* forthcoming; Joseph LaPalombara and Myron Weiner, "The Origin and Development of Political Parties," in *Political Parties and Political Development* (Princeton: Princeton University Press, 1966); and Sigmund Neumann (ed.), *Modern Political Parties* (Chicago: University of Chicago Press, 1955).

Given the salience of the political party or parties in the recruitment process, it is necessary to consider the internal procedures by which the party recruits its own candidates. In particular one might ask what groups in the party are allowed to participate in the selection process, and from what groups the candidates themselves are selected. Party activities may be characterized by a "closed" nomination procedure, in which members of the party elite determine which names are presented to the party membership for ratification. Or, at the other extreme, the nomination may be open to a competitive election process of its own, as in the open primaries in various states in the United States. More common, perhaps, than either of the foregoing procedures is a process of consultation involving various relevant factions and groups in the party. Those involved in such consultation may range from a select few to a large number of groups.

In a one-party system the selection of the party's candidate, by whatever means, determines the individual recruited. The general election has a primarily symbolic, propagandistic significance. But in a multiparty system the electoral process makes the final recruitment choice. The role of party activities in elections has been the object of many studies,[18] and we cannot begin to note even the primary points here, except to recognize that usually many activities are aimed at reinforcing the support of followers rather than at attracting new or opposition voters. But the shaping of party platforms to attract broader electoral support is a factor to which we shall return in a moment.

Aside from the internal selection procedures, general patterns of party recruitment in a society may be characterized as either *hegemonic* or *turnover*.[19] In hegemonic recruitment patterns, the same party or the same coalition of parties hold dominant positions over an extended period of time. Turnover

[18] See, for example, Sections IV and V of Harry Eckstein and David Apter (eds.), *Comparative Politics* (New York: The Free Press of Glencoe, 1963), pp. 247–389; and Campbell, Converse, Miller, and Stokes, *The American Voter* (New York: John Wiley & Sons, Inc., 1960), Chaps. 3, 6, and 7.

[19] The classification is that of LaPalombara and Weiner, *op. cit.*

situations are those in which there is a relatively frequent change in the party that governs or the party that dominates a coalition. Mexico, India, and Japan offer examples of hegemonic party recruitment, as do Germany and Italy, with the Christian Democrats holding power alone in the former case and dominating a shifting set of coalitions in the latter. Turnover systems characterize Great Britain, the French Fourth Republic, and for the most part the United States.

The importance of a hegemonic or a turnover pattern relates particularly to two problems. First of all, it is clear that for most political parties the possibility of gaining political office is a major force sustaining support. Where one party cannot attain office, for whatever reasons, it will usually disappear unless sustained by other factors, such as by the distribution of patronage through its elites, by strong ideological commitments, or by performance of integrative social functions for the members. Thus, a strongly hegemonic pattern may well discourage the maintenance of a responsible opposition party. The opposition may disappear, or may move to radical extremes in an effort to garner support.

Closely related to this question is the effect of hegemonic recruitment on interest aggregation. It has long been held that one of the most important roles of a political opposition is that it forces the party in power to consider the interests of all important groups in making policy. If important elements are neglected, the opposition party can espouse their causes. Thus the impetus is given to the sort of pragmatic-bargaining process of the Downs model.[20]

Parties and Political Socialization. Students of political parties have in the past concerned themselves primarily with the role of parties in recruitment and decision making. Only during recent years, with the emergence of totalitarian systems and now of the developing areas, have party structures been recognized as powerful agents for political socialization. The political party is one of the few social structures even potentially capable of involving large numbers of people in political action on a sustained and controlled basis. Involvement may encom-

[20] Downs, *op. cit.*

pass both communication and participation. Such political stimulation either reinforces existing political attitudes and beliefs, or inculcates new ones.

The preceding statements imply a certain relationship between attitudes and actions: that while actions stem from various sorts of beliefs, so also do actions shape beliefs. Where an individual must engage in activities which are in conflict with his beliefs, a considerable strain is created. A stress is produced towards reduction of the conflict.[21] Thus, a white segregationist in the southern United States who obeys school desegregation laws (either because he places a higher value on law and order, or because he has no physical alternative than compliance) may encounter a severe internal conflict between the knowledge of his action and his segregationist beliefs. Unless additional aggravating circumstances are present, the consequence is usually a reduction of the conflict by a lessening of intensity of the unpracticed belief. This force towards internal consistency means that any large-scale continuous participation in politics must affect beliefs about politics — must initiate a degree of political socialization. The influence over attitudes may be an unintentional side effect of political actions, or it may be a carefully controlled effort to break down traditional orientations and to inculcate new ones.

We may distinguish, then, between two kinds of political socialization performed by political parties. The first is a reinforcement of the existing political culture, providing continuity in performance. The second is the initiation of significant change in existing political-culture patterns. Although the phenomenon of reinforcement does not seem to have been subjected to extensive comparative analysis, even a superficial look generates several interesting questions. In the first place, the reinforcement of existing political culture may be either functional or dysfunctional for the political system. In a nation like France the party structure reflects and sometimes reinforces the fragmented political culture. The parties have often controlled

[21] See Leon Festinger, *A Theory of Cognitive Dissonance* (Stanford: Stanford University Press, 1957); and M. J. Rosenberg *et al., Attitude Organization and Change* (New Haven: Yale University Press, 1960).

newspapers; they benefit from traditional family attitudes towards them; and they provide rather comprehensive organizational contacts, at least in the case of the Communists, the socialist Left (to a lesser degree), and the Catholic political movements on the right. The individual may be exposed to few of the kinds of "cross-pressures" that moderate his rigid political attitudes.[22] Thus the fragmentation of political culture is sustained as diverging political attitudes tend to be reinforced by party activities. In a nation such as the United States, on the other hand, the two-party structure cuts across particularistic regional and class lines. The parties draw upon long-established and accepted political symbols — recognized by both parties — which reinforce the underlying national agreement on the "rules of the political game." Unfortunately, many of the parties appearing in nations with strong traditional and ethnic subcultures seem to be reinforcing divisive particularism. This seems to be the trend among the Indian opposition parties at all levels, and constitutes a justification often given for one-party systems.

The party activities, at least in the American and British context, also can provide a kind of reinforcement which helps to resolve one of the standing problems in a democratic polity: how to maintain a responsive polity and yet delegate enough power to the central government to make possible effective performance. One solution in a democracy is limited political activity on the part of most citizens sustained together with a high degree of awareness of the potential for active participation.[23] This protects the responsiveness of the system without subjecting the polity to the intense stresses and strains of a continuous, full-citizen involvement in the political process. The retention of political awareness is critical, however, and it is in this endeavor that the party structures assist in main-

[22] American voting studies have shed considerable light on this phenomenon. Some of the studies are noted and the analysis extended with some excellent survey data in Campbell, Converse, Miller, and Stokes, *op. cit.*, pp. 80–88.

[23] For a more complete discussion of this problem see Gabriel A. Almond and Sidney Verba, *The Civic Culture* (Princeton: Princeton University Press, 1963), Chap. 15.

taining the balance. Unless the particular interests of the individual are at stake, he does not have to engage in extensive and continuous articulation of his demands. The party assures him that his general interests will be safeguarded with minimal personal involvement. Yet a steady level of party activities, culminating in the electoral process every few years, keeps the citizen in constant contact with the polity, ready to participate actively if the need should arise. Not only is the vehicle of participation potentially at hand, but through voting and other political actions the orientation to activity has been socialized and reinforced.

A more dramatic, though not necessarily more important, example of the role of political parties in the socialization process is to be found where the parties are engaged in the initiation or maintenance of new patterns of political culture. Such party activities may be present, of course, in Western societies. It is clear that the parties of the political Left, the Socialists and Communists, had enormous influence on the patterns of political culture which emerged in nineteenth-century Europe. One may observe the effect of the Fascist and Communist parties in Europe during the Depression, when their tight, monolithic organizations and powerful political symbols provided political coherence and direction for millions in a time of distress and social disintegration.

As these examples suggest, when socio-economic conditions are in a period of flux and disruption, parties which can offer political solutions discontinuous with long-standing cultural patterns are in a favorable position to woo adherents. Moreover, it is because historical patterns of thinking have been shaken or dislodged by new conditions that party elites are able to introduce, and often to reinforce through modes of participation, new expectations and norms of political behavior. This situation appears today in many of the so-called underdeveloped or transitional areas of the world. Under conditions of radical, social, economic, and political change — extending from one end of the society to the other — the role of political parties in socialization is of great importance.

The degree to which elites in the underdeveloped areas rely

upon the political party to control and order the process of political change, particularly to provide new standards of legitimacy and orderly patterns of mobilized political participation, has been noted by almost all students of the African and Asian nations. David Apter, for example, describes the phenomenon as follows:

> Political movements are directly akin to religious ones. They allow people to feel purified and personally better organized, by virtue of membership. And membership itself is an informal matter. It is a matter of feelings more than party cards, loyalty rather than organization. And, because of the weak articulation of the movement, it tends to be very fragile, breaking up when some of its primary objectives have been accomplished. It is in the transformation of the movement into a party, whether of representation or solidarity, which quite often determines the constitutional future of a country and the nature of its polity; because in the institutionalization of loyalty and the institutionalization of authority, political leaders in a movement seek to transform the restless sweep of public energy, liberated by and flooding through the political sector of social life, into something more stable and permanent, so that organized beliefs about authority and government are defined and made to stick.[24]

Obviously, the ways in which political parties affect the development of political culture depend upon a large number of factors, including the nature of the traditional political orientations, the general conditions and issues of salience in the national environment, and the performance of other agencies of socialization, particularly the mass media and schools. But several general ways in which party activities may influence political socialization can be mentioned here.

Political party activity may shape political culture in each of three dimensions: the cognitive, the affective, and evaluative. Even with increasingly penetrative mass media, the informal personal lines of communication engendered by party activity can be important sources of information — accurate or otherwise — about national issues and problems, political elites and

[24] David Apter, *The Politics of Modernization* (Chicago: University of Chicago Press, 1965), Chap. 6.

their conduct, channels of grievance and redress, and the means by which the individual may relate actively to his polity. Through a local party organization the peasant or worker may discover the procedures of applying for unemployment benefits or for free medical care. He may encounter people, ideas, and experiences far beyond the customary range of his daily life. Participation in party activities, moreover, can increase the sense of loyalty and identification between elites and followers; thus we see the affective dimension. The symbols of "party" and "leader" are capable of imposing a coherence and an order upon the frightening newness and instability of a transitional society. They may satisfy underlying emotional needs for security and identification engendered by the breakup of traditional society.[25]

Finally, in addition to its impact on cognitive and affective dimensions of political culture, the party can become a factor in determining evaluative orientations. Parties can supply both goals and criteria against which to measure existing political and economic realities. Awareness of standards in other societies — democracy in Britain, or economic development in the Soviet Union — may establish new yardsticks for judging the polity at hand. Also fundamental is the awakening of expectations of change itself. In a traditional society relatively stable patterns of political, social, and economic behavior prevail over long periods. Natural and economic disasters may occur, but these are seen as the hand of fate and far beyond any human control, except possibly through the always-uncertain placation of the gods. For the members of such a system, the idea that life may be substantially changed for the better through human effort is momentous. Party activities may introduce this idea or reinforce it.

In addition to stimulating awareness about other modes of existence, the party may present a specific ideology with goals for the future and a program for achieving them. Such an ideology defines the proper behavior of mass and elite alike,

[25] See, for example, Lucian Pye's account of the Westernized elites in Burma in *Politics, Personality, and Nation Building* (New Haven: Yale University Press, 1962).

setting forth particular criteria for political legitimacy and prescribing political tactics. Adherents to the ideology are rewarded by a sense of order, a sense of identity, and a respite from the emotional confusion brought about by change. Fulfilling such needs can be a powerful factor in mobilizing support for a regime and a political system. Thus, the ideological party supplies a complete scale of evaluation for the political culture.

The party may also play an important role in harnessing charisma as a foundation for stable authority. In times of stress an individual leader may arise who exerts enormous influence over men's behavior, providing a model for a new way of life or touching deep-seated psychological needs in a way which provokes widespread response. An individual possessing these extraordinary personal qualities can transform social behavior and attitudes. But unless he can tie the attitudes and goals he espouses to more stable and enduring institutions, they are unlikely to long outlive his own existence.

> Only parties can organize enthusiasm on the basis of a solidarity of interests with citizens outside the government. The routinization of charisma in political parties becomes possible as the leader makes consistent use of that organization, speaks in its name, and lends it his mantle.[26]

If the party can assume the aura of legitimacy surrounding the charismatic leader, it can guide and direct support during his life, and preserve and promulgate his ideas after his death.

The dominating mass political parties in the developing areas are frequently oriented around a political ideology and a charismatic leader. This orientation can make them agencies second to none for the controlled transformation of a political way of life. In India, Egypt, Ghana, Guinea, Tanzania, and on across the roster of the new nations, political parties conducting political socialization activities have been abundantly in evidence.

[26] Manfred Halpern, *The Politics of Social Change in Middle East and North Africa* (Princeton: Princeton University Press, 1963), p. 285. And see Weber, *op. cit.*, pp. 245–252.

The effectiveness with which political parties carry on social-ization activities depends upon the internal characteristics of the party as well as on conditions of the political and social environment. The style of adherence to the party subculture, the nature of the party organization, the solidarity of party leaders, and other factors could be considered at this juncture. By the same token, the party is not only an "independent" variable in the process of development and change. Parties have their own dynamics of development and will be greatly shaped by the culture in which they must operate. But an examination of these factors and a more detailed considera-tion of the whole fascinating question of parties and political change is a matter beyond the scope of this treatment.

CHAPTER VI

Governmental Functions and Structures

IN THE LONG TRADITION of political theory, the problem of differentiating and classifying governmental functions has been a central one. Aristotle, Polybius, Cicero, Hobbes, Locke, Montesquieu, the writers of the *Federalist Papers,* and many others have all treated this problem, though in somewhat different terms. The classic theory of separation of powers, which emerged out of this tradition, divides the governmental process into three functions: legislative, executive, and judicial.

In the last decades there has been a rather thoroughgoing critique of this separation-of-powers doctrine. A generation of students of political parties, pressure groups, and the media of mass communication found this threefold classification inadequate but still sought to accommodate their findings within this theoretical framework. Thus they spoke of pressure groups as a "third chamber of the legislature," and of the press as "the Fourth Branch of Government." Chapter IV and V treating the functions of interest articulation and aggregation and Chapter VII on communication and politics represent efforts at drawing the implications of this research for the theory of political functions. We employ a sixfold classification of conversion functions rather than a threefold one. A second casualty was the tendency to identify structure with function. While the version of separation-of-powers theory advocated in the *Fed-*

eralist Papers specifically provided for some mingling of "powers," this was done in "checks and balances" terms. The justification for these checks and balances was to preserve the relationship between the legislature and rule making, the executive and rule application, and the courts and rule adjudication. A generation of students of the courts, Congress, and the executive have established a division of labor quite different from this classic separation of powers–checks and balances doctrine. They pointed to the judiciary as a principal lawmaker and law-vetoer, to the executive and bureaucracy as the principal source of rules, and to the legislature as an aggregator of interests, as a legitimator of rules, and not much of a rulemaker at all.

We take this into account in our conception of the multifunctionality of all political structures. The relation of function to structure in particular political systems is something that has to be determined by empirical observation. It is possible, however, to make a few general points about the interdependence of the functions of rule making, application, and adjudication before we turn to an analysis of specific governmental functions and structures.

If human beings are to live in close proximity to one another, certain rules imposing obligations and limiting conflict are inevitably needed. In the most primitive societies such primary rules may be found regulating sex relationships, limiting the use of violence, and imposing obligations of leadership and obedience in the hunt in order that the community may survive. These rules are given by custom and tradition and not subject to regularized procedures of change or adaptation.

But even in such societies the reliance upon primary rules alone, backed only by a common willingness to obey and enforce them, would be inefficient and uncertain. A set of secondary rules is needed to provide a regularized basis for the recognition of the primary rules, to determine whether they have been violated, and to enforce them in cases of disobedience.

The distinction between primary and secondary rules is suggested by L. A. Hart. Primary rules require that human beings perform certain actions or abstain from certain actions, whether they wish to or not — primary rules impose duties or prohibitions. Secondary rules provide for operations leading to the creation or variation of these restraints and obligations — they confer authority to initiate, change, enforce, or adjudicate them. A constitution, if it has meaning in a system, is largely such a set of secondary rules.[1] Some such secondary set of rules exists which designates certain roles as having the authority to perform these functions. Thus, certain roles have the responsibility for maintaining the tribal traditions and seeing that they are passed from generation to generation. Or, a shaman or chief may have the authority to decide that a rule has been violated and to mete out punishment.

The existence of such a set of secondary rules designating certain structures as having authority to initiate, to discover, to apply, or to judge the violation of the primary rules of the society characterizes all political systems. And although the authority to initiate primary rules on a regular basis may be late in developing, it is typical of human societies that institutionalized ways of resolving disputes, such as the feud and the duel, appear very early in history. These rule-application and rule-adjudication processes are not to be confused with random outbursts of violence; they are recurring social processes with well-understood rules and modes of enforcement. As such, they constitute the most primitive political structures, undifferentiated, diffuse, and intermittent, but yet invoking the ultimate sanctions of the society.

The significance which rules have for the system is determined in large measure by the ways in which they are implemented. Laws on the statute books mean nothing if they are not enforced, and the most grandiose, authoritative plans for social reorganization and change can be rendered meaningless if the resources to carry them out are not available and effectively utilized. If, indeed, those charged with applying the rules consistently refuse to do so, or if they warp the form of application, then the application structures may be said to

---

[1] L. A. Hart, *The Concept of Law* (London: Oxford University Press, 1961), Chap. 5.

have taken over the rule-making function to some degree. However, this possibility does not mean that rule application has become rule making. Rather, such a shift means that the basic "rules of the game," the secondary rules allocating authority to utilize primary rules in various ways, have been altered. Hart, in spelling out this distinction, uses a pure game analogy:

> Up to a certain point, the fact that some rulings given by a scorer are plainly wrong is not inconsistent with the game continuing: they count as much as rulings which are obviously correct; but there is a limit to the extent to which tolerance of incorrect decisions is compatible with the continued existence of the same game, and this has an important legal analogue. The fact that isolated or exceptional official aberrations are tolerated does not mean that the game of cricket or baseball is no longer being played. On the other hand, if these aberrations are frequent, or if the scorer repudiates the scoring rule, there must come a point when either the players no longer accept the scorer's aberrant rulings or, if they do, the game has changed. It is no longer cricket or baseball but "scorer's discretion"; for it is a defining feature of these other games that, in general, their results should be assessed in the way demanded by the plain meaning of the rule, whatever latitude its open texture may leave to the scorer. In some imaginable condition we should say in truth the game being played was "scorer's discretion" but the fact that in all games the scorer's rulings are final does not mean that that is what all games are.[2]

Hart's analogy relates most directly to what we should call rule adjudication. (He is, in fact, rejecting the statement that the law is always just "what the courts say that it is.") But the point applies to both rule application and rule adjudication. They may be distinguished from the function of rule making in just this fashion; when bureaucracies or courts take it upon themselves to change the rules of the game, as, for example, the Supreme Court did in 1954 with regard to race relations, they have become engaged in rule making. Since the nature of rule making is so fundamental a component of political systems and

2 *Ibid.,* p. 141.

processes, it is crucial that in comparative analysis we discern which structures actually make the rules.

THE RULE-MAKING FUNCTION

We refer to "rule making" rather than "legislation" for the simple reason that the term "legislation" seems to connote some specialized structure and explicit process, whereas in many political systems the rule-making function is a diffuse process, difficult to untangle and specify.

If we look at primitive and traditional political systems, we can distinguish rule-enforcement and rule-adjudication processes from other social interactions even in the very simplest ones. It is more difficult to explicate the processes which formulate the general political rules themselves. It is the very essence of traditionality that rule making be problematic and extraordinary. The codes of law of ancient times were imputed to great lawgivers such as Hammurabi, Moses, or Solon, who either codified the traditional rules — in other words, "declared" them — or transmitted laws charismatically as intermediaries for deities or as men of extraordinary virtue and wisdom. The making of laws was viewed as an extraordinary event.

The politics of ancient Israel is illustrative of the process. As the Hebrew kingdoms deviated from the desert tradition with the adoption of court life, with the pursuit of policies of expansion and military defense, and with the development of secular diplomacy, the prophets declared and reaffirmed the Sinaitic tradition and rejected the rules and practices of the royal courts and priesthood. The royal courts, the priesthood, the prophets, and the persisting tribal and clan leaderships were the chief structures engaged in the political, or rule-making, process in ancient Israel.

There was no fully legitimate right to make new general rules. The legitimate rules were all given in the tradition and were viewed as the product of revelation. According to Biblical scholars, the book of Deuteronomy, which contains a codification of Hebrew law, was actually written in the later period of the Kingdom of Judah. However, this codification was legitimated by alleging that this "book of the law" written by Moses had been discovered by the priests when they were restoring the temple under the reign of King Josiah. In other words, they did not make the law; they rediscovered it. After the fall of the Kingdom of Judah, the rabbis and scribes took over the task of studying and declaring the law. New legislation was treated as sublegislation, as "building a fence around the law." As this process became entrenched, the role of prophet or charismatic legislator became more suspect. The words of Jesus of Nazareth, "It is written . . . but I say unto you . . ." represent the prototype of charismatic appeal. It was an appeal bitterly opposed by the more traditional codifiers of the law.

The more gradual processes of declaration and administration of the rules may, of course, lead to changes as substantial as those induced by the charismatic. Skinner tells the story of the enforcement of the inheritance law among the Mossi of the Upper Volta in Africa. Under the Mossi law, property was to be distributed among sons and other male relatives. The practice, however, had developed of including the daughters in such legacies, particularly if the father had been wealthy. In the specific case referred to, a daughter had been excluded, and the case was brought to the district chief for adjudication. The district chief applied the more liberal practice, rather than the more restrictive rule. Over time a series of such adjudications of inheritance law and practice would result in substitution of the practice for the original law.[3]

Thus, rule making in traditional and primitive political systems tends to be either a charismatic process or a slow, incremental process of the accumulation of tradition, which is in part a derivative of the day-to-day rule enforcements and rule adjudications of the systems. It is possible for us to distinguish the rule-making function in such political systems and to describe the kinds of structures which engage in it. Members of most traditional or primitive societies, on the other hand, would not admit the legitimacy of a rule-making function as we understand it. They might acknowledge the legitimacy of

[3] F. P. Skinner, *The Mossi of the Upper Volta* (Stanford: Stanford University Press, 1964), pp. 84 ff.

a prophetic representation of the will of the deity, or of a magical communication with extranatural powers, but they would not acknowledge the legitimacy of a process whereby new rules are made by secular political institutions.

It is quite clear, however, that while the differentiation and full legitimation of the rule-making function is a relatively recent development, rule-making processes are present in some form in all political systems. One of the tasks of comparative political analysis is to characterize this rule-making function even though it may be a rudimentary process, a charismatic process, or a derivative of the other governmental functions of rule application and adjudication.

THE EMERGENCE OF DIFFERENTIATED
RULE-MAKING STRUCTURES

In the simpler types of intermittent political systems, the structures or institutions which are involved in the making of rules may be the group of adult males in the band or village, or the lineage elders intermittently meeting as a council, or specialized roles such as those of the village head or the magical leader. These groups and individuals are the codifiers and repositories of the political system's traditions, which they bring to bear on problems arising out of the activities of the community or out of its interactions with other communities. Each action involves bringing out of memory the appropriate set of rules, and each time such rules are invoked in specific contexts, something may be added and something left out so that the rules are adapted and changed.

Schapera in his discussion of the activities of tribal governments argues that in all tribes the chief has the power to make laws. But then he goes on to say that this is a rarely exercised prerogative and that he finds only a few examples of lawmaking among the Bantu. Most new legislation seems to have been made through executive or judicial action.[4]

In the case of patrimonial kingdoms, the rule-making structures may consist of political rulers such as kings, councils of

[4] I. Schapera, *Government and Politics in Tribal Societies* (London: Watts, 1956), pp. 67 ff.; Cf. Adamson Hoebel, *The Law of Primitive Man* (Cambridge: Harvard University Press, 1954), p. 285.

officials, and individual officials, who either declare what the law is or adapt and modify it as they confront specific cases. In these political systems there may also be prophets and law-givers active primarily in times of conflict and threat, who may reaffirm traditional rules or transmit new rules attributed to extranatural forces.

In his treatment of the historical bureaucratic empires, Eisenstadt uses the pursuit of autonomous goals on the part of the rulers as one of the criteria defining these systems. In this larger scale, differentiated political system, which Eisenstadt [5] views as transitional to modern political systems, one begins to get a differentiated rule-making function. Similarly, in some of the ancient and medieval city-states, there was an explicit legislative process lodged in a legislative body or bodies. In Athens the Assembly annually reconsidered the statutes, reenacting those it favored and rescinding those it opposed.

In thirteenth- and fourteenth-century England, the more important rules were declared by the king in an assembly of bishops and barons called the Magnum Concilium. In addition to these extraordinary council meetings, the king had in constant session a permanent council made up of his chief officials, to whom he looked for advice and counsel on the daily decisions of government.[6]

The rule-making function in Britain as such did not become fully differentiated until the fifteenth and sixteenth centuries.[7] The Magna Carta represented an effort on the part of the nobility to maintain the validity of the ancient feudal freedoms and customs against the efforts of King John to develop new powers of taxation and regulation. It was justified as a declaration of the law, rather than an enactment.

As we consider the interaction between kings and parliaments in Britain in the course of the thirteenth, fourteenth, and fifteenth centuries, we observe the gradual differentiation

[5] S. N. Eisenstadt, *The Political Systems of Empires* (New York: The Free Press of Glencoe, 1962).

[6] F. W. Maitland, *The Constitutional History of England* (Cambridge: Cambridge University Press, 1963), pp. 90 ff.

[7] See, *inter al.*, Carl J. Friedrich, *Constitutional Government and Democracy* (Boston: Ginn & Company, 1950).

of a general rule-making function. The process began as a series of bargains in which the king acquired the right to impose specific tax measures in exchange for the redress of specific grievances. In this centuries-long interplay of demand and response, the power of Parliament to enact statutes slowly became legitimate, an appropriate function to be performed by "the king in Parliament." Similar struggles over the process of differentiation of a rule-making function are to be observed in the history of continental European countries such as France and Prussia, although the process and the institutional results differed substantially from the British pattern.

One of the most important turning points in the development of political systems was the shift from traditional to constitutional restraints on political action. It is the nature of traditionalism to resist the very idea of rule making, since this grants legitimacy to the "changing of the rules." As a consequence, one of the most important mechanisms of change in political structure and in public policy in traditional systems is the charismatic mechanism. Constitutionalism, on the other hand, represents a secularization of the limits on political action and political power. Constitutionalism accepts the legitimacy of the rule-making function as a secular process, but it sets legal limits to it. That is to say, rules must be made in certain ways and by specific institutions and within certain kinds of limitation. Their enforcement and adjudication is also subject to limits.[8]

---

[8] It is possible to combine the theoretical insights of Eisenstadt and Friedrich into a hypothesis about stages of political development. Eisenstadt treats the bureaucratic empire as a kind of traditional stage from traditional to modern political systems. The political system is modernizing when it develops a ruling elite which formulates goals that are separate from those of the constituent feudal or patrimonial components, and when these ruling elites develop instrumentalities (bureaucracies) which enable them to regulate the society and to mobilize human and material resources in the pursuit of these autonomous policies and goals. The political process in Eisenstadt's bureaucratic empire was a struggle between what he calls the "strata" (earlier tribal and status elites) and the central elites and their bureaucracies. Centralization, differentiation and secularization were primary issues in the struggle: Was it legitimate for a king to resort to new modes and objects of taxation, to mobilize

The problem of distinguishing the rule-making function in all political systems arises from the fact that the very idea of rule making as an everyday event is modern (with the exception of those city-states which have much in common with modern political systems, and some of the bureaucratic empires which Eisenstadt views as transitional). It presupposes a legitimation of change by means of secular institutions and processes which are in conflict with the concept of tradition.

RULE-MAKING STRUCTURES

The long history of the emergence of the British Parliament is one of struggle over the location of the rule-making power and over questions having to do with which elements in the society ought to be represented in the rule-making process. The struggle between king, lords, and commons continued until the eighteenth century, when the statutory power of the houses of Parliament was formally legitimated and established. But if the struggle was settled formally, it continued politically as the king and powerful aristocrats sought to control the House of Commons. In the nineteenth century the center of gravity shifted to the House of Commons, and the contemporary pattern of rule making by cabinet and House of Commons appeared.

Throughout this long history, however, the houses of Parliament, with rare though important exceptions, tended to be

---

the labor of his people, or to regulate their conduct and behavior in novel ways? Eisenstadt also observes a more modern form of political struggle in the conflict over goals and policies that arise between the rulers of bureaucratic empires and the various components of their civil and military bureaucracies. Friedrich names this stage of development "centralization," and he argues that in the development of European political systems the centralization stage preceded what he refers to as the "constitutional stage." In the constitutional stage the political struggle turns on the issue of the limits on the power to make and enforce rules, a power which has now been centralized in the ruler and his bureaucracy.

Actually what Eisenstadt and Friedrich locate in the larger scale, more centralized political systems is to be encountered in a rudimentary form even in the simpler patrimonial systems. Here, too, there is a constant struggle between the central rulership and officialdom and the constituent tribal, village, or status components. A rudimentary process of conflict over policy and rule making is also present within the officialdom of patrimonial systems.

legitimators and modifiers of general rules rather than rule makers or rule initiators. In the early period the initiation and formulation of statutes came from the king and his officials, and these were modified and authorized in the houses of Parliament. In the later period the initiation and formulation of general rules came from the upper levels of the bureaucracy, from the ministers, and from the cabinet. Thus, in a sense, the bodies which we think of as being the specialized legislative structures have never been the rule makers in the full sense of that term. American legislative bodies have been more active rule makers than has the British Parliament, but even in the United States the trend has been toward the initiation and formulation of general rules by the political executives — presidents, governors, and administrative officials — with the legislative bodies acting predominantly as modifiers and as legitimators of rules initiated elsewhere.

The difference in this respect between modern democratic systems and totalitarian ones, though of very great importance indeed, is a difference in degree. The rules in Communist countries are formulated and initiated by political executive agencies such as party presidiums, central committees, party secretariats, and the upper levels of the governmental bureaucracy, with the elected legislative chambers serving as legitimating and declaring agencies. In democratic systems, while the political executive and the bureaucracy are the main sources of the rules, there is a real and often exercised power of the legislative bodies to reject legislation proposed to them, and to modify it substantially as well as to legitimate it.

The political executive agencies themselves must not, of course, be viewed as necessarily unified and hierarchical structures. When we refer to *the* rule makers or to *the* decision-making structures, we are using only a kind of analytical shorthand. In most political systems, but particularly in modern democratic ones, the performance of rule making, like that of articulation and aggregation, will be dispersed and delegated, focusing perhaps around the role of the chief executive but not residing in it. For various reasons some executive agencies may be able to serve as autonomous participants in the rule-making process, initiating and affecting various component rules. Under the leadership of a strong and capable Cabinet officer, for example, an agency in the American executive branch may be able to use congressional connections, administrative discretion and competence, and the technique of ignoring undesirable presidential requests, to attain a highly autonomous position. Richard Fenno has provided us with a fascinating account of the "political fiefdom" established by Jesse Jones, as the head of Roosevelt's Reconstruction Finance Corporation. Within limits Jones was able to ignore certain of Roosevelt's proposals, to overcome financial cuts which the Bureau of the Budget attempted to impose over the RFC, and generally to operate the RFC as an independent force in its own area of competence.[9] Such tendencies are not uncommon in the most rigidly controlled of political systems, though they may not come to light until a political coup or a power struggle suddenly shifts the formal as well as informal center of rule making.

The degree of centralization of the structures involved in rule making is a matter for empirical investigation. There may well be considerable variation from issue area to issue area. The central decisions and rules made in a foreign policy crisis, such as the Cuban missile confrontation, may be largely the product of a single structure (such as the President and his immediate subordinates). In other issue areas, such as tax legislation, welfare, tariff policy, or budget expenditures, a wide range of rather autonomous rule-making structures may be involved. Faced with such an intricate problem as budget formation, the President and his subordinates can at best engage in selective decision making in a few areas or in shaping broad outlines. Such an extremely important but complex problem may be resolved largely through a process of decentralized accommodation, rather than through rational and systematic analysis of alternative courses of action by a single rule maker. This point becomes clear in Wildavsky's description of the American budgetary process:

[9] Richard F. Fenno, Jr., *The President's Cabinet* (Cambridge: Harvard University Press, 1959), pp. 234–247.

Since there is no one group of men who can necessarily impose their preferences upon others within the American political system, special coalitions are formed to support or oppose specific policies. Support is sought in this system of fragmented power at numerous centers of influence — congressional committees, the congressional leadership, the President, the Budget Bureau, interdepartmental committees, departments, bureaus, private groups, and so on. Nowhere does a single authority have power to determine what is going to be in the budget.[10]

Thus, the problem of identifying the rule-making structures in political systems is one of specifying the whole set of agencies and institutions involved in the process, determining the kind of things they do, the way they do them, and how they interact to produce general rules. When we have worked out this part of the puzzle, we can relate it to the processes and agencies of interest articulation, aggregation, and communication, which precede it; and to the processes of rule application and adjudication, which follow it. This whole system of interdependent conversion structures and processes can in turn be related to the political socialization and recruitment processes, which give the system its character or propensities; and it can also be related to the kind and level of performance of the political system in its domestic and international environments, in other words, to its capabilities.[11]

PATTERNS OF RULE MAKING

As we have seen in Wildavsky's description of the American budgetary process, various more or less autonomous structures may have complex interrelations in rule making. If, for various reasons, the formal or tacit consent of each is required to make

[10] Aaron Wildavsky, "Political Implications of Budgetary Reform," in Francis E. Rourke (ed.), *Bureaucratic Power in National Politics* (Boston: Little, Brown and Company, 1965), p. 143. Also see Wildavsky, *The Politics of the Budgetary Process* (Boston: Little, Brown and Company, 1964).

[11] For example, for a discussion of the implications of centralized "synoptic" decision-making patterns as opposed to those of "partisan mutual adjustment," see David Braybrooke and Charles E. Lindblom, *Strategy of Decision* (New York: The Free Press of Glencoe, 1963); and Charles E. Lindblom, *The Intelligence of Democracy* (New York: The Free Press of Glencoe, 1965).

the policy in a given issue area, then different forms of bargaining and different patterns of accommodation and interaction may emerge. In his study of New Haven city politics, for example, Robert Dahl suggested five alternative patterns of arriving at policy agreement: (1) covert integration "by Economic Notables"; (2) an executive-centered "grand coalition of coalitions"; (3) a coalition of chieftains; (4) independent sovereignties with spheres of influence; and (5) rival sovereignties fighting it out. And in fact Dahl found four of these five patterns existing in various policy areas at various time periods in recent years in New Haven.[12] While clearly a wider range of patterns would be needed to analyze rule-making relationships among diverse national structures, Dahl suggests that in the American case a pattern of accommodation roughly corresponding to the "coalition of chieftains" may be found within Congress, while much general rule making (at least under the Roosevelt and Truman administrations) follows the "executive-centered 'grand coalition of coalitions.' "[13] By the same token, although one would have to distinguish different issue areas with great care, it could be said that the British pattern corresponds closely to pattern 2, and that the Italian and the French Fourth Republic patterns are akin to types 3, 4, and 5. (The instability of these systems accounts in part for the ambiguity.)

Of course, in describing and explaining the patterns of rule making in a society, we must consider the importance of individual leadership and of the cultural environment. As in the consideration of the performance of the other political functions, the discussion of the emergence and functioning of particular political structures involves the roles of individuals who may utilize their skills, resources, and energy to shape the direction of political events. It is all too easy to forget the relative fluidity and impermanence of many political structures and performance patterns, and their dependence upon the particular coherence and direction given by the leadership of a

[12] Robert A. Dahl, *Who Governs?* (New Haven: Yale University Press, 1961), pp. 184–189 ff.
[13] *Ibid.*, pp. 186–187.

single individual. Moreover, the patterns of political culture
in the society, or among the leaders in particular, may shape
and perhaps limit the sorts of rules and decisions which are
made. A traditional or ideologically-oriented set of attitudes
will tend to close off certain alternatives of political decision
making. Secularization, on the other hand, will increase the
range of means available to solve political problems and to
promote the rational and pragmatic evaluation of these means.
But even in a highly secularized system, an accepted pattern of
policy making tends to acquire considerable inertia, to become
traditional in its own right, so to speak. It has been suggested
that the American system took at least half a decade to break
free of traditional patterns of policy making and to confront
the full range of alternatives for coping with the depression of
the '30's.[14]

THE RULE-APPLICATION FUNCTION

THE EMERGENCE OF DIFFERENTIATED
RULE-APPLICATION STRUCTURES

The presence of differentiated and well-developed structures
for rule application greatly expands the capability of a political system to manipulate its environment. As a political system
expands in size, or faces an increasingly complex environment
or a widening range of tasks, the pressures to develop specialized rule-application structures are inexorable. The sheer volume of rules to be enforced, resources to be gathered, and
information to be processed and transmitted requires the rule-
making structure, be it monarch, legislature, or common assembly, to seek assistance in application. It becomes imperative
that the system develop capabilities to meet new goals or pressures; effective rule application is a necessary prerequisite to
such development.

One must return, in fact, to very small, primitive, or decentralized systems to find examples of undifferentiated rule-application roles. In the segmentary-lineage system of the Nuer,

14 David Easton, *A Systems Analysis of Political Life* (New York: John
Wiley & Sons, Inc., 1965), p. 161, and in general see the discussion on pp.
454 ff. on "Decision Rules."

there are almost no specialized political roles. Traditional customs regulate conflict, determining, for example, the suitable kinds of weapons and extent of the bodily injury appropriate in duels within the lineage group. These conventions are enforced by bystanders, who may separate the combatants when the proprieties have been exceeded, or by the elders of a particular group, who may intervene in a duel. Yet, even in the Nuer, there is a point at which a feud or dispute may threaten the cohesion of the community and recourse may be had to a specialized role, the "leopard skin chief," to mediate the argument. He not only adjudicates the dispute by determining whether a custom has been violated and the appropriate form of redress, but may also threaten to curse the disputing parties if they do not abide by his decision. In a society where there is a lively belief in the supernatural, the threat of a traditional curse may verge on authoritative compulsion or coercion. To this extent the leopard skin chief constitutes a specialized application and adjudication role.[15]

In more developed traditional societies, such as the Ouagadougou, a nineteenth-century African kingdom in the Upper Volta region, an elaborate rule-application structure may emerge. The Ouagadougou kingdom was divided into provinces, the provinces into districts, the districts into villages, and the villages into compounds where the extended families lived. Each level was subject ultimately to the power of the king and his chief ministers. The kingdom collected a variety of taxes and requisitioned a substantial quota of personal services. The lower echelons functioned under the order of the higher ones, although the communication process was so intermittent that these lines of control often became tenuous. Without this elaborate and differentiated rule-application structure, the Ouagadougou kingdom, uniting about a million persons residing in an area of some twenty to thirty thousand square miles, could hardly have managed to function as a single political system.[16]

Needless to say, not all the differentiated rule-application

---

[15] See Lucy Mair, *Primitive Government* (Baltimore: Penguin Books, Inc., 1962), pp. 35 ff.

[16] Skinner, *op. cit.*, pp. 78 ff.

structures which can be found in primitive and modern political systems operate with the same style and level of effectiveness. They may differ in complexity, in hierarchical structure, in degree of autonomy, and in impartiality of rule enforcement. For example, it is often claimed that India has had an important advantage over other transitional nations in initiating programs of development because of the legacy of the British civil service. The relatively high degree of administrative capability provided by such an organization provides an important boost in the system's efforts to control its environment.

It can, in fact, be argued that in most modern systems the bureaucracies — the structures charged with rule application — have come to play an almost dominant role. By their very preponderance of size and effectiveness and by virtue of the crucial position of the rule-application function, these structures come to be involved in all the process functions of the system. Let us then consider the role of bureaucratic structures in political systems as they perform first the function of rule application and then the other conversion functions.

THE BUREAUCRACY

Though all commentators stress its importance, something may still be said about bureaucracy to illuminate its significance and the reasons for its predominance. Max Weber treats "bureaucratization" as the very essence of the political modernization process.

> The decisive reason for the advance of bureaucratic organization has always been its purely technical superiority over any other form of organization. The fully developed bureaucratic mechanism compares with other organizations exactly as does the machine with the non-mechanical mode of production.[17]

Carl Friedrich tells us that "the vast bureaucratic structure of modern states with their tens of thousands of officials make

[17] Max Weber, *From Max Weber: Essays in Sociology,* ed. Hans H. Gerth and C. Wright Mills (New York: Oxford University Press, 1958), p. 214.

them the core of modern government." [18] Eisenstadt gives as one of the major criteria of his class of empires the existence of a differentiated bureaucracy.[19]

Bureaucracy, of course, is a characteristic of organizations. Hierarchy of command, differentiation of roles and functions, and written records, which are among its distinguishing features (according to Weber), may be found in churches, parties, labor unions, and baseball clubs as well as in government. In all such organizations the structural hierarchy stands beneath the top decision makers, serving their information and resource needs as well as implementing their decisions on a regularized day-to-day basis. In this book, when we speak of bureaucracies we are referring to the relatively elaborate organization through which rulers or rule makers seek to implement their decisions. In the United States, for example, the various administrative departments, the military services, the federal regulatory agencies, and similar organizations make up the federal bureaucracy.

The problem of how important bureaucracy is and why it is important, in a positive sense, has not often been directly confronted in political science. We have viewed it as "very important" or as "too important," and have discussed and analyzed different ways of subjecting it to popular control or different ways of making it more efficient or more honest. Modern political theory, whether it be democratic or Marxist-Leninist, has been preoccupied with the problem of making bureaucracies instrumental to political purposes and responsive to ideological norms. Perhaps because government and its instrumentalities emerged prior to the development of Enlightenment political theory, this theory has often been ambivalent in relation to bureaucracy. Thus, we have been more concerned in western Europe, and particularly in Britain and the United States, with speculating on how to reform and control bureaucracy than with establishing what it is. In Marxism-

[18] Carl Friedrich, *Man and His Government* (New York: McGraw-Hill, Inc., 1963), p. 464. See also Friedrich, *Constitutional Government, op. cit.,* pp. 37 ff.

[19] Eisenstadt, *op. cit.,* Chap. 2.

Leninism this ambivalence is carried to the ultimate extreme. The Communist wants to totalize governmental and bureaucratic authority in order (so his ideology claims) that he may ultimately eliminate it totally.

The Emergence of Bureaucracies. Before we try to come to grips with the place of bureaucratic structures in political systems, it may be useful to discuss varieties of officialdoms and bureaucracies and to illustrate them with some concrete cases. The simpler types of political systems are characterized by an almost total lack of officialdom. There may be a headman of a band or a village; there may be a magical leader. But these are part-time roles operating within face-to-face groups rarely exceeding more than a few hundred in number. We can, of course, view the varieties of self-help such as seizing stolen property, dueling, and feuding as examples of part-time, occasional, or intermittent administrative roles. In traditional political systems where the headman or the chief has no administrative staff, he must rely upon prestige, persuasion, or material inducement as a way of having his orders carried out or his requests fulfilled. This would appear to be the case with the headman in the Anuak village, where the young men of the village may band together to serve as the chief's retainers and to clear his fields, but where these services are supplied only as long as he is able to provide them with beer and food from his own resources.[20]

This would appear to be an even less differentiated rule-application system than the ones encountered in the Biblical patriarchates, which seem to have been the cases which Max Weber had in mind in his treatment of patriarchal authority. The household of Abraham was evidently a quite complicated one, numbering in the hundreds of members. These were either kin or servants, and we know that there was some division of function among them.[21]

Patrimonial administration is built on the model of the patriarchal household. The patrimonial ruler, like the patri-

20 Mair, *op. cit.,* pp. 71 ff.

21 Reinhard Bendix, *Max Weber: An Intellectual Portrait* (Garden City: Doubleday & Company, Inc., 1960), pp. 331 ff.

archal head, owns and controls the *patrimonium,* whether it be on the scale of a small Sudanic kingdom, or that of the whole of Pharaonic Egypt. In the relatively pure type of patrimonialism, military and civil officials are the servants of the patrimonial ruler and are supplied from his storehouses.

The preliterate Sudanic kingdoms in Africa had quite elaborate administrative staffs and hierarchies. In Ouagadougou the king's central administrative staff was controlled by a prime minister and five provincial ministers who functioned as a kind of executive-legislative council. There were in addition corps of palace guards, police, and tax officials. The district chiefs had their own administrative staffs. They were paid from fees levied against the king's revenue in cowrie shells and produce, which were transmitted from throughout the kingdom by the district chiefs to the central royal court. The kingdom of Buganda was similar to the Sudanic kingdoms in its administrative organization, except that the district chiefs were not chosen from noble clans and had no hereditary rights to office.[22] In the Sudanic kingdoms they were chosen from aristocratic clans.

These examples of patrimonial officialdoms of eighteenth- and nineteenth-century Africa may seem to be exotic, but they are not so different from the early history of the civil service in England. Tout points out that the early Norman kings carried their whole administrative organization around with them as a part of their court as they moved from royal domain to royal domain. In the twelfth and thirteenth centuries,

> the king's clerks, accountants, and administrators belonged to the same category as the king's cooks, guardians, grooms, and valets. The public service of the state then was hopelessly confused with the domestic service of the court.[23]

[22] Skinner, *op. cit.,* pp. 52 ff.; and Mair, *op. cit.,* pp. 146 ff. See also M. G. Smith, *Government in Zazzau* (London: Oxford University Press, 1960), pp. 42 ff., for an excellent characterization of the officialdom of a patrimonial kingdom in northern Nigeria during the nineteenth century.

[23] T. F. Tout, "The Emergence of a Bureaucracy," in Robert K. Merton *et al., Reader in Bureaucracy* (New York: The Free Press of Glencoe, 1952), p. 69.

The first administrative office to be distinguished from the king's court and to acquire a separate status of its own was that of the Exchequer. It acquired this separate status during the reigns of Henry I and Henry II. The second office to acquire a separate administrative status outside of the king's household was the Chancery, which developed out of the secretarial staff of the king. As the king's correspondence became more voluminous and as the chief secretary (Chancellor) became the most trusted of all the king's ministers, he became in effect the prime minister with a staff of Clerks of the Chancery. The office acquired increasing importance because succeeding chancellors moved from the simple task of writing and filing the king's correspondence to the actual drafting of royal orders and communications. This led to increasing participation in the making of the policies transmitted through these orders and communications.

> By the days of Edward III the Chancery like the Exchequer since Henry II had become a government office, self contained, self sufficing, with its own staff, traditions, and methods, and plainly separated from the court.[24]

Under the Tudor monarchy these steps toward establishing separate administrative services with increased functional specialization took on added momentum, particularly under the reign of Henry VIII and his chancellor, Thomas Cromwell. In his efforts to establish national authority, Cromwell appreciated the importance of central organization, adequately staffed and with considerable functional specialization, as a means of increasing the extractive and regulative capabilities of the government.

> The polity which Cromwell envisaged and largely achieved needed national government. Both household and national governments were of course the king's governments. But household methods meant that the king stood actively at the center of things; they demanded a great deal of personal effort from the holder of the crown and relied on his immediate entourage for the driving power behind the machinery. National bureau-

[24] *Ibid.,* p. 71.

cratic methods on the other hand, while they still depended in that age of monarchy on the existence and power of the king, were freed from the personal activity of either king or entourage.[25]

This brief discussion of the emergence of bureaucracy in British political history brings us to the general category of what S. N. Eisenstadt refers to as the "bureaucratic empires." Eisenstadt points out that in most of the bureaucratic empires which he included in his study, the emergence of a relatively autonomous bureaucracy outside the household of the ruler was usually associated with the development of autonomous goals among the bureaucratic officials. The bureaucracies sought to protect and expand their particular fields of competence against interference by the king or ruler on the one hand, and efforts on the part of the aristocratic strata on the other. He attributes the relatively effective centralization of these bureaucratic empires, their increase in magnitude, and their persistence through time, to the development of such autonomous bureaucracies and to their success in avoiding a reassimilation into the court of the king or a subordination or colonization by the aristocratic strata.[26]

Bureaucracies and Types of Political Systems. One of the most valuable analyses of types of bureaucracies has been suggested by Merle Fainsod.[27] Fainsod's classification is based upon different relationship patterns between bureaucracies and the political agencies. He suggests five patterns: (1) representative bureaucracies; (2) party-state bureaucracies; (3)military-dominated bureaucracies; (4) ruler-dominated bureaucracies; and (5) ruling bureaucracies.

The first type, representative bureaucracies, he describes as characteristic of political systems in which the ultimate political authority is determined by a competitive political process.

[25] G. R. Elton, *England Under the Tudors* (London: Methuen & Co., Ltd., 1955), pp. 180–181.

[26] Eisenstadt, *op. cit.*, pp. 160 ff.

[27] Merle Fainsod, "Bureaucracy and Modernization: The Russian and Soviet Case," in Joseph LaPalombara (ed.), *Bureaucracy and Political Development* (Princeton: Princeton University Press, 1963), pp. 233 ff.

"The initiative which representative bureaucracies exercise must be adjusted to an underlying political consensus; the dynamics of change are regulated by the competitive political process." [28] The functions of these bureaucracies are *conditioned by* the operations of the party system. Where the party system is unable to produce stable and homogeneous rulership or coalitions, the bureaucracy may acquire an especial importance. In the case of the French Fourth Republic, the fragility of party coalitions and the instability of cabinets gave special importance to the performance of the bureaucracy in rule making in different policy areas. The weakness of the party system, moreover, made it possible for powerful interest groups to colonize the bureaucracy and to utilize it for their purposes. In other words, the French bureaucracy was not able in any significant way to use its power to pursue a coherent and directed political course. In Britain, on the other hand, the existence of two relatively cohesive parties alternating in control of Parliament and cabinet has resulted in a situation in which the bureaucracy functions as a relatively effective rule-application instrument of the political agencies — cabinet, majority party, and Parliament.

Fainsod describes party-state bureaucracies as the "by-products of totalitarian regimes and other one-party-dominated political systems." [29] These types of political systems are characterized by the superimposition of a political bureaucracy upon a functionally differentiated and technically competent governmental bureaucracy. Thus, the control of the Soviet governmental bureaucracy by the Communist party is attained through the development of a substantial body of professional party officials controlled by the secretariat, which in turn is controlled by the top leadership of the party.

While this form of tight control of governmental bureaucracies by a political bureaucracy is unique to totalitarian systems, it is important to keep in mind that there are similar tendencies in democratic systems. For example, in recent decades in the development of the American political system,

[28] *Ibid.*, p. 235.
[29] *Ibid.*, p. 235.

it has been found that the only way in which the executive and legislative branches of the American government can exercise relatively effective control over the bureaucracy is through the development of their own specialized bureaucracies. The development of the White House staff in recent decades represents a situation in which the President's immediate bureaucracy, so to speak, provides an instrumentality which enables him to penetrate, control, and direct the specialized bureaucracies of the various departments. Similarly, the efforts on the part of the House of Representatives and the Senate to oversee and influence the performance of the bureaucracy are connected with the development of legislative bureaucracy in the form of the various staffs of the congressional committees and the staffs of the individual congressmen and senators. However, we should avoid pressing these comparisons too far, since there is a monocratic element in the Soviet political system which is not present in the bureaucratization of democratic political systems. In the American system the various departmental bureaucracies and the presidential and legislative staffs may and do overtly pursue different policies, and are, of course, responding to a very different set of input structures and patterns.

The party-state type of bureaucratic system grades off into political systems where there may not be a single party but rather a one-party-dominant pattern, as in the case of India. The Indian Congress party has been in office ever since the attainment of independence. There is a considerable overlap in personnel between the upper echelons of the Congress party and the upper echelons of the Indian government and administrative services. But, again, the Indian Congress party is not the disciplined, homogeneous party that the Communist party of the Soviet Union tends to be. The Congress party itself is a coalition of interest groups, and hence its control over the administrative services is less homogeneous and less centralized.

Fainsod's category of military-dominated bureaucracies describes systems in which one component of the bureaucracy — members of the officer corps — takes control over the civilian bureaucracy. This is a common pattern historically, and also in the contemporary world.[30] Fainsod characterizes these systems as being either conservative or modernizing, depending on the training and ideology of the officer corps.[31]

Ruler-dominated bureaucracies coincide with Eisenstadt's bureaucratic empires. What Fainsod has in mind here are political systems in which an autonomous ruler imposes his rule through a bureaucracy or officialdom. His final category is one in which the bureaucracy itself provides the ruling element in the political system. This would be comparable to a military-dominated bureaucracy, except that a civil bureaucratic clique possesses the authority. The examples Fainsod gives of this form of bureaucratic system are certain cases of colonial rule in which the colonial administrators in the field function with "minimum direction from a metropolitan center and with more or less absolute authority over the local inhabitants." [32]

Fainsod's classification of political systems according to the role played by the bureaucracies in them is a useful starting point for our discussion of the importance of bureaucracy. We suggested at the outset that while political theorists stress its significance and importance, we lack a good theory which can help us explain its importance.

The Significance of Bureaucracies. When we consider even the simplest political systems, it is quite clear that quantitatively most of the roles in these systems are administrative ones. But when we consider the states of the modern era, we find that bureaucracies overwhelmingly outnumber the other subsystems of the polity. In these systems bureaucrats outnumber judges and legislators on the order of more than a thousand to one. While we cannot measure significance or importance in numbers, surely the quantitative aspect is relevant to the question of importance. Not only are there vastly more bureaucratic roles than there are legislative or judicial roles, but modern bureaucratic roles, unlike legislative roles and unlike

[30] See, *inter al.*, Morris Janowitz, *The Military in the Political Development of the New Nations* (Chicago: University of Chicago Press, 1964); and John J. Johnson, *The Role of the Military in Underdeveloped Countries* (Princeton: Princeton University Press, 1962).

[31] LaPalombara, *op. cit.*, p. 236.

[32] *Ibid.*, p. 236–237.

some judicial roles, are full-time occupations and professions characterized by permanence of tenure. If we add to these facts the additional points that bureaucrats are technically proficient in particular areas of public policy, that they are in continuous contact with particular areas of public affairs, and that they are in possession of information which is essential to the making and enforcement of public policy, we begin to appreciate why political scientists quail before the task of generalizing about the importance of bureaucracy, and why they seem to be more concerned with devising ways for controlling it and for preventing it from getting out of hand.

If we wish to come to grips effectively with the question of the significance of bureaucracy in political systems, we have to ask functional system questions — we have to ask questions having to do with the things that bureaucracies do in the conversion processes of political systems. More particularly, we have to come to grips with the question of what different kinds of bureaucracies do in different kinds of political systems, and of how these different bureaucratic patterns affect the over-all characteristics of these political systems.[33]

In order to understand the peculiar role of bureaucracy, we have to start with the output side of the political system. We would like to argue the thesis that bureaucracies tend to monopolize outputs. Only bureaucrats enforce laws, policies, or decisions. There are, of course, instances in political systems where policy makers occasionally take the law into their own hands. In the Soviet Union the trial and execution of Beria is alleged to have been carried out by his colleagues in the Presidium, although it is not clear who actually fired the shot. But this is the kind of exception that proves the rule. Surely, the administration and enforcement of rules is largely a monopoly of the bureaucracy. The development of "counterbureaucracies" within party or legislature is the only effective check, given the complexity and technical nature of the activities of modern political systems. The decisions of political leaders or of judges are enforced by bureaucrats and administrators.

[33] Along these same lines see the chapters by LaPalombara, Eisenstadt, and Riggs in *ibid.*

In addition to having this monopoly of rule enforcement, bureaucracies are typically of great importance in the processes of rule making. In the modern era most legislation is of a very general kind; in order that it may be effectively enforced, administrative officials must work out regulations or regulatory codes elaborating the policy which has been adopted by the political branches of government. Usually the extent to which a general policy is carried out is dependent upon the interpretations which bureaucrats give to it, and upon the spirit and effectiveness with which they enforce it. Thus, much of the substance of policy is a matter of decision by bureaucrats, and the effectiveness of policy is the consequence of the spirit and the will of bureaucrats.[34] In addition we know that a great deal of the adjudication carried on by modern political systems is carried on not by independent courts, but by administrative agencies, whether they be organized as independent regulatory bodies or as units in regular operating departments.

But our discussion of the significance of bureaucracy is not complete by simply examining its role in the performance of what we call the governmental functions of rule making, rule adjudication, and rule enforcement. We have already pointed out that bureaucratic agencies may perform important functions as articulators and as aggregators of interests. Thus, for example, agriculture departments, labor departments, defense agencies, and welfare and education agencies may be among the most important spokesmen for interest groups in the society. Bureaucratic agencies have many resources and channels of access to make them extremely significant in interest articulation. A good example of the pressure which can be generated through bureaucratic administrative discretion in conduct of regular affairs is furnished by the tactics of Postmaster General Authur Summerfield. "He gave orders to curtail mail deliveries one day a week . . . when Congress was showing reluctance to appropriate some funds which Mr. Summerfield said were necessary to prevent deficiencies in his agency. Despite outraged cries, Congress gave Mr. Summerfield the money. After

[34] Also see the discussion of bureaucratic agencies as autonomous rule-making structures on pages 138–139 above.

all, people wanted their mail on Saturdays." [35] It has often been argued that foreign offices are the spokesmen for the demands of foreign nations. Bureaucratic agencies may also function as significant aggregators of interests, as, for example, when a department of agriculture attempts to get agreement among different agricultural pressure groups in the field of agricultural policy, or when a labor department attempts to draw together competing trade unions around some common policy or approach.

Finally, bureaucracies are of enormous importance in the performance of the communication function in political systems. Even in democratic political systems, the bureaucracy is one of the most important sources, if not the most important source, of information about public issues and politically significant events. Newspapermen and radio and television newscasters are constantly knocking at the doors of administrative officials in search of the latest information in all spheres of foreign and domestic policy. While an aggressive press in a modern democratic society has considerable leverage in forcing information out of the bureaucracy, it is quite clear that bureaucrats have some control over the amount of information which is transmitted and the way in which it is interpreted. The decisions made by political elites, whether they be executives or legislators, are also based in considerable part on the kind of information which they are able to get from administrative agencies. Similarly, interest groups, political parties, and the public are dependent on information transmitted by administrative officials.

We do not wish to overemphasize the role of bureaucracy in the conversion processes of political systems, but surely Friedrich is right when he speaks of the bureaucracy as the core of modern government, though the term he uses is suggestive rather than explanatory.

While the enormous importance of bureaucracy is suggested by our analysis of its role in the various conversion processes

[35] J. Leeper Freeman, "The Bureaucracy in Pressure Politics," in Rourke, *op. cit.*, p. 34. Freeman also provides an excellent short discussion of other forms of bureaucratic interest-articulation activity.

of modern political systems, the discussion may suggest a monster which at least in some measure is imaginary. An historical note may be in order. The bureaucratic empires described by Eisenstadt and the absolutist regimes in Europe described by Friedrich are characterized by the development of bureaucracy and its penetration into the periphery of the society. Political development subsequent to the Age of Absolutism in western Europe may be viewed in part as a process of growth of agencies intended to direct, control, or limit central bureaucracy.

For the bureaucracy to occupy a dominant position, the minimum requirement is that there be a ruling and directive group. Without such a group, bureaucracy may be involved in a range of political functions, but in an incoherent and decentralized fashion, as in the French example discussed above. Two of the types of political-bureaucratic systems described by Fainsod are ones in which the bureaucracy itself provides either a military or a civil clique as the ruling element in the political system. What Fainsod means here is that there is some group within the formal limits of the bureaucratic organization which, working through the subordinate echelons of the bureaucracy, takes on the role of central directing and policymaking agency. In the absence of a central directing and controlling agency, whether in the bureaucracy in the formal sense or outside it, there are characteristic inertial and centrifugal tendencies in bureaucratic systems as each component of the bureaucracy moves in the direction of its own goals, or comes to a halt. Internal fragmentation and conservatism is a tendency in all bureaucracies, whatever the formal hierarchy.

The Communists attempt to solve the problem of bureaucratic direction and control by imposing on top of the governmental bureaucracy a party bureaucracy under the control of the top party elite. In the American political system the problem of coordinating and directing the enormous federal bureaucratic establishment is a constant and acute one. The concern is more with making bureaucracy an effective instrument than with fearing its domination of policy formation. We have sought to solve the problem by giving the President access to an increasingly large personal administrative and advisory staff, which supplements his constitutional power to appoint and remove the top stratum of the various administrative services. Even with these corrective measures the problem of political control over American bureaucracy is a complex and difficult one, and each President solves it differently. Arthur Schlesinger, Jr., gives us a dramatic account of the efforts of President Franklin D. Roosevelt to make the American administrative system work in the fulfillment of his purposes.[36] Roosevelt seems to have solved his problem by refusing to give clear-cut delegations of power to his various administrative heads, and by encouraging competition in the recommendation of policy among his various advisers and administrators. In the British system the control and the direction of bureaucracy is solved in part by drawing the ministers in charge of the various departments from the leaders of the majority party in the House of Commons, and by imposing on top of the ministries a smaller cabinet which constitutes the chief policy-making agency of the British government.

In the absence of such a central, directing, policy-making agency, the trend toward inertia and decentralization appears to be inevitable, for in the nature of the case the bureaucratic monster is a technical-instrumental monster. The history of many of the bureaucratic empires which Eisenstadt analyzes is marked first by a movement toward effective centralization and then, as the effectiveness of the central ruling component declines, by the decline of power and energy at the center and the transformation of satrapies and provinces into independent political systems. Another pattern of decline of bureaucratic empires is in a feudal direction, as components of previously centralized political systems become transformed into relatively autonomous fiefs.

The conception of bureaucracy which we have been elaborating is one of multifunctionality. And while all political structures are multifunctional, the specialized officialdoms and bureaucracies of differentiated political systems are more multi-

---

[36] Arthur Schlesinger, Jr., *The Coming of the New Deal* (Boston: Houghton Mifflin Company, 1959), especially pp. 521 ff.

functional than almost any of the other types of structure. Bureaucracies dominate the output end of the political conversion process; they are indispensible in the rule-making and adjudication processes as well as influential in the political processes of interest articulation, aggregation, and communication. Other governmental structures, such as political executives, legislatures, and courts, must be viewed in relation to the functioning of bureaucracy. They cannot be functionally effective save through bureaucracy. Thus, political executives — whether they be kings; military or civil bureaucratic cliques; presidiums and secretariats; prime ministers, cabinets, and ministers; presidents, their staffs, and departmental heads — may be viewed as initiators of policy which may only be enforced by bureaucracies, as energizers and catalysts of bureaucracy, or as monitors of bureaucratic performance. Similarly, legislative structures must be viewed in relation to the bureaucracy, as catalysts of bureaucracy, regulators, and modifiers, or as legitimators of bureaucratic activity. Finally, if interest groups, political parties, and media of communication are to attain their goals, they must come to grips with (and in some degree to terms with) the governmental bureaucracy. For the bureaucracy is the only structure which has a near monopoly of a crucial political function, that of rule application or enforcement. It guards the "output gate" of the political system. The art of modern rulership consists not only in the prudent search for appropriate goals and policies, but also in learning how to interact with this massive and complex set of instrumentalities, and in knowing how and when to press it and coerce it, how and when to flatter it and reward it, how to teach it, and how to learn from it.

THE RULE-ADJUDICATION FUNCTION

The primary rules of the political system impose authoritative restraints or obligations on individuals. These rules may apply to specific classes or strata of the society, as do laws governing welfare distribution or law enforcement, to groups or individuals in specified circumstances, or to all members of the system. But in any case, some provision must be made for the possibility that the rules will be violated. Penalties for violation of the rules and enforcement procedures for these in various rule-application roles are commonly provided by the rules. However, serious conflict is inevitably generated over the issue of whether or not a rule has been violated in any given instance. The citizen accused of a traffic violation or the minor official accused of embezzlement, for example, will attempt to find reasons why the law should not or does not apply in his special case. At some point it must be decided whether or not a rule has actually been violated and to what degree, with appropriate penalties provided by the rules. The performance of the adjudication function involves this process of making the authoritative decision as to whether or not a rule has been transgressed in a given case. As such, it almost invariably involves the resolution of conflict.

THE EMERGENCE OF RULE-ADJUDICATION STRUCTURES

In modern Western societies it is common to associate adjudication with courts. In fact, of course, other structures may and often do engage in adjudication, and courts perform other functions. The rule-application structures themselves may make the adjudicative decisions. The secret police in a totalitarian system, for example, may pursue an individual, accuse him of violating a rule, decide that he is guilty with or without allowing him to defend himself, and execute a sentence.

Yet it is remarkable to note that in spite of the difficulty in making the distinction between rule application and adjudication in many instances, separate rule-adjudication structures often emerge as early as the differentiated rule-application structures. Even where the same officialdom or structure may perform both functions, they are often separately handled. That is, there is some clear indication of a shifting from one process to the other, either by changing the location of the action, by setting aside special times for these purposes, or by employing different procedural forms. Thus the Katikiro of the kingdom of Buganda was not only the king's prime minister, but was also the highest judge under the king himself.

However, when the Katikiro tried cases among disputing parties, he moved to a separate building where the judicial function was usually performed.[37]

The powerful tendency for specialized adjudication structures to emerge creates a strong presumption that the performance of this function has important implications for the political system. Moreover, political theorists have often been deeply concerned with the development of an independent judiciary to perform this function autonomously and impartially.

From the perspective of the political system as a whole a specialized adjudicative structure provides a means of resolving conflict within the system without expanding the pressure on the rule makers to make new laws or to become intimately engaged in the administration of old ones. Moses' father-in-law, Jethro, advised him to delegate his adjudicative functions, when he found him in the wilderness, wearied by a multitude of disputes requiring his decision and unable to find time for the creative tasks of leadership. As David Easton points out, the adjudication process accepts a certain set of settled or presumed rules and applies these to conflict situations in the society.[38] Resort to these processes implies a willingness to abide by the decision. Those who are accused of rule violation have this opportunity to protest their innocence. Thus, a channel is provided which can often process certain kinds of demands very effectively, but which neither increases pressure on the rule makers nor challenges the fundamental rules of the system.

If there is dissatisfaction over the effect of any law as its application impinges on an individual or group, two kinds of demands for redress may be made. If the demand seeks new rule making, then the appeal is to one of the authoritative rule-making structures. This is the familiar interest-articulation, aggregation, rule-making cycle which we have been discussing in the last few chapters. But if the rule itself is accepted and the dispute relates to the propriety of its application in a given case, then changes may be sought through a demand

[37] Mair, *op. cit.,* pp. 145 ff.
[38] Easton, *op. cit.,* pp. 264–266.

to the adjudication structure. The burden of decision making for the rule makers is eased; and they do not have to become bogged down in handling divorce cases, disputes over contracts, criminal cases, and charges of irregularity by minor officials. The various courts can handle these demands.[39]

THE PERFORMANCE OF RULE ADJUDICATION

In modern Western systems, a norm of impartiality has grown up around the performance of the adjudicative function. The courts are supposed to insure not only that the enforcement and the rules will continuously be juxtaposed, but also that in determining each case the adjudication should be performed in as impartial and detached a fashion as possible. Although students of the law are aware that absolute impartiality is an ideal not attainable in reality, the myth of the fair-minded judge has a powerful effect on citizen and judge alike. The belief that adjudication will be performed in an impartial style greatly encourages the resolution of conflicts through this somewhat "insulated" channel. By the same token, the availability of an impartial adjudication structure encourages activity *within* the political system. Even if the laws are acceptable, demands may take violent and anomic forms if the officials enforcing the laws are thought to be unpredictable or biased.

However, if impartiality of style is meaningful in some systems, it is because antonomy of structure has accompanied differentiation. When the courts and other adjudicative structures are subjected to close supervision and control by various other political structures, as were the courts in Nazi Germany, it is difficult, if not impossible, to maintain more than a sham of impartiality of style. In cases pitting police against the individual, the case is always prejudiced against the individual. Since the differentiated judicial structure is controlled by other structures, it is unable to force secret police, army, or bureaucracy to bring all cases before the courts and to subject

[39] The rule makers may choose, of course, to retain sole adjudicative authority in some cases. Thus, courts may be denied jurisdiction over sensitive political issues, national security cases, and the like.

them to authoritative review of the propriety of their rule application. Political prisoners are tried in circumstances very unlike those under an autonomous judiciary either formally, or through a process of *ad hoc* judgment. The individual disputant has no real chance to make his plea, and he finds no refuge from the all-embracing arms of the rule-application structures.

Thus, where the special structures which perform much of the adjudication for the society are autonomous and differentiated in structure and impartial in style, they constitute an important check upon the performance of rule application. There is an independent point of reference in considering whether or not the rule has been violated in a given case. In providing such a check they have a powerful influence on the system and on the potential of the individual to gain its responsiveness.

Once autonomous rule-adjudication structures have been established, the political system moves to a higher level of complexity. Independent courts, in the nature of the case, become involved in rule making and rule application. No statute enacted by any rule-making agency can anticipate all the situations to which it may apply. And where there are different classes of law as in the United States (*e.g.*, constitutional, statutory, and administrative), the courts may acquire quite significant rule-making and implementing functions, giving modified and new meanings to constitutions, statutes, and regulations. Similarly, courts may function as articulators and aggregators of interests as they interpret the intent of rule makers — the framers of constitutions and the enactors of statutes and regulatory codes. They may also perform an important communication function as they declare the meaning of the law and by their decisions transmit information to interested groups.

From the point of view of political culture the development of autonomous courts brings with it a form of competence among the rank-and-file members of the political system. If the law is explicit and known, and enforceable by agencies relatively insulated from the often capricious, vindictive, or self-interested motives of elites, then the subject, though surely not a free man, at least has a calculable domain of relatively safe operations.

This relatively secure "subject competence" is the product of a secular body of law and an independent judiciary. It reflects the attainment of a high level of neutrality, universalism, and control over the use of violence and coercion in the relations between rulers and ordinary men, between the strong and the weak. It represents the fulfilment of an impulse already manifest in the primordial processes of simpler and more primitive political systems — in the rites of trial by fire and by water, or in the *post hoc* judgment of a prophet as he condemns a king for the theft of a subject's vineyard.

CHAPTER VII

The Communication Function

THE ANALYSIS AND COMPARISON of the performance of political communication is one of the most interesting and useful means of examining different political systems. Political leaders and political theorists alike have long recognized the implications of communications for the system. Every citizen and office-holder is dependent upon the information he receives and the effectiveness of the messages he transmits. Democratic theorists have insisted on the necessity of freedom of press and of speech in order that the people may check the activities of their rulers. Totalitarian leaders have invariably attempted to dominate such institutions and to manipulate the information available to the citizens. The great historical empires, as well as modern large states, have been characterized by the appearance of specialized communication structures and by the expenditure of important resources to facilitate communication flows. The Mongol hordes of Genghis Khan, for example, were linked by an elaborate system of mail riders (much like the American Pony Express) which could cross the steppes of Asia with remarkable speed. From the drummers, runners, and smoke signals of primitive tribes, through medieval heralds, to the presidential press conference and bureaucratic "memo," political systems have created special communication structures to accomplish their purposes.

It is possible to take many different approaches to the analysis of communication in a society. Communication is so pervasive an element in all human life that it is encountered within every facet of social activity. There are those who suggest that all of political science be reconceptualized in terms of communication, and of the factors which generate messages and determine their impact.[1] As one writer has suggested, the body of potentially relevant literature for the study of communication and comparative politics is almost unlimited.[2] General systems theorists, economists, sociologists, students of the mass media, and many political scientists have considered communication problems.[3]

Rather than recasting all political thought in communication terms or only considering communication activity as a factor in understanding other political functions, it seems most useful for our purposes to take a middle road. We can attempt to focus on the most general and significant flows of information in political systems. The structures performing these communication activities can be analyzed and compared. In this fashion, the communication analysis gains utility as a focus integrated into our framework. The performance of the communication function does not include all the other politi-

[1] For instance, Karl W. Deutsch, *The Nerves of Government* (New York: The Free Press of Glencoe, 1963).

[2] Richard R. Fagen, *Politics and Communication* (Boston: Little, Brown and Company, 1966).

[3] See for example, David Easton, *A Systems Analysis of Political Life* (New York: John Wiley & Sons, Inc., 1965); Norbert Weiner, *The Human Use of Human Beings: Cybernetics and Society* (New York: Doubleday & Company, Inc., 1954); Adrian M. McDonough, *Information Economics and Management Systems* (New York: McGraw-Hill Book Co., Inc., 1963); M. DeFleur and O. Carsen, *The Flow of Information* (New York: Harper & Row, Publishers, 1958); Peter M. Blau and W. Richard Scott, *Formal Organizations* (San Francisco: Chandler Publishing Co., 1962); Wilbur Schramm, *Mass Media and National Development* (Stanford: Stanford University Press, 1964). Among other political science works see Karl W. Deutsch, *Nationalism and Social Communication* (New York: John Wiley & Sons, Inc., 1953); Daniel Lerner, *The Passing of Traditional Society* (New York: The Free Press of Glencoe, 1958); J. G. March and Herbert Simon, *Organizations* (New York: John Wiley & Sons, Inc., 1958); and Lucian W. Pye (ed.), *Communication and Political Development* (Princeton: Princeton University Press, 1963).

cal functions, but it constitutes instead a necessary prerequisite for performance of other functions.

Communication performance can hinder or enhance the development of other kinds of system activity. Thus, underlying interest articulation is the opportunity for individuals to exchange thoughts freely, which greatly enhances the likelihood of their forming groups and making demands upon the political system. Information obtained from newspapers or television about conditions in the political system or about actions of political leaders may determine the types of support rendered and demands initiated. The implications of communication performance for other functions can also be examined. The making and implementing of political decisions, for instance, is clearly dependent on accurate information and on the successful communication of messages to subordinates, military or civilian, throughout the system.

The analysis of the performance of the communication function, by various structures and in various ways, can also suggest some of the endemic problems which various systems are likely to encounter in maintaining or sustaining general performance levels. In this way communication analysis leads to predictions and understanding of system development, as well as to further refinements in distinguishing between different systems.

In this chapter we deal with the following aspects of communication and politics: (1) the various types of communication structures; (2) the differentiation and autonomy of the media of communication; and (3) the implications of communications patterns for the performance of other political functions. The principal examples used are taken from contemporary democratic, totalitarian, and modernizing nations. Illustrations of communication patterns in primitive and traditional political systems are to be found in Chapters IX and X.

TYPES OF COMMUNICATION STRUCTURES

All forms of human interaction involve communication. The mass media, such as radio and television, make up only the most specialized and differentiated communication structures in a society. For comparing and analyzing political systems, it is useful to classify the types of structures which may perform communications functions. The presence or absence of these types of structures, the volume of information passing through them, and the freedom from control they may enjoy have important implications for the political system. For our purposes we may distinguish five types of structures: (1) informal face-to-face contacts, which spring up more or less independently of other societal structures; (2) traditional social structures, such as family or religious-group relationships; (3) political "output" structures, such as legislatures and bureaucracies; (4) political "input" structures, including trade unions and similar interest groups, and political parties; and (5) the mass media.

The role of *informal face-to-face contacts* in any political system should not be underestimated. Modern social science research has emphasized the degree to which informal channels pervade the most developed communications systems. In studying the mass media and public opinion, Katz and Lazarsfeld found that the mass media did not make a direct impact on most individuals.[4] Rather, certain persons who for one reason or another had greater interest in following political events, and who communicated information and opinion to friends, neighbors, and co-workers, served as "opinion leaders." It was they who interpreted the information received through the media and other contacts, and who directly shaped the knowledge and beliefs of others. Social status and personal gregariousness were the two characteristics singled out by Katz and Lazarsfeld as most significant in determining whether a person would assume such an opinion-leadership role in the United States.

The significance of informal personal contacts suggests, for example, the impact which a high level of mobility may have in a society. As a person moves out of the countryside and into the city, he establishes a whole new set of personal communications patterns, and exposes himself to a new set of interpreters as well as to new information sources such as newspapers and political parties. In such circumstances the new information

[4] Elihu Katz and Paul F. Lazarsfeld, *Personal Influence* (New York: The Free Press of Glencoe, 1955).

becomes cumulative in its impact on older orientations and beliefs.

The continuing prevalence of intermittent face-to-face communications, as well as the prevalence of traditional kinds of interaction such as those of the family, is another example of the "pre-modern" elements which we have noted so often before in modern societies. It exemplifies the cultural and structural dualism typical of developed societies.

In a modern political system it is easy to overlook the communications role played by *traditional social structures.* But in traditional and developing societies their influence is very marked. Tribal heads and councils of elders, the extended family, and religious leaders may play a powerful role as initiators and interpreters of information for large sections of the nation. The role of the Buddhist monks in Vietnam in shaping popular attitudes may be viewed partially in this light. So may the role of Islam in the Middle East. Jean Grossholtz has emphasized the role of traditional community leaders in the Philippines, particularly where a language barrier hinders more direct communication from the outside.[5] The traditional community leaders stand between the national elite and the people, and may hinder or ease the transition to national unity. The impact of family ties, even among the modernized elite, is usually remarked upon by political observers of the developing nations.

The formal structures in a political system constitute a particularly important channel of information. The *governmental structures,* particularly the bureaucracy, make it possible for the political leaders to communicate directions for rule implementation to various political officeholders in an efficient and unambiguous fashion. The lifeline of communication holds the entire governmental structure together and makes possible coordinated implementation of laws and the mobilization of societal resources. Many of the communications linking political leaders and the general public also flow through these structures. The courts and various governmental agencies are the

[5] Jean Grossholtz, *Politics in the Philippines* (Boston: Little, Brown and Company, 1964), Chap. 9.

major agencies through which redress of grievances or regis-
tration of demands is undertaken. The major role of the courts,
and more recently of the Justice Department, in the civil rights
movement in the United States provides an example. The governmental structures also supply large amounts of general
information to the public. Not only is information regarding
the formal laws, such as social security regulations, dissem-
inated through special agencies, but news releases from governmental agencies constitute one of the chief information
sources for the mass media in most societies. The accuracy of
such information is a more complex question, closely related
to the issue of autonomy, which shall be touched upon below.

The *"input" structures,* such as interest groups and parties,
constitute yet another significant information channel. By their
very nature they are engaged in transmitting popular and
special-interest demands to the political leadership. The existence of such structures, at least in systems where they are permitted to operate free from government control, provides the
average citizen with a large number of channels of access to
the political elite. With access to such organizations and the
freedom to form new ones, the citizen can easily voice his demands. Moreover, organized interest groups and parties constitute an important channel for disseminating information
about the activity of elites. Lobbyists in the capital not only
seek to influence political activities and to express the demands of their clients, but they also make sure that elite activities affecting their interests are subjected to careful scrutiny. In
a similar fashion, the opposition party is eager to expose the
mistakes or scandals of the incumbent administration. Parties
and organized groups also can establish networks of personal
contact with the people, and can utilize their organizations to
press an ideology or a set of issues upon the populace. Such
potential for mobilizing the consciousness and activity of the
voter constitutes the primary reason for the development of the
mass political party in modern democratic systems.

The *mass media,* including newspapers, television, radio,
magazines, and books, constitute the last class of communication structures. They are the most specialized and differenti-

ated of such structures, existing primarily for the purpose of communication rather than depending upon it in the course of other activities. Given appropriate conditions of technical development and literacy (in the case of the press), the mass media are capable of transmitting information to very large numbers of people at low cost and with minimum distortion. The radio broadcaster cannot be certain that his audience will interpret his words in the desired manner, but he knows that the process of transmission and reception will not alter the words. Rumor and word-of-mouth transmission is substantially more uncertain.

The emergence of the mass media in a society provides the political elites with a tremendous potential for arousing the interest and influencing the attitudes of the citizens. By the same token, the free circulation of information through a mass media structure creates a great potential for popular action on the basis of widespread and accurate knowledge about political events. Independent mass media offer the average citizen opportunities to express his grievances and to call upon both the leaders and his peers to join him in seeking change. By enabling all groups and political elites to present their cases to the public in a direct and economical fashion, the media can check and regulate the performance of all political functions. In the democratic West, the freedom of the press has long been held to be integrally linked to the maintenance of free government. In our concluding section we shall explore this problem in more detail.

THE AUTONOMY OF COMMUNICATION STRUCTURES

In discussing the various kinds of communication structures, we have referred to the level of autonomy and control which may be exercised over such structures. An autonomous structure is one that is free of domination either by political leaders or by particular interests in the society. Thus, to a large degree, the interest-group and party communication structures in the United States are free of tight political control. They can — and must — be receptive to information and demands reaching them from their members, and they are disposed to transmit these demands on to the political officeholders. The mass media are similarly free to disseminate information to everyone and to transmit almost all information received from multitudinous sources.

In a totalitarian system these structures are subject to a high degree of control by the elites. They are receptive to demands and information upward through the hierarchy only as permitted by those at the top. They disseminate only that information permitted and ordered by the top elite. In other systems a particular interest, such as the Catholic Church in Spain, landowners in certain Latin American nations, caste groups in India, or the Communist party in areas of France and Italy, may dominate some or all of the communication structures in a given area or in the nation as a whole. The reception and dissemination of information and demands is shaped accordingly.

IMPLICATIONS OF COMMUNICATION PATTERNS

The development of a science of comparative politics depends initially upon the accurate description and classification of political processes in different societies. Much of the significant work in the last decade has contributed to the development of the concepts and techniques to make such description possible. In most of our discussion the emphasis has been upon introducing these concepts and illustrating their application. Relationships among different factors, such as the role of bureaucracy in rule application and the implications of its performance for the extractive capability, have been suggested but not spelled out in detail.

However, if the study of politics is to fulfill its promise, political scientists must develop and test hypotheses which will link the descriptive variables in dependent relationships. The analysis of political communication patterns is particularly suggestive of such relationships, because of the dependence of other functions on communications processes. The students of organizations and of comparative politics, as well as communications theorists as such, have built a considerable body of knowledge in this area. We can focus upon some of the general relationships suggested by their work to illustrate both the utility of our concepts and the possibilities for development of scientific political theory.

We know, for example, that hierarchical patterns of communication tend to inhibit or distort the information passed upward through the hierarchy.[6] It is also clear that the presence or absence of intervening structures and the attitudes of local "opinion leaders" greatly affect the impact of mass media on popular orientations.[7] There are limits, too, to the volume of information which a given communication structure can pass on in a given period of time without conscious or unconscious "filtering out" of part of the message. Certain types of information seem to be less amenable to accurate transmission, or are more influenced by the prejudices and attitudes of the individual conveying them. Obviously, the presence or absence of certain communication structures greatly affects the possibility of effective interaction, and the limitations upon available information affect rational, directed activity.

These very general statements about communication patterns take on a substantial reality in the political context. Thus, distortions may be introduced into the flow of information to political elites when a hierarchical bureaucracy is the only communication channel. Or, the attitudes of traditional local leaders may affect the impact of national leadership appeal through the mass media in the rural areas. Or, in an overcentralized system the sheer volume of relevant information may overwhelm the decision makers or their communication channels. These relationships suggest in turn that the performance of political communication in a system may lead to changes in the performance of other political functions, or may limit and inhibit the development of certain types and levels of system capability. The dynamics of political change, as well as the interdependence of functional performance, can be considered in terms of the role of communication. We shall suggest a few such relationships between communications patterns and other functions of the political system, using

6 Blau and Scott, *op. cit.,* pp. 134 ff. and 139.
7 Katz and Lazarsfeld, *op. cit.*

as illustrations political socialization, system capabilities, rule making, and interest articulation.

Maintenance and Adaptation Functions: Political Communication and Political Socialization. A fragmented political culture in a society results from the different socialization experiences of various subgroups. In different areas or classes, the family, church, and school may introduce individuals to very different perceptions of the political system. Such primary socialization patterns may be reinforced or broken down by the general pattern of political communication.

In a nation such as India the information being received by various elements in the society varies radically among different geographic areas, between urban and rural areas, and among class and caste groups within areas. In the rural areas in most underdeveloped nations, the influence of the mass media is markedly limited by the low volume of newspaper circulation and the low number of radio receivers. At the same time the influence of traditional social structures and traditionally oriented opinion leaders in interpreting the information which does reach these areas is likely to be very great. This heterogeneity of information reinforces the differences in orientations and attitudes among groups exposed to very different primary socialization from family and peers.

However, political communication structures may also be developed, or may emerge, which can break down these differences in attitude and orientation. In a system like that of Great Britain, for example, the flow of information is relatively homogeneous. The top government leaders may have special information sources through particular bureaucratic agencies; some newspapers may aim at a particular class or political group; and news interpretation by informal face-to-face channels will certainly vary between upper class and lower class. However, compared with the problems of India or Nigeria, the level of homogeneity in communication is extremely high. All groups have access to a relatively homogeneous and autonomous flow of information from the mass media. Barriers of language or of cultural orientation are minimal. The masses can be aware of elite actions and can exercise a considerable degree of control over them. The elites can be aware of popular demands and of the consequences of all types of governmental actions as seen from "below." The continuous circulation of homogeneous information builds and sustains a set of common beliefs about politics and the nature of the political game.

In most transitional areas the political leaders see development of modern mass media as a force for enhancing national unity, as well as a force for shaping and encouraging modernization. Breaking down language barriers and differences in knowledge, belief, and custom, communication expansion serves to bridge systems previously characterized by very heterogeneous communication flow. As Jean Grossholtz suggests in the Philippines:

> Radio has become a popular medium and the speed with which popular songs spread through the islands is indicative of its effectiveness. . . . Information programs lag far behind entertainment in communicating with the rural people, which is true of all the media. The entertainment aspects of radio, however, are as useful in building national identities and goals as the duller and more informative programs of the government. Commercial radio programs utilize traditional Filipino art forms and humor that satirize modern life and social types who have counterparts in the barrio community. Filipinos can thus identify with a larger community that is recognizable and relevant. These programs contribute . . . a sense of a shared culture. At the same time, they highlight the similarities rather than the differences between urban and rural life and between upper and lower classes and help to overcome fundamental and potentially dangerous splits in the population.[8]

Yet, the issue of building a national identity is a complex one. Despite the positive force of the national mass media, the development of a stable and homogeneous political culture will depend to a great degree upon the directions developed by the intervening communication structures of parties, interest groups and opinion leaders, which contact the citizen in a more immediate sense. It is no simple task to persuade an indi-

[8] Grossholtz, *op. cit.,* pp. 206–207.

vidual to switch reference groups, to turn from those persons and structures to which he habitually looks for emulation and for interpretation of political matters. If these reinforce one another and are at odds with the national system, the impact of national radio or television will be minimal.

The case of France is particularly instructive in this regard. France is a nation with a well-developed sense of national identity. French citizens identify themselves with pride as Frenchmen, not as members of some divergent subgroup. Moreover, the national television network is controlled by the central government and oriented to its wishes and needs. Nonetheless, France is also a nation with a heterogeneous communication flow which tends to reinforce a fragmented political culture. The distinct sets of communication subsystems, made up of informal contacts, party and interest-group organizations, traditional social structures such as the Catholic Church, and the various group and party newspapers, can provide the Communist worker or the Catholic peasant with special worlds of information. Their beliefs can be sustained within these subsystems with limited danger of pressures from other information sources.

Of course, some information, particularly from the mass media, will cut across the geographic and class boundary lines. But two characteristics of attitude change limit the impact. First, interpretation of information through the mass media will probably be carried out by opinion leaders. The opinion leaders will themselves be highly influenced by other face-to-face contacts, which research has consistently shown to be a more powerful means of persuasion than mass media. Where a strong organization exists to sustain a given pattern of belief — or, even better, several strong reinforcing organizations such as church and party — the impact of independent mass media is highly limited. It is for this reason that modernizing states often attempt to combine media control and organization reinforcement.[9] In its extreme form, this strategy of combining

[9] See, among others, the analysis by Ithiel de Sola Pool, "The Mass Media and Politics in the Modernization Process," in Pye, *op. cit.*, pp. 234 ff.

mass communication with party organization, particularly at the grass roots level, has been pioneered by the communist movement.

System Capabilities: Communications Expansion and Social Mobilization. The complex impact of the mass media upon the political system is, in fact, a problem of which students of the underdeveloped areas are well aware. Before atittudes of national unity are consolidated, the great variety of economic, geographic, and ethnic groups becoming aware for the first time of their relationship to the rest of the nation and to the political system can generate a host of demands which create severe conflicts. As Deutsch suggests, the rapid expansion of communication may

> promote the consolidation of states whose peoples already share the same language, culture, and major social institutions; while the same process may tend to strain or destroy the unity of states whose population is already divided into several groups with different languages or basic ways of life.[10]

There seems to be no escape from the problems of information expansion, from the host of conflicting demands and needs generated by exposure to modernity and by the beginning of secularization. The developing nations of Asia, Africa, and Latin America are engaged in a desperate struggle to improve their economic and social conditions, and to create a better life for their people. These goals of development have emerged from many forces. They stem from a gradual awareness of better conditions in other nations, from the rallying cry which led to independence, from the efforts of politicians to unite a new and fragmented nation with themselves at the head, and from the initial experience with economic development. Whatever the motives, the leaders, and an articulate — if small — part of the population in these areas, are firmly committed to developmental goals. In those areas where such goals have not emerged, it would seem to be only a matter of time before the

10 Karl W. Deutsch, "Social Mobilization and Political Development," in Harry Eckstein and David E. Apter (eds.), *Comparative Politics* (New York: The Free Press of Glencoe, 1963), p. 580.

possibilities of modern economic improvement seep through barriers of traditionalism and fragmentation.

A government interested in promoting rapid development — particularly in a great expansion in the output capabilities of the political system — must encourage and assist social changes which are fundamental to the mobilization of human and natural resources. Karl Deutsch has defined social mobilization as

> the process in which major clusters of old social, economic, and psychological commitments are eroded or broken and people become available for new patterns of socialization and behavior.[11]

A traditional agricultural society cannot develop the level of societal resources upon which to base a high extractive capability. High levels of either welfare distribution or economic investment are clearly impossible without a considerable level of extraction. The deliberate efforts to increase mass media penetration, to build strength of a dominant political party with which to reinforce new attitudes and control their direction, and to launch massive educational efforts, are largely based on this need for the social mobilization which must precede development of political and economic capabilities.

Social mobilization is in large part a communications phenomenon. Urbanization, literacy, secularization of traditional ties and beliefs, employment in a wage economy, and other concomitants of mobilization are inextricably involved with exposure to new structures and processes of communication. It is this exposure to modernization which creates the "revolution of rising expectations." Its dilemma is that political aspirations and expectations rise much faster than the system can develop the capabilities to meet them. The resulting discontents make for a political instability often encouraged by the extravagant hopes built by political leaders.

The dilemma is not to be resolved easily. Every success seems to sow the seeds of vast new problems. When India achieved her independence, for example, the groups which had entry to the political system were rather few, very largely included

11 *Ibid.,* p. 583.

in the Congress party and the highly developed legacy of British bureaucracy. The elite was united by the independence movement and by the personality of Nehru. But in the decades since independence, the very success of the changes in Indian life has brought more and more groups into the political arena and has radically altered the nature of the political elite. The resultant strains on the political system, and on the Congress party in particular, have constituted a grave danger for the cohesion of the Indian nation and for the viability of its political system.[12]

Conversion Functions: Political Communication and Rule Making.[13] Various patterns of communication have great impact on conversion functions such as rule making, as well as on socialization and on system environment. Making effective decisions requires accurate and relevant information. The decision maker must be aware of a variety of factors, such as local physical conditions, the attitudes of people involved, and the material available for action. History is filled with the memorable, but often ludicrous or tragic, results of decisions made on the basis of inadequate information. Steel plants have been built in an underdeveloped nation hundreds of miles from iron and coal reserves, with only a dusty mountain trail linking the two sites. Examples of similar waste and error are innumerable.

Information distortion can, of course, stem from many sources. But two characteristics of communications structures which have been well established in small-group research lend themselves to broad hypotheses. The first of these is that a given communication structure can process only a given level of information in a given period of time. When the volume and complexity of incoming information passes a certain point, either distortion or a considerable time lag will set in. The second hypothesis suggests that information which flows

[12] See Myron Weiner, *The Politics of Scarcity* (Chicago: University of Chicago Press, 1962), especially pp. 238 ff.

[13] One pertinent discussion of these problems may be found in Deutsch, *Nerves of Government, op. cit.*, pp. 219 ff. Also see Easton, *op. cit.*, Chaps. 8, 9, and 26 in particular.

through a hierarchical structure tends to be distorted by the desires and sensitivities of the individuals with greater status, and by the intimidation of those lower in the heirarchy.

Effective activities by the elites in a large, centralized, and complex political system are hampered by the problem of the sheer volume of information which may be processed upward through the bureaucracy. Any political system in which the central government engages in a very wide range of activities occurring within a rapidly changing environment encounters this problem. A large business organization, unwilling to de-centralize, is confronted by the same difficulty. The organiza-tion's refusal to grant autonomous decision-making authority to individuals at lower levels means that all information rele-vant to all decisions must be communicated up the hierarchy. In more decentralized systems, only a more limited set of in-formation, only that relevant to particular leadership decisions, must be communicated to the top level.

When a central decision maker is responsible for evaluating all information and making all decisions, rather than for mak-ing basic policy choices alone, his effectiveness in a large and complex system is diminished by several factors. First, he can read or hear and understand only a limited quantity of infor-mation. All large organization leaders complain of the volume of relevant communications crossing their desks and of the impossibility of handling it all. It is inevitably necessary to decentralize at least to the extent of letting a presidential staff, or its equivalent, dispose of much of the incoming material that seems irrelevant or unworthy of the chief functionary's time.

Furthermore, as the information "chain" of a centralized decision-making structure involves more steps, the likelihood of error and distortion becomes multiplied. Not only do lower level officials have their own interests at stake, but human error is always a possibility. In addition, any communication chan-nel is limited in the sheer amount of information it can receive and pass on in a given span of time. If the volume is too high for every bit of information to be passed on, some things will be intentionally or inadvertently filtered out. Otherwise there will be serious time lags in the flow of information. Just as the ticker tape on the New York Stock Exchange may run minutes and hours behind the price shifts as the volume of business mounts far beyond its accustomed level, so, too, may human information systems lag.

A final problem in centralization is the increasing technical complexity of much relevant information. The leader cannot be, even though he may be expected to be, a genuine expert in all fields of military technology, cost accounting, political maneuvers, monetary inflation, urban transportation, or medical care. At various points the "raw data" from the environment must be put in a form that can be interpreted by the top elite. This process may involve many steps, including scientific or statistical interpretation of information, analysis by experts, and "translation" into layman's terms. Each stage involves a potential for error. In such cases the top official is almost totally at the mercy of his experts except in those few fields where he possesses special competence.

As a consequence of high volumes of information, and of the technical nature of much information, a very large and complex system is pushed inescapably either towards a degree of decentralization, or towards inefficient and nonrational actions. Events within large democratic societies have emphasized these decentralizing forces. Students of governmental regulation of business in the United States and of the nationalized industries in Great Britain have, for example, noted the tendency of regulatory agencies or national administration boards to slip from government control, to become the captives of those whom they seek to administer. The sheer magnitude of the industry and the technical expertise of the "old-hand" business managers and advisers overwhelm the official from the outside. In similar fashion, students of congressional control over the Defense Department or the Bureau of the Budget have increasingly commented on the impossibility of effective control over a massive bureaucratic organization by small leadership groups, which can hardly manage to struggle through all the material prepared for them by the agency itself let alone exercise really independent checks. Thus, decentralization takes

place more or less inadvertently, often through the development of counterbureaucracies such as congressional staffs.

In totalitarian nations there have been efforts to maintain
control and centralization at all costs. But the price paid has
been considerable. Reports of bureaucratic inefficiencies in the
Soviet Union are commonplace. This is due not only to the
systematic distortions in hierarchical upward information flow,
but also to the common inefficiencies which result in any organization where the volume of problems and information is
great and the decision maker is too far removed from the scene
of action. Various individuals in the upward information chain
delete or dismiss information which turns out to be most
relevant to the local problem. Unable to rely on centralized
planning, the local officials, held responsible for their output,
turn to the "fixer" to unsnarl the clogged communication
channels and to unearth necessary supplies and information.
But these private arrangements have their own inefficiencies,
unchecked as they are by the cost-reduction pressures of
competition. Thus, boatloads of coal may pass each other on
the river, each fulfilling a private deal with a manufacturing
plant in the port of origin of the other. It should also be recalled that the elaborate, multiple information-and-control
systems developed in totalitarian nations — bureaucracy, party,
police — all require time and resources to fulfill their communications functions. Insofar as the information is duplicated,
this too involves great inefficiency in government activities.

Some measures seem to be under way to alleviate the costs
of centralization, both through limited and selective decentralization and through initiation of technological improvements in information processing (such as the use of computers).
Suspicious totalitarian rulers, however, are not readily willing
to relinquish their decision-making monopoly. Moreover, in
highly interdependent systems, some degree of centralized organization is needed to keep various parts in balance, such as
the maintenance of fiscal and monetary policy to prevent and
check inflation or depression. Thus, the emergence of such
compromise decentralization measures as giving autonomy only
in applying carefully drawn policy, building a large and

trusted staff of experts, or distributing authority among several top-level agencies, is likely to be one of the most probable responses to communication problems of this type. An irreducible element of inefficiency is likely to remain for the indefinite future, as all such centralized systems balance their perceived needs of coordination and control against their needs for free-flowing and accurate communication and efficiency.[14]

The problems of volume load and transmission error may affect elite ability to make laws which are effective and also responsive to social demands. The long-standing arguments about the virtues and defects of direct representation of small areas and population groups in national government may be viewed as having this important communications component. First, of course, it is argued that unless the local people have direct control over the election of a representative, he will be unlikely to be receptive to the demands that they make. But it may also be argued that because of the sheer volume of demands and information as to local conditions pouring out of large national systems — or even out of large sub-units like a state — some more specialized representation is necessary to ensure particular local interests of a communication channel through which their interests are assured of attention. Thus, the people of New York City might argue that if they had no direct representatives in Congress, their demands and complex problems might well be overlooked in the flood of Eastern Seaboard problems and demands. The struggle over state redistricting also involves a strong component of a communications problem, as rural citizens argue that if they are given the same proportional representation as city dwellers, their special needs cannot receive adequate attention. They suggest that rural problems are more distinctive and that geographic size as well as number of persons is a factor shaping the volume of information reaching a representative. On the other hand, if more and more diverse demands receive careful attention, the volume of information to be processed in collective decision making may hinder and overload that process.

[14] See the comment by Blau and Scott, *op. cit.*, pp. 242 ff., on this perennial organizational dilemma.

Sheer volume and complexity of information is only one of the problems which faces elites of complex and centralized political systems. The distorting effects of bureaucratic hierarchy may also create considerable problems of information for effective decision making. All large decision-making systems must depend to a considerable degree upon the bureaucracy to obtain and interpret information. In a bureaucracy, hierarchy and discipline are to some degree necessary for coordination of action. But a bureaucratic official is responsible to his superiors and is often dependent upon their favors for advancement. He often develops great sensitivity to the needs and wishes of his superiors. He has an inevitable tendency to tell powerful generals, cabinet ministers, or presidents that which they wish to hear or that which will reflect favorably on his own career. Active and innovating Presidents of the United States, such as Franklin Roosevelt, have been highly sensitive to this danger of distortion and have endeavored to supplement all formal information channels with a vast networks of informal contacts with individuals at various points in the hierarchy.[15]

In open political systems, with many autonomous political structures and channels of communication, the elites can also utilize other information sources to help balance distortion by subordinates. Leaders read the newspapers, make personal appearances, and have polls conducted by autonomous organizations, in an effort to get an unbiased understanding of popular attitudes, and various sides of complex issues. However, in matters of security, in complex technological questions, and in times of crisis in particular, these normal channels may cease to operate or to be relevant. The United States' Cuban policy, for example, has tended to be shrouded in secrecy from the beginning, and many observers suggest that political leaders have been dangerously dependent on such secret agencies and information channels as the CIA. Not only the desire to please, but also the special prejudices and orientations of any single agency, may distort information.

[15] Richard W. Neustadt, *Presidential Power* (New York: John Wiley & Sons, Inc., 1962), pp. 156 ff.; and Deutsch, *Nerves of Government, op. cit.*, pp. 224–225.

Although the differences are easy to exaggerate, the totalitarian systems face these problems of information distortion
in a particularly complex fashion. Observers of closed political
systems, such as Nazi Germany or Stalin's Russia, have remarked on the constant, but often unsuccessful, efforts made
by the ruling elites to obtain information about what is happening throughout the system. The immense scale of government activities and the efforts to accomplish far-reaching goals
of economic development and military victory, or simply to
maintain top rank within the system in the face of changing
and unstable conditions, create an insatiable need for information. Yet the communications patterns which tend to emerge
in these systems are closed, nonautonomous patterns, because
the elites wish to prevent the possibility of popular knowledge
and activity which might lead to subversion, and because the
lower officials are receptive only to pressures from above, and
not from below.

These closed communication structures seem to have in-
herently pathological tendencies, particularly in stress situations. Such tendencies appear as a partial consequence of
threats and use of violence and force in order to maintain
control over lower officials and citizens. In such cases the lower
officials who staff the communications line to the elite are confronted with a difficult set of alternatives. If they deliberately
distort information and are discovered, the consequences are
likely to be costly. But, reporting unpleasant facts is likely to
be nearly as dangerous. The man who dares hint that the
leaders may have erred badly in their assessment of a situation
is apt to have his career, if not his life, abruptly cut short in
favor of those who convey more compatible news. The tendency of tyrants to surround themselves with "yes men," who
confirm the existing beliefs of the ruler is well known. Boulding explains this phenomenon in the following terms:

> The case is somewhat analogous to that of the schizophrenic
> or the extreme paranoid. His sense receptors are so much
> "afraid" of him that they merely confirm the products of his
> heated imagination. The terrorized information sources of the

tyrant likewise tell him only what they think will be pleasing to his ears. Organizations as well as individuals can suffer from hallucinations. It is the peculiar disease of authoritarian structures.[16]

Needless to say, the situation is reinforced by the average citizen's reluctance to tell even the lower officials anything but the formal "party line." Information about popular attitudes is likely to be distorted. So are reports of the inefficiency or ineffectiveness of the actions of the reporting subordinates. Even general "scientific" information may be heavily slanted, as is apparent in the work of social scientists in the Soviet Union — and which has even been the case in the continuing support (until recently) of biological theories which have been long discredited in the West. It was through such tendencies that Hitler's conduct of the war in the last days became totally divorced from reality.

Barrington Moore has emphasized the strenuous efforts made by totalitarian leaders to lessen their dependency on any single information source.[17] In the Soviet Union, Stalin used the secret police, the party, and the bureaucracy as checks on one another, relying on each separate organization to inform him of errors and deviations of the other two information channels. But, as Apter and others have suggested, in times of stress the multiple channels are apt to reinforce distorted information rather than to correct it.[18] In fact, this is likely even in much more autonomous systems.[19] If it is clear that the leadership is convinced of a set of facts, the information channels will find substantiations rather than denials.

These characteristic problems induced by closed communication systems suggest the limits on the performance of governmental functions in highly controlled authoritarian and

[16] Kenneth Boulding, *The Image* (Ann Arbor: University of Michigan Press, 1956), p. 101.

[17] Barrington Moore, Jr., *Terror and Progress USSR* (Cambridge: Harvard University Press, 1954), pp. 176 ff.

[18] David Apter, *The Politics of Modernization* (Chicago: University of Chicago Press, 1965).

[19] See Ole Holsti, "The 1914 Case," *The American Political Science Review,* June, 1965, pp. 365–378.

totalitarian systems.[20] The increase in control reaches a point of diminishing returns as the distortion of information and the costs of maintaining multiple information channels cut into effectiveness and efficiency. Rulers facing very uncertain situations, requiring high degrees of adaptability and quick response to new conditions, take a particular risk if they seriously limit autonomous information flow into the system.

The Conversion Functions: Political Communication and Interest Articulation.[21] Popular control over political leaders is the sustaining myth of democracy. The claim of a democratic system is that "the people" can make their wishes known to officeholders, and can, at regular intervals, "throw the rascals out" if the job is not being properly done. We have already suggested that the availability of autonomous interest groups, parties, and mass media communication structures is vital in insuring that the "will of the people" is communicated to the leaders in continuous and unambiguous fashion. But a second aspect of communications in popular control or influence has also been of concern to students of democracy. Without accurate knowledge of the actions of officeholders and without an understanding of the relationship between those actions and popular goals, a meaningful articulation of interests and exercise of political checks is impossible.

In theory the presence of autonomous mass media, autonomous interest groups, and informal personal contacts in a society would make possible popular awareness of the consequences of elite activity. It is the effort to block or restructure such awareness which underlies the unanimous efforts of totalitarian systems to control the communication structures.

But several factors complicate the availability of information which would make popular control possible. The first of these is the difficulty of establishing definite cause-and-effect relationships in the world of politics. The number of factors in-

20 See also Karl W. Deutsch, "Cracks in the Monolith: Possibilities and Patterns of Disintegration in Totalitarian Systems," in Eckstein and Apter, *op. cit.*, pp. 497–508.

21 For a provocative treatment of this problem, see Murray Edelman, *The Symbolic Uses of Politics* (Urbana: University of Illinois Press, 1964).

volved in any set of political events is likely to be so complex that responsibility is difficult to assess. Students of political science are aware, for example, of the difficulties encountered in tracing down explicit responsibility for the failure of Congress to pass a strong civil rights bill in the late 1950's. Was it the fault of the administration, which drafted a complex but very limited legislative proposal? or of the Southern senators, who crippled the legislation in committee? or of the liberal Northerners, who did not care enough to override their Southern colleagues? or of the whole "temper of the times," the level of popular awareness, pressure, and demand, which did not make a sufficiently strong impression on the leadership? Or, was the law itself drawn well enough to do the job, but made ineffective because of lax implementation? This is not to say that the answers to these questions could not be unraveled, but the problem is obviously a complex one. The diffusion of responsibility in the American system complicates the problem, but even in a system such as the British, where the governmental process is more unified, the relationship between a particular government action and its popular consequences may be difficult to trace.

The problem is intensified by a second factor, which is becoming of increasing importance in modern society: the technological complexity of governmental activities and the specialized knowledge necessary to understand them. How is the public to assess the issues involved in the government's decision to build a Polaris submarine, but not to develop ever-faster manned bombers? How many people can judge whether the decision to build a river dam on one site rather than another is based on sound technical and economic analysis, or on the consideration of land interests in the area? The issues involved in many public activities may well be so complex and specialized that the public is in no position to judge whether what was done was better or worse than any alternatives.

And a final problem is the sheer remoteness of many vital issues for the society. About an event which touches his daily life, an individual is likely to hold strong opinions, and to assign blame to someone if things go wrong. Whether or not the blame is justified, the sheer fact that someone will bear the responsibility exercises a restraining effect on the political leadership. But in many cases the decisions may affect the life of the individual only peripherally. Even if the mass media proclaim the importance of the issue, the individual is usually uninterested and often lacks any realistic standards of judgment. Since most men think in concrete and pragmatic rather than in abstract and theoretical terms, a remote event is beyond the individual's scope of interest, or, if he does judge it, he may utilize symbolic and emotional arguments which have little relation to the factual issues at hand.

Congressmen and other political leaders are acutely aware of the differing salience of political issues. Thus, a Southern senator may have great freedom of choice in stands on foreign affairs, though he must accede to the demands of his constituents on matters of civil rights. Although organized groups help to alleviate this problem of the uneven salience of political issues by closely watching activities affecting their interests, they are often incapable of arousing or sustaining general public interest and their specific pressure activities may also be well removed from the "public interest." Moreover, general groups, such as consumers, lacking a strong, immediate organized group to press their interests, may suffer in the struggle.

The argument that those who feel most strongly about various issues will be informed about them, and hence will exercise needed checks on matters involving their rights, has much merit. But many areas of vital national interest may be too remote or too complex to arouse strong, immediate interest. Decisions on deficit spending and on foreign aid are examples of such issues. In these areas the elites may enjoy great freedom to act unchecked, or even to manipulate the flow of news to shape opinion about the matters, a procedure which deviates very far from the old model of citizen awareness.

It may be, of course, that a high degree of elite flexibility in pursuing policy is a beneficial circumstance for the political system. Under such conditions it may be possible for the leaders to make and implement policy which is necessary for development but which is detrimental to the short-run interests of particular groups. That is, it may be possible for the elite to take a longer perspective than they would be allowed if the public were involved. The capability of an elite to satisfy popular demands with symbols (such as, in the "name of the revolution," continuing minor land distribution or promises thereof, or expropriating foreign property) may provide time for a decade or so of great resource investment at the expense of popular consumption. Mexico's industrialization in the 1940's and 1950's, when the personal income of the lowest social groups actually declined as the economy boomed, was supported by just this approach.

But it must also be recalled that the promise to act in the best interests of the people, even if they do not perceive these interests, has been the eternal claim of authoritarian and totalitarian rulers. Substituting symbols for action, at least in part, has the advantage that it usually puts a time limit upon the process. People will not eat symbols forever when real development is going on all around them. If communications flow is more or less autonomous, elite flexibility will be circumscribed eventually. But the immediate process is an "unresponsive" one and may develop habits of elite dominance which are not easily altered when the people demand a more active role in policy making.

In raising again the old problems of elite guidance versus democratic participation, this time in terms of the information issues involved, we have come full circle to the most traditional problems of democratic theory. We are touching upon some modern dimensions of the problems of traditional political theory. Technological complexity and the obscuring of cause-and-effect relationships in the interdependent and intricate processes of modern society make it much more difficult for even the informed modern citizen to evaluate elite performance. But the basic question of the proper relationship between individual and society is among the most significant, as well as among the oldest, problems in political science. It is a measure of the pervasiveness of the communications process that an analysis of its function leads us directly to these problems as they present themselves in modern guise.

CHAPTER VIII

The Capabilities of Political Systems

EMPIRICAL STUDY of what political systems actually do in their social and international environments represents something of an innovation in political theory.[1] Plato and Aristotle dealt with the performance of political systems, just as did later political theorists, but the main stress of their treatment was on the "ought" of performance rather than on its reality. Thus, in both Plato and Aristotle distinctions were drawn between "lawful" and "unlawful" forms of political rule, according to whether kings, aristocracies, or majorities used political power for the good of the rulers or for the good of the general society. Plato discussed at great length the question of what kinds of policies good rulers ought to follow. Aristotle developed in some detail the question of how the structure of a given society, in particular the distribution of wealth, affected the structure

[1] There are, of course, important exceptions to this generalization. Karl Deutsch writes of the effects of social and economic change on "the stability and capabilities of governments," though he does not develop any precise notion of what capabilities may be. And David Easton considers "the capacity to handle demands" of political systems and discusses types of "authoritative performances" at some length. But neither develops a systematic analysis of capabilities. See Karl W. Deutsch, "Social Mobilization and Political Development," in Harry Eckstein and David E. Apter (eds.), *Comparative Politics* (New York: The Free Press of Glencoe, 1963), p. 583; and David Easton, *A Systems Analysis of Political Life* (New York: John Wiley & Sons, Inc., 1965), p. 119 and pp. 355 ff.

and process of the polity and how this in turn affected the kind of public policies these political systems pursued.

The liberal political theorists of the eighteenth and nineteenth centuries similarly treated the performance of political systems in ethical or normative terms. They argued that republican and democratic forms of government would and should follow certain lines of public policy. The classical liberal political theory, which argued that "that government is best which governs least," spoke in favor of a political system which limited itself to maintaining basic order in a society and to defending the nation. Beyond this, social systems other than the state, such as the economy, the religious community, and the family, were to have the major role.

Marxist theory presented the argument that the class structure of a society determined the structure and process of the political system, and its performance in society and in the international environment. Marxist theorists believed that the capitalist form of society produced a political system dominated by the bourgeoisie, acting in its own interests and following a policy of international aggression in order to maximize markets and profits.

The above discussion illustrates some of the ways in which political theorists have attempted to understand the performance of the political system in its domestic and foreign environments. The novelty in the capabilities approach lies in our insistence that the problem of what political systems do is one of empirical inquiry. It is not correct to say that democratic systems follow a particular course of domestic and foreign policy. We know that some democracies have followed social welfare and economic nationalization policies, while others have hewed more closely to the line of nonintervention in economic and social life. Furthermore, we know that democracies have changed their patterns of public policy from one era to the next. Before the depression of the 1930's the United States followed a policy of limited intervention in the economic sphere, while after this period a "welfare" democracy developed in the United States, and is, indeed, still developing.

There are at least two ways in which analysis of capabilities enables us to treat political phenomena more precisely and more comprehensively. First, it enables us to classify and compare political systems more effectively. Until this time we have classified political systems according to the rules and practices affecting their internal operation (*e.g.*, according to the characteristics of their party systems, whether their governments are parliamentary or presidential in form, or whether their courts are relatively autonomous). When a capability analysis is introduced, we can include the performance level, the patterns of interaction with the social and international environments.

The capacity for greater precision also enables us to make our comparative analysis more relevant to the debates over the ethics and benefits of different types of political systems. Although political performance is obviously a major concern of much political debate, we tend to generalize about the policy and performance dimension. The classifications of systems commonly suggested have been of little aid in providing a systematic basis for comparison of this dimension of politics.

Students of French politics, for example, have been tormented by the effort to evaluate the significance of the fall of the Fourth Republic and the import of the Gaullist regime which followed it. Adding a capabilities dimension to process analysis enables us to put such normative speculation on an empirical basis: at the cost of certain changes in political structure and process, which we can specify, the French political system has registered some changes in both responsiveness and output performance level which we can also specify. The evaluation of these various changes requires, of course, a weighing of their relative worth and importance, but such ethical analysis is precarious without a precise idea of just what changes, in what spheres, *have* taken place.

By the same token, conservative Americans have been troubled by the socialist orientation of the British political system, particularly under Labour governments. If we really wish to come to grips with the differences in policy orientation between American and British democracy, we have to examine the whole pattern of performance of the two systems. The

British system may allocate a larger proportion of its resources to social security, welfare, and medical programs than does that of the United States. But if the impact of educational expenditures in creating a greater level of equality of opportunity in the United States is considered, it might be argued that the distributive capability of the American system, viewed in broader terms, may reflect as much "collectivism." We are suggesting, in short, that the question is a complicated one which needs to be approached in a systematic fashion, utilizing the best empirical measures of performance available.[2] Unless various aspects of performance are accurately and systematically compared, what are now often pointless polemics about the properties of political systems cannot be reduced to precise analysis.

The study of the performance or capabilities of political systems also enables us to deal more directly and effectively with the problem of political change. We know that the stimulus for political change can come from three sources: from the political system itself (that is to say, from its elites), from social groups in the domestic environment, and from political systems in the international environment. Usually these three sources of political change interact with one another. For

[2] The *World Handbook of Political and Social Indicators* suggests some of the following relevant statistics for comparison of American and British system performance. A much more precise treatment would be necessary, of course, for full understanding of their performance.

Indicator	United States	United Kingdom
Expenditure of central government, social security, and public enterprises as a percentage of GNP	21.0	38.8
Expenditure of central government as a percentage of GNP	20.4	29.9
Primary and secondary school pupils as a percentage of population aged 5-19	81	80
Students enrolled in higher education per 100,000 population	1983	460

See Bruce M. Russett *et al.*, *World Handbook of Political and Social Indicators* (New Haven: Yale University Press, 1964), pp. 63, 60, 218, 215.

example, pressures coming from the political elite which affect changes in the capabilities of the political system may produce changes in the society or in the international political system which in turn may change the pattern of demand and support. When we look at the political system at the level of interaction with its environment, our attention is drawn to changes in magnitude and content of the flow of inputs and outputs, and these changes in magnitude and content may be the stimuli of political change. Thus, if we look at the flow of demands into the political system, we can make judgments about the load on the system, whether it is beyond the capacities of the structures and processes of the political system to handle. If it is, we can make some estimate of the probability that the system will have to change its structure and process patterns and its capabilities (or both) if it is to continue carrying the load.

Similarly, if we examine the outputs of the political system to observe how they are changing the domestic social environment or the international environment, we can make some judgments about how these changes may affect the flow of inputs into the political system (whether they are likely to reduce the flow, to increase it, or to change its content).

When we introduce the capabilities level of analysis, we enhance not only our capacity for scientific prediction and explanation, but also our capacity to talk about policies as they may affect political change in desired directions. Suppose we were called upon to advise statesmen on the question of how they can increase the rate of investment in economic growth and modernization. With a capabilities form of analysis we can break down these public policy goals into specific capability or performance levels. We can spell out the extractive, regulatory, and distributive measures needed to increase the rate of economic growth by a given increment. We can say that to increase the rate of economic growth by a given increment, one will have to increase the pattern of performance of the political system by given increments. We can then address ourselves to the question of how one can affect the performance of the political system in the desired direction. Here as students of politics we would be able to spell out the structural and cultural requisites of different levels and patterns of capability. We can also relate these aims to the socialization and recruitment requisites of different levels of capability. What kinds of citizens, politicians, and administrators does one need in order to operate pressure groups, political parties, legislatures, bureaucracies, and courts in such a way that they will sustain the kind of output that is required for a policy of economic growth?

THE EXTRACTIVE CAPABILITY

The extractive capability of a political system refers to the range of system performance in drawing material and human resources from the domestic and international environments. The capability to obtain such resources underlies the other capabilities, and limits or expands the possibilities of attaining various goals for the system and the society.

In characterizing the extractive capability we can first consider the amount of resources which flows into the government at various levels (national, state, local). The support aspect of extraction can also be ascertained — the ratio of extractions levied to those obtained, and the willingness of a population to provide resources under different sets of circumstances. In addition, it is important to know who pays for the resources extracted. Are soldiers conscripted from a particular group or stratum, or does the system rely on mercenaries? What groups bear the burden of taxation?

We should also want to know what means are used to obtain the extractions. Are there threats of force and coercion, with armed bands accompanying the tax collectors? Is it necessary to mount a powerful patriotic appeal accompanied by material reward, as when a system attempts to issue war bonds? Does the attainment of resources involve a promise to repay — with interest, as in the case of bonds, notes, and foreign loans — or is it without future obligation?

The structures and procedures of extraction are also of interest in analyzing the extractive capability. Does the system rely on an efficient bureaucracy, capable of continuous, equitable, and effective activities over long periods of time? Or does it rely on "tax farmers" who keep all they can get after the central government has been paid a particular amount? These are a few of the questions which may be asked in characterizing the extractive capability. In some cases it may be useful to probe even deeper in explicating the basic extractive resources. For example, a system such as Venezuela or Kuwait is largely dependent on a single resource — oil. Other nations may be dependent on a single agricultural crop. The failure of this crop or a drop in prices may seriously undermine the extractive capability.

THE REGULATIVE CAPABILITY

The regulative capability refers to the political system's exercise of control over behavior of individuals and groups. By common definition, this is the distinguishing capability of political systems, the employment of legitimate coercion to control behavior. In characterizing regulative performance one must consider what individuals and groups are being subjected to regulation, what areas of individual and collective life are affected, and what frequency or intensity of intervention is exercised.

In a political system such as the United States, for example, the political system regulates many sectors of economic life — it protects consumers from monopoly pricing and dangerous food handling, businessmen from unfair practices, unions from suppression, and so forth. Not only are such clearly deviant social activities as murder and assault regulated, but property rights and certain types of interpersonal relationships such as marriage and parental responsibility may also be regulated. The whole realm of contract which underlies so much of economic and personal interaction may be government regulated.

But there are also certain limitations on the intensity of regulation in a system such as the United States. In most cases the conduct of regulation is carried out in terms of and limited by certain procedures which protect the individual as long as he stays within the clearly defined boundaries of the law. The style of regulation is legal rather than customary or arbitrary. Moreover, although many areas of life, from driving a car to employing workers, are in some measure regulated by the political system, the initial presumption is still that what is not clearly defined as in the public sphere is not subject to governmental control.

In a hypothetical case of extremely high regulative capability, the political system would endeavor to control every aspect of the lives of its citizens. The central government would run all business and services and would attempt to direct all resource allocations. It would attempt to eliminate the family as we understand it, and to become directly involved in procreation, child care, and religious belief. All interpersonal contacts would be subject to constraint. Speech, movement, association, and press would all be regulated. Of course, there are limitations upon the degree to which such controls could be pushed, limitations imposed by the complexities of information flow, concentration, and cost, and by the problem of regulating the regulators. Nonetheless, Hannah Arendt and George Orwell have provided us with images of such extreme regulation [3] — all the more total because it is arbitrary as well as completely penetrative — and Stalin's Russia provided something like an approximation.

It is indeed in the arena of political life that regulation becomes particularly significant for the individual. If this area of life is relatively open, then other regulations can be fought and protested. But if political activities are prohibited, if news is heavily censored, and if freedom to associate and to travel is restricted, then the individual is truly at the mercy of the system.

Regulation, like extraction, obviously underlies much of the performance of the other capabilities. These two capabilities are in themselves interdependent. A system needs resources in order to regulate, but it is through the use of control, and of coercion or its threat, that resources are obtained.

[3] Hannah Arendt, *The Origins of Totalitarianism* (New York: Harcourt, Brace & World, Inc., 1951); George Orwell, *1984* (New York: Harcourt, Brace & World, Inc., 1949).

THE DISTRIBUTIVE CAPABILITY

The distributive capability refers to the allocation of goods, services, honors, statuses, and opportunities of various kinds from the political system to individuals and groups in the society. It is the activity of the political system as dispenser or distributor of benefits among individuals and groups. The most relevant measurements of distributive capacity must involve the quantity and importance of the objects distributed, the areas of human life they touch, the particular sections of the population receiving various benefits, and the relationship between individual needs and governmental distribution to meet those needs.

Some aspects of distribution can be measured with considerable ease. Governmental expenditures constitute, for the most part, distributions of particular kinds.[4] These can be characterized according to both the *area of life* and the *groups in the population* which receive the expenditures. We might distinguish, for example, among expenditures designed to meet material needs of individuals, such as expenditures on social welfare; expenditures designed to assist them in their economic activities, such as farm subsidies; and expenditures designed to provide health and safety, such as community sewage projects and police protection. Further categories could easily be suggested. At the same time, types of governmental expenditures must be considered in terms of the groups and individuals who receive the benefits. The different occupational and income groups; the different sectors of the economy (farmers, mineworkers, small businessmen); regional groups; ethnic or religious groups;[5] and all sorts of interesting special institutional

---

[4] This must be qualified in certain respects. For example, some of the revenue and expenditure figures in budgets of governments which operate nationalized industries may simply reflect the day-to-day costs of carrying on these industries — the costs of pig iron in the steel industry, for example — and may inflate figures without reflecting appreciable changes or even specific government controls over these monetary flows. The ambivalence in treatment of the "trade sector" by different government budgets reflects the complexity of the problem.

[5] *E.g.*, are government funds distributed to Catholic primary and secondary schools? Or, do Negroes benefit from government welfare and educational expenditures?

groups, such as the military, the clergy, landholders, or the political elite itself, must be considered. In some general sense we think of the distributive capability of a political system increasing as its expenditures increase in amount and as the range of individuals and groups receiving benefits broaden. The distributive capability of a bureaucratic empire, for example, may be limited to a moderate total level and be largely confined to the members of the elite itself. This would contrast with a nation such as Sweden, where the government distributes an enormous range of goods and services to every member of the society.

However, it is important to remember that the expenditures of a political system represent only a part, although perhaps a major part, of its distributions. Government jobs, for example, may be seen as distributive, quite apart from the sheer fact of the salaries. The taxation structure has its distributive aspects as it levels income distribution and wealth in the society. Such benefits as education may be highly important distributions, involving and expanding the impact of the political system upon the entire social stratification system of the society. Regulations, too, may be viewed in their distributive aspect. What constrains one individual or group may benefit another. The political system may also distribute honors and statuses by conferring knighthoods or medals of honor.

THE SYMBOLIC CAPABILITY

The symbolic capability is the rate of *effective* symbol flow from the political system into the society and the international environment. Symbolic outputs include affirmations of values by elites; displays of flags, troops, and military ceremony; visits by royalty or high officials; and statements of policy or intent by political leaders. These may be seen, of course, as a kind of distribution, but they take on a special character since they have little immediate cost for the elites yet are highly dependent on tapping popular beliefs, attitudes, and aspirations for their effectiveness.

The effectiveness of symbolic outputs of this kind is difficult to measure, but political elites (and journalists and scholars) often attempt to do so by counting crowds and audiences, by recording the strength and duration of applause, or by conducting surveys of attitudes. Of course, symbolic output is not the same thing as symbolic capability. The output of symbols may cease to be edifying, menacing, or credible, or may even stop being received. Royalty or high officials may be reviled, statues may be thrown down from high places, television and radio sets may be turned off. Or, as in the case of new nations, the symbolism may have little if any resonance. Symbolic messages may be transmitted but not received. The symbols of local authority may be the only ones granted legitimacy, while the central symbol output may have little meaning or effect. Thus, the activities of governments in making displays, building statues, and making speeches to the nation are not in themselves indicative of the capability level.

The significance of a high symbolic capability for a nation should not be underestimated. Through the judicious creation and exploitation of a set of powerful and popular symbols, the political elites may be able to gain acceptance of policies which they deem necessary but which are painful or unpopular. Reserves of support may be created or mobilized, as by Churchill's speeches during World War II. Symbolic capability can magnify the impact of certain governmental distributions or regulations far beyond their physical effect on individual citizens. Thus, signs on highways may be used to increase compliance with traffic regulations. Similarly, the distributive and symbolic capabilities can be used to reinforce one another. The redistribution of land in Mexico during the regimes of presidents Cárdenas and Camacho, for example, had an effect in building support for the government which was many times greater than mere promises of redistribution could have been. But it also appears to have had an impact many times greater than would seem to be justified by the actual amount of land redistributed and the minimal improvement in actual peasant living conditions it brought. The actual government distribution was enhanced by great symbolic attachment to the ideal of land redistribution. The land redistribution in the 1930's, combined with the enhancement of strong nationalist symbols by such actions as the government's expropriation of the

American-owned oil industries in 1938, helped create a public mood which brought the regime through the difficult economic development periods of the 1940's and 1950's with a strong reserve of support.

THE RESPONSIVE CAPABILITY

While extractive, regulative, distributive, and symbolic capabilities are ways of describing the pattern of outputs of the political system into the internal and external environments, the responsive capability is a relationship between inputs and outputs. Responsiveness is of great concern for political scientists in their normative, explanatory, and predictive analyses of political systems. Certainly many of the judgments we commonly make about dictatorships and democracies, tyrannical progressive governments, are founded on some estimate of responsiveness. Indeed, most modern political elites make elaborate claims to be giving the people "what they want," regardless of how responsive they may appear to observers. Some sort of claim to ultimate responsiveness has come to replace custom or religious belief as the legitimating grounds for popular support and obedience.

In a sense every political system is "responsive" to something. The political system must be responding to some set of internal or external pressures and demands. The more salient questions are: To whom is the system responsive? In what policy areas is it responsive? How does it manage to sustain a pattern of responsive behavior? Thus, in a bureaucratic empire the governmental activities may be at the whim of the king or emperor or of his immediate staff, with little concern to demands and pressures — if they exist — from other sources. The political elites would then constitute almost the sole source of political inputs. We would commonly characterize such a system as having a low responsive capability, although the specific sources of elite inputs would still be a matter for interest and study.

In contrast, a political system with a highly developed set of interest groups and political parties to which elites are sensitive and responsive in policy making would represent a case of a highly developed responsive capability. But, of course, there is a vast range of responsiveness falling between these two extremes, and we can only suggest a few of the possibilities in this discussion.

We should be first concerned with considering what groups are engaged in making demands on the political system and what sort of responses the elites usually make to them. Thus, demands may be confined to a small group of landholders, first families, military officers, and members of the political elite, such as has been traditionally the case in Latin America. Or there may be a broad range of demands from most groups in the society, but particular regional, ethnic, or religious groups may be excluded from the political input process. Such is the case of the Bantu in South Africa, who make up more than two thirds of the population, and such was long the case of the Negro in many parts of the United States.

Closely related to this question is the whole problem of the mechanisms and channels of demand processing, which we have discussed above. The structures and cultural attitudes underlying the performance of the internal conversion processes of the political system have great influence on the responsive capability. If certain well-organized, well-financed groups have special channels of access to the political elites, then it is likely that the system will be primarily responsive to their demands and not to those of the masses. The masses may have to become aroused to the point of violence and demonstration before an impact is made.

One final point must be made about system responsiveness. A political demand for certain needs may be met by the political system in the form of a response which not only provides certain immediate benefits, but institutionalizes the responsiveness of the system in that area. That is, the political elites concede that the political structures have the responsibility for meeting a certain kind of want or need, and set up specific political roles and structures to meet the need on a continuing basis. Subsequent response then becomes automatic. It may be that the individuals or groups in question may still have to request that government intervention be initiated, or may have to show that they meet certain criteria, such as having been unemployed for six weeks to obtain unemployment compensation. Or the response may be geared directly to some given measure of need and the bureaucracy obtains the information showing that performance in that area is necessary. The policemen on the beat or the food inspectors of the Department of Agriculture keep at their regulatory activities even if no specific complaints are made — although they generally continue to be responsive to demands, and perhaps more zealous in their activities, because of them. But the point is that responsiveness may be institutionalized so that new demands are not necessary to insure continued output response to a need.[6]

DOMESTIC AND INTERNATIONAL CAPABILITY

We have referred constantly to the fact that political systems interact both with their domestic societies and with political systems in the international environment. We need to look at political systems, then, not only in terms of their domestic performance, but also in terms of their international performance. At least in the beginning we can use the same categories of capability to analyze the international behavior of political systems. Thus, we can speak of the international extractive capability as meaning such things as income from international trade or foreign tourists, profit from the investment of capital abroad, tributes and reparations drawn from foreign countries, and even levies on the services of foreign peoples, as aspects of the international extractive capability of a political system. Similarly, we may speak of the international regulative capability of a political system, meaning the extent to which a political system penetrates another one and controls its politics and public policy. There have been enough cases of puppet and satellite regimes in recent decades to make clear that the pene-

[6] Sidney Verba, in fact, suggests four stages in an "ideal type, short-range crisis" cycle: a change in the environment of the political system, designation of that change as political in its consequences, government performance in response to the newly defined political problem, and institutionalization of the response pattern. Unpublished manuscript, 1965.

tration of one political system by another is a common phenomenon.[7]

The international distributive capability might take the form of subsidies, grants, and loans, and technical assistance such as is provided by American, British, French, Russian, and Chinese governmental agencies. The international symbolic capability is a measure of the effectiveness of the flow of symbols, images, policy statements, and the like from one country to other countries. Agencies of the American government are constantly concerned with the question of American prestige abroad. The foreign press is carefully read and the foreign radio broadcasts monitored; surveys of public opinion are made in foreign countries and a kind of prestige barometer is read periodically. American concern with its prestige abroad is at least in part based on the assumption that other components of our international capability are dependent on foreign opinion and foreign attitudes, and that these are affected by what we do and say. We assume that voting support in the United Nations, support of our diplomacy, and even military support, are in some measure related to our international symbolic capability.

We have also to concern ourselves with the input aspect of international capability. The international extractive, regulative, distributive, and symbolic capabilities of one political system may take the form of inputs of demand and support into another political system. The relation between inputs emanating from other political systems in the international environment and outputs of a given political system into the international environment may be viewed as the international responsive capability of that political system. Examination of the flow of action from the British system into the international environment and from the international environment into the British system will enable us to characterize its international capability according to a variety of dimensions. Thus, an accommodative international capability would be one in which

[7] The extreme case would be James Rosenau's example of the "penetrated polity." "Theories and Pre-Theories of International Politics," unpublished manuscript, 1965.

demands made on other political systems are in some proportion to compliance with demands which other political systems make upon it. The study of the different patterns of interaction among political systems according to these categories of capabilities should enable us to be much more discriminating than has been the case in the past in characterizing and distinguishing between the foreign policies of different political systems.

Just as we have suggested that there is an important set of relationships between one order of capability and another in relation to the domestic environment, so also must we appreciate the fact that there is some relationship between patterns of domestic capability and patterns of international capability. A system with a high resource extraction capability at home, may also be able to demand much from other nations. But, again, we must be very cautious in thinking of the relationship between domestic and international capability. The Romans extracted resources from their empire and distributed food and entertainment to their unruly urban population. Totalitarian systems which are not at all responsive to demands emanating from their own societies may, when their security is at stake, be moderately responsive to the demands which other political systems make upon them. What we are suggesting is that international capability cannot be directly inferred from domestic capability, nor can the domestic capability be inferred from the international, although there may be important links between the two. We have to look at the actual flow which takes place and ascertain what these relations really are in given cases and given types of circumstances.

FACTORS AFFECTING CAPABILITY

The goals and actions of the political elites are a major factor in shaping capability patterns. Political structures do not fluctuate blindly in response to pressures and demands. The human beings who perform elite roles have goals and fears, perceptions and beliefs. Elite responses to societal and international inputs of demand and support are a major factor affecting levels and patterns of capability. Broadly speaking, elite responses to inputs or demands may take the form of repression, indifference, substitution, or accommodation. Repression of demands will require an increase in the regulative capability of the political system. Indifference or lack of awareness may result in a buildup of pressure on the political system, producing more intense demands which may make later responses more difficult. Substitutive responses may take the form, for example, of diverting groups from their demands for increased participation or welfare by gratifying their needs and demands for national identity through an aggressive foreign policy. Another substitutive response might take the form of providing increases in welfare without gratifying demands for increased participation and democratization. Accommodative responses on the part of the elite take the form of either outputs or structural changes which in some measure satisfy the demands on the political system. We are not treating these varieties of elite response to demand in any detail, but simply referring to them as a way of demonstrating the great importance of elite reactions to demands in the development of political system capabilities. We are concerned here with the role of the politician and of the statesman in shaping the performance and process of political systems.

A second factor affecting capabilities are the material resources required for the performance of the political system. The extraction of services from the population depends on the size of the population, its skills, and its motivation. Planes and ships cannot be built if there is no iron or coal. Political systems have engaged in wars just to obtain such resources as iron and oil reserves or waterways. Obviously, if a system faces the depletion of a crucial material resource, its capabilities are likely to be affected. In a nation where 90 per cent of foreign exchange depends on a single agricultural product or mineral resource, it may be impossible to maintain a stable extractive capability, which may in turn weaken other capabilities.

A third factor affecting capability is the organizational apparatus of the political system. A system with a well-developed and effective bureaucracy, for example, can sustain levels and ranges of performance impossible in a system depending on a more primitive officialdom. One of the characteristics of modern political systems is that the presence of differentiated and specialized political structures and of secular cultural patterns makes it possible for such systems to attain and sustain high capability levels in many areas. In modern systems not only is capability level higher on a day-to-day basis, but the range itself is greater. The system may be characterized as having a high level of versatility. It can shift its outputs to deal with various sorts of fluctuations in the environment without major structural and attitude changes. Such was the case when Britain met unemployment with corresponding levels of social welfare distribution. The modern political system has much more flexibility in dealing with the various problems which it may confront. Needless to say, particular patterns of socialization and recruitment are needed to maintain the trained personnel for such organizational resources.

Finally, levels of support affect the performance of the political system. The system needs to be able to draw on popular support for its activities if it is to sustain them at given levels of effectiveness and efficiency. Low levels of support or compliance reflected in tax evasion or civil disobedience hinder the development of high levels of capability. By the same token, decline in support levels for certain activities affects capabilities. The military effectiveness of an army declines with great rapidity when the soldiers decide to desert or simply not to fight. One of the great problems faced by the "transitional" nation is that loyalties are given to tribe or clan and not to the national system and its goals. This makes it very difficult to achieve goals such as agricultural improvement without first thoroughly resocializing the peasantry and perhaps using coercion in the process.

CAPABILITIES AND POLITICAL DEVELOPMENT

The analysis of the capabilities of political systems, including potential capability and the support bases of capability, provides a useful conceptual tool for the study of political development. There is a logic to the process of development. A system must have adequate capabilities of extraction and regulation before it can begin to distribute resources. At an even more basic level, we suggest that structural differentiation and secularization are prerequisites to the development of higher levels of extraction and regulation. The development of structures to perform the conversion functions — interest groups and parties to convey demands, and bureaucracies to implement them — links together the different levels of development of system performance.

But in addition to allowing us to study political development in these very general requisite terms, the analysis of capabilities also enables us to explain and even to predict cycles of short-range and long-range change in response to various kinds of environmental pressures. Without undertaking a systematic analysis of all the causes and sorts of change, let us conclude this discussion by examining two cases in which capability analysis might lead us to predict new crises for the system and the possible system responses in developing new capability levels.

First, we might consider the case of a system such as that of Venezuela, which is highly dependent on the export of a single commodity, petroleum, for the maintenance of its extractive capability and of its living standards. Let us suppose that geological reports suggest that, at the projected use rates, the oil will run out in twenty years. Such a prediction suggests that unless new sources of national wealth are found, the system will face a severe crisis. The extractive capability of the political system will drop sharply, forcing a cutback in various welfare and land-redistribution programs. At the same time, incomes will decline and unemployment will rise. The economic system, in other words, will be unable to maintain its present level of performance. As a consequence, important pressures will be placed on the political system to meet these economic problems at the same time that its own extractive capability is declining. Since the Venezuelan system is at present functioning under considerable pressure and threat, which requires a high level of responsiveness and distribution, we can predict that the present level of performance will not be adequate to deal with new pressures unless some solution for the basic economic problem can be found.

Capability analysis suggests several possibilities of coping with the problem. The system might cut back on its distributive activities but step up its flow of symbolic activities, resorting to a propaganda of nationalism and anti-Americanism. Or it might increase its regulative capability very markedly, suppressing demands for government action and suppressing anomic or organized violence with force. Finally, the system might face a complete restructuring of its conversion functions as well as of its capabilities. That is, the present form of government might be overthrown and a Communist or rightist authoritarian regime based on a new set of structures be put in its place.

If we had a good analysis of the capabilities of the Venezuelan political system, we could perhaps predict the probability of any of these various developments. An analysis of the depth and quality of support, for example, might suggest the probability that people would be willing to tighten their belts to accept symbolic outputs in place of economic and distributive performance. If this did not appear to be the case, then the elites would be well advised to seek other ways of increasing their capability levels. They might seek to diversify their economy, to increase their police and military forces, to seek sources of international aid, or any combination of these approaches. Capability analysis can improve our capacity to anticipate loads or pressures on political systems, and can help us understand how different elite responses might cope with these pressures and how these responses in turn might affect the structure, culture, and performance of political systems.

A second case for analysis is provided by the process of urbanization and social mobilization which is taking place in many of the underdeveloped or transitional nations of the world today. In these nations, as individuals are moving from rural to urban areas, they are being exposed to new sets of values and new possibilities of life and comfort. Traditional patterns of behavior — social, economic, religious, familial, and political — are being broken down in the process. New needs are created as thousands of human beings move into situations of close personal contact for which their childhood training has not prepared them. The cities need water, sewage disposal, police, and food-distribution systems. The inhabitants need to adapt to new patterns of life for which their old habits have provided little preparation. Although family and kinship ties have often to some extent survived, the way of life which they have handed down from generation to generation is no longer so appropriate as it once was. And in many cases the family and all the old bonds of social control and regularized interaction have been destroyed. At the same time that new needs emerge, so too do new aspirations. Not only is there exposure through word of mouth and media of mass communication, but the new urbanite can see with his own eyes the life of the wealthy. The contrast between the slum and other areas is painfully clear.

The phenomenon of urbanization, industrialization, and exposure to modernity has enormous consequences for the political system. On the resource and organization side, the process creates potential capability and support if these free-floating individuals, their traditional ties and habits loosened by their experiences, can be trained and utilized for a host of modern secular activities. But at the same time, this shifting environment is likely to place demands on the system far greater than can be accommodated in the short run. The new needs and new aspirations confront the political system with a set of intense demands, for the other social systems are no longer capable of meeting the stresses placed on them. The family, if it exists, is not capable of training the young for their new life; the old ways of trade and of agriculture are not suitable for the urban industrial economy, and the old forms of community life cannot meet urban community needs. Because of this, there is great pressure on the political system to build schools, to create a modern economy, to provide community services, and to distribute food and shelter to the poor. The political system is confronted by an intense and cumulative load.

Although we cannot in general predict the precise magnitude and impact of the pressure, the social indicators of mobilization [8] predict almost certainly that these pressures will emerge or will intensify. Our analysis of the capabilities of a transitional political system indicates the degree to which it will be able to cope with these pressures at its present levels. If it has great resources and a well-developed distributive program geared to meet increasing demands, if it has pilot community-organization programs and trained personnel, if it has educational facilities geared to expansion, if it has strong police and military forces, if it has a pervasive and sensitive political infrastructure (such as a well-organized political party), if it has a strong and acceptable set of national symbols (usually including a magnetic leader), then we might predict that the present system may be able to cope with the environmental pressures without discontinuous or revolutionary change.

In practice, of course, most transitional nations do not have these actual and potential capabilities. They do not have them *because* they are transitional, because to develop such capability levels requires the structural differentiation and cultural secularization, the resources, skills, and motivations, characteristic of modern societies. It is one of the advantages of a nation such as India that her British experience left her a trained bureaucracy, a well-educated and well-trained political elite, and a strong party organization with a charismatic leader. Even so, the forces impinging on the Indian political system threaten to load it faster than its capabilities, structures, and processes can adapt. Since many of the new nations have to cope with similar problems without these initial advantages,

8 Deutsch, "Social Mobilization," *op. cit.,* utilizes the following indicators: Gross National Product, Gross National Product per capita, population, percentage of population in radio audience, percentage literate, percentage of work force in nonagricultural occupations, and percentage of population in urban areas. He examines shifts and rates of growth in these indicators and combines the last four to derive an index of "exposure to modernity." See pp. 393 ff. Russett *et al., op. cit.,* use the following indicators to suggest "stages of economic and political development": G.N.P. per capita, per cent population in cities over 20,000, per cent of literate adults, higher education per 100,000 population, inhabitants per physician, radios per 1,000, per cent voting in elections, per cent of the 15-to-64 age population in military, central government expenditure as a per cent of G.N.P. See pp. 293 ff.

it is no wonder that their political systems tend to be so unstable. They find it most difficult to develop capabilities which
can cope with the increasing pressures, even with the help of
loans and aid from the international environment.

One of the common patterns of political instability among
the new and modernizing nations has been to shift from a
capability pattern emphasizing distributiveness and responsiveness to one emphasizing regulation and symbolic satisfaction. The political changes which took place in Ghana in the
last years before Nkrumah's overthrow can be viewed from this
perspective.[9] A nation's elites may believe that they can achieve
a more stable equilibrium and can better sustain their position
through authoritarian repression and symbol manipulation.
They may dispair of trying to juggle the nation's slender extractive resources so as to satisfy present welfare demands while
still investing in economic growth to provide for future demands The shift to an authoritarian pattern must be recognized as one of the typical developmental patterns of the new
nations. From the point of view of democratic aspirations, the
costs of this shift may be great. Elite and popular attitudes may
be developed which will make it difficult to reverse the pattern
to one of greater responsiveness. However, given the overwhelming load to which these systems are subjected, attaining
any stable equilibrium, let alone a responsive one, is apt to be
a prolonged and difficult process.

[9] See the discussion of Ghana in Chapter X, pp. 287–291.

CHAPTER IX

Types of Political Systems:
Primitive and Traditional

WE COME FINALLY to the age-old concern of political science with the varieties of political systems and with their growth and development. Most political theorists from Plato and Aristotle on have dealt in some way with these two problems. Aristotle's classification of forms of political authority has been repeated again and again with variations by many political theorists.

Aristotle proposed a sixfold classification based upon two dimensions. He distinguishes between rule by one man, rule by the few, and rule by the many. He further distinguishes between rule in the interest of the whole society and rule in the interest of the ruler or ruling group. Thus, in *monarchy* the king uses his power in the interest of the whole society, and in *tyranny* the ruler uses his power for his own interests. In *aristocracy* the few act in the interest of the whole society (in other words, are virtuous), and in *oligarchy* the wealthy or those of "high" birth use their power in their own interests. In *polity* the many act in the interests of the whole society, and in *democracy* the many (usually the poor) act in their own interests and suppress the rights of the minority. He refers to political systems which combine oligarchic and democratic elements as "mixed constitutions."

213

Aristotle then goes on to discuss the dynamics of change from one form of political system to another. He offers ingenious arguments and some evidence from history as to why monarchy turns into aristocracy; aristocracy degenerates into oligarchy; oligarchy, into tyranny; and tyranny, into democracy.[1] This Aristotelian scheme of political classification and theory of political development must seem rather simple to modern students of politics, but the fundamental questions which Aristotle asked and sought to answer are still the ones that each generation of students of politics must seek to answer. As Robert Dahl quite correctly points out, each generation will answer them in its own way.

Dahl complicates the Aristotelian classification by adding "subsystem autonomy" as a dichotomized dimension. He is concerned with distinguishing between structurally differentiated systems in which the subsystems (political parties, pressure groups, courts, and the like) have autonomy, and those in which the subsystems are subordinated and controlled. His scheme ends up with sixteen cells. Dahl's scheme and the one used here have much in common.[2]

When Aristotle wrote his *Politics,* he was seeking to work out a conception of political systems and political change based upon the experience of the relatively civilized Greek city-states. Though he does treat the forms of kingship in the Orient to a limited extent, his scheme is almost entirely based upon Greek experience with the small city-state. Students of politics in the contemporary world cannot avoid a more universal confrontation encompassing all of man's experience with politics in all parts of the contemporary world as well as in the past. The independent nation has become a nearly universal phenomenon. The past several decades have seen a national explosion on the continents of Asia and Africa. This has

[1] Aristotle, *Politics,* Rackham translation (London: Wm. Heinemann, Ltd., 1932), Book 3, pp. 259–260. Actually, Aristotle's classification of political systems is more complicated than this. Thus, he isolates four varieties of oligarchy and five varieties of democracy based on the economic characteristics and stratification of the population. See Book VI.

[2] Robert A. Dahl, *Modern Political Analysis* (Englewood Cliffs: Prentice-Hall, Inc., 1963), pp. 25 ff.

produced an extraordinary confusion of cultures, and mixtures of archaic and modern institutional forms. In some way this confusion must be brought to order, and the capacity to explain and predict must be reaffirmed. Our contribution to these themes is an eclectic one — it draws heavily on the work of Aristotle and others of the classic tradition of political theory, on Max Weber, Carl Friedrich, S. N. Eisenstadt, Robert Dahl, Edward Shils, David Easton, James Coleman, David Apter, and Seymour M. Lipset, as well as many others. It also draws on contemporary sociological and systems theory, on Talcott Parsons, Marion Levy, Jr., and Karl Deutsch.

What we will suggest is a classification oriented around the themes of increasing structural differentiation and cultural secularization. We will not repeat the naïveté of Enlightenment theorists regarding the evolutionary progression in political systems from traditional patterns to constitutional and democratic forms. Rather, we shall argue that the earlier historical experience of political systems as well as the environmental challenges to which they are currently exposed affect their propensities for change and set limits on the ways in which they can change.

In the same sense, when we talk about different kinds of political systems, we are not arguing that one class of political system is "better" than another. We are simply arguing that one political system differs from another in certain specified ways and that these differences are subject to measurement in the empirical sense of the term. What ethical judgments one wishes to make about the differences in the properties of political systems is a second and very important question. Indeed, it is so important that we would require another book to deal with it adequately. What we would suggest is that a good book on the ethical analysis of political systems needs to be informed by solid research on the properties of political systems.

We propose to divide political systems into three classes, according to the degree of structural differentiation and cultural secularization. These classes are (1) systems with *intermittent political structures,* in which there is a minimum of structural differentiation and a concomitant diffuse, parochial culture; (2) systems with *differentiated governmental-political structures,* characterized on the attitudinal side by the spread of what we have called a "subject" culture; and (3) systems in which *differentiated political infrastructures* (political parties, interest groups, and media of mass communication) have developed along with some form of participant political culture. Within each major category several subcategories further distinguish the systems according to degree of structural differentiation, structural autonomy, secularization, and the like. These will be spelled out in detail subsequently, but the table on page 217 sets forth the three classes and their subclasses, with examples of each type of system in parentheses.

In this chapter we shall discuss the first two classes of political systems, examining for illustrative purposes some examples of the more important and widepread subcategories. Rather than expanding the analysis of the typology at this point, we shall discuss the various categories and the distinguishing and related characteristics as we proceed. It is clear, however, that this classification scheme, like any such scheme, states the differences more sharply than reality would warrant. It would not be correct, for example, to say that Classes I and II have no political infrastructure. We shall show in this chapter how the Eskimo communities, the patrimonial kingdoms, and the bureaucratic empires have handled problems of communication, interest articulation, and interest aggregation, and describe the structures which perform these political functions in these primitive and traditional systems. The important point to stress about the first two classes of political systems, however, is that political functions are handled intermittently and diffusely by social structures such as kinship or status groups, or by governmental roles and structures such as sub-chiefs, village heads, district chiefs, and councils of various kinds.

The classification scheme itself is closely related to the problem of political development and change. Not only is the classification based on a pair of more or less continuous major variables which are closely associated with one another — differentiation and secularization — but the changes in these vari-

CLASSIFICATION OF POLITICAL SYSTEMS ACCORDING TO DEGREE OF STRUCTURAL DIFFERENTIATION AND CULTURAL SECULARIZATION

I. PRIMITIVE SYSTEMS:
   INTERMITTENT POLITICAL STRUCTURES
   A. Primitive Bands (*Bergdama*)
   B. Segmentary Systems (*Nuer*)
   C. Pyramidal Systems (*Ashanti*)

II. TRADITIONAL SYSTEMS:
    DIFFERENTIATED GOVERNMENTAL-
    POLITICAL STRUCTURES
    A. Patrimonial Systems (*Ouagadougou*)
    B. Centralized Bureaucratic (*Inca, Tudor England, Ethiopia*)
    C. Feudal Political Systems (*Twelfth-century France*)

III. MODERN SYSTEMS:
     DIFFERENTIATED POLITICAL INFRASTRUCTURES
     A. Secularized City-States:
        Limited Differentiation (*Athens*)
     B. Mobilized Modern Systems:
        High Differentiation and Secularization
        1. Democratic Systems:
           Subsystem Autonomy and Participant Culture
           a. High Subsystem Autonomy (*Britain*)
           b. Limited Subsystem Autonomy (*Fourth Republic France*)
           c. Low Subsystem Autonomy (*Mexico*)
        2. Authoritarian Systems:
           Subsystem Control and Subject-Participant Culture
           a. Radical Totalitarian (*U.S.S.R.*)
           b. Conservative Totalitarian (*Nazi Germany*)
           c. Conservative Authoritarian (*Spain*)
           d. Modernizing Authoritarian (*Brazil*)
     C. Premobilized Modern Systems:
        Limited Differentiation and Secularization
        1. Premobilized Authoritarian (*Ghana*)
        2. Premobilized Democratic (*Nigeria prior to January 1966*)

ables are associated with a whole pattern of development of capability and response to various environmental pressures and internal aspirations. Although historical appearance was not itself a basis of classification, it is no accident that most systems in Classes I and II are historical systems, and that Class III is largely composed of modern or modernizing systems. The reason for this loose dichotomization seems to be that the capacity of intermittent systems to deal with complex problems, including expansion of neighbors, is very limited. Nor can systems of Class II, with differentiated output structures only, cope well with the internal demands rising from economic secularization and differentiation or from the example of prosperity and participation in other systems. Only in a few cases have such systems managed to survive in today's world. The Ethiopian case is a rare one, and it is generally agreed that the winds of change have not yet begun to blow behind her frontiers.[3] We shall, however, return to this problem in more detail in Chapters X and XI.

(I) INTERMITTENT POLITICAL STRUCTURES: PRIMITIVE POLITICAL SYSTEMS

Primitive political systems, such as those of the Eskimos, the desert Bedouins, or the Bergdama bands of southwest Africa, are characterized by minimal role differentiation and cultural secularization. There may be a headman, or a headman and a shaman, but both of these are diffuse multisystem roles. The headman, for example, may combine the roles of economic, political, and religious leader. Intermittent political systems are usually small enough to be constituted of direct face-to-face groups. The minimal degree of role differentiation in political

[3] Thus Donald N. Levine found, in a 1959–1960 survey, that 67 per cent of Ethiopian secondary school seniors identifying themselves as Amhara — the ruling people and dominant culture — maintained that *"one should always obey the order of a superior."* The reasons given emphasized that unquestioning obedience to a superior was a virtue, a duty, and a religious imperative. The dominance of such traditional subject attitudes among even educated youth is as indicative of Ethiopia's unusually undeveloped and isolated position as her lack of associational interest groups, political parties, and modern communications media — and it helps to explain the absence of a differentiated infrastructure. See Donald N. Levine, "Ethiopia: Identity, Authority, and Realism," in Lucian W. Pye and Sidney Verba (eds.), *Political Culture and Political Development* (Princeton: Princeton University Press, 1965), pp. 251 ff. Also see the discussion of efforts to develop Ethiopia without building a specialized infrastructure — Chapter V above.

action is paralleled by minimal role differentiation in economic and religious action.

To illustrate, let us imagine a Bergdama band sitting around an evening campfire somewhere in the mountains of southwest Africa after the completion of the evening meal.[4] The group might be discussing plans for hunting-and-gathering activities during the following day, a discussion in which the headman may take the leading role but in which other adult males take active part. In this context the headman and the adult males may be making economic decisions. They may invoke spirits to insure the success of the next day's operations. In this connection they would be acting as the religious subsystem of the society. Finally a disagreement among the adult males about the appropriate course of action, or a quarrel about a woman, may bring the political subsystem into operation. Here, when the order of the society is threatened by a quarrel, there may be a threat, either overt or implied, of compulsion against the offending member or members.

These primitive bands tend to be omnifunctional social systems. There are no clear boundaries between the economic, the political, and the religious systems of action. To be sure, religious, political, and economic action differ in substance and in structure; but changes in the division of labor and in orientation appropriate for these different forms of social action are intermittent. The boundaries between them are not drawn with any clarity, nor is there any clear awareness among the members of these societies of the shift from one form of action to the other.

Conversion Functions. Nevertheless, one can characterize even so simple a system as this according to our three-level scheme of functional analysis which we discussed at an earlier point. Thus, we can speak of the conversion functions, the system maintenance and adaptation functions, and the capabilities of intermittent political systems.

An illustration of the conversion processes of an intermittent political system can be found in the execution of an incorri-

[4] See I. Schapera, *Government and Politics in Tribal Societies* (London: Watts, 1956).

gible offender against customary rules of behavior in Eskimo communities.[5] There is a rule in Eskimo society that persons who engage in repeatedly disruptive activities such as acts of violence or theft against other members may be dealt with by an executioner or a group of executioners. The process by means of which this rule has been adopted in Eskimo society has been a long and gradual one. Over time, the group as a whole has come to formulate the kinds of action which are subject to this form of sanction and the methods appropriate for enforcing it.

If in a particular Eskimo community an individual emerges as a habitual thief, a point might be reached at which the application of this rule becomes appropriate. But before this occurs, there is something like an adjudicative process as the adult members of the society deliberate with one another about the behavior of the disruptive member. An executioner may be designated or may volunteer, and on the appropriate occasion may enforce the rule by killing the offending member. If we were examining this process closely, we would observe all the functions of the political system being performed. The processes of communication, of articulation of different points of view, and of aggregation of these points of view into alternative courses of action might be distinguished; and we might observe processes leading to the adjudication and the enforcement of the decision.

It is, of course, a subtle matter to tease out these different processes in simpler societies where there are relatively few specialized roles. The important thing to keep in mind is that these very simple political systems are susceptible of being analyzed with the same kind of conversion scheme that one uses for the most highly differentiated and secularized political systems. Thus, one can speak of the Bergdama band and the modern democratic political system as both being political systems, just as one can speak of the amoeba and the vertebrate as both being biological forms.

System Maintenance and Adaptation. It is also possible to

5 Adamson Hoebel, *The Law of Primitive Man* (Cambridge: Harvard University Press, 1954), pp. 67 ff.

describe these simple societies in terms of their system maintenance and adaptive characteristics. The recruitment processes
are minimal, of course, since there is relatively little role differentiation. Nevertheless, there is some differentiation of roles
in the economic, religious, and political subsystems of the
society according to sex and age. There are well-understood
ways for recruiting the headman or the shaman. Thus, among
the Eskimos the headman is selected quite informally on the
basis of his ability in organizing hunting and fishing activities.
The incumbents of this role may change with some frequency,
according to differences in the abilities of the adult males in
the group. It is also possible to describe how members of primitive and traditional societies are socialized into the particular
sets of orientations and attitudes appropriate to their roles in
the political system.

Capabilities. One can also analyze intermittent political systems according to their performance, or capability patterns.
Thus, one can describe the extractive capability of the Bergdama band as they engage in their hunting-and-gathering operations. The headman may be entitled to a larger share of the
yield, but he may decide on distributing the portions among
the other members of the band. The headman and the adult
males may regulate their own behavior and the behavior of
the women and the younger children. They may regulate marriage and marital relations, make and enforce plans for hunting and gathering, and make decisions about defense against
attacks from other bands in the same area. In the processes of
decision making, the headman and the adult males may sound
out opinion of other members of the society and may take
these opinions and demands into account. Thus, one can recognize a form of the responsive capability in these intermittent
political systems.

One can say of primitive political systems that though they
have all the capabilities which are to be found in the more
elaborate and complicated types of political systems, they have
relatively little ability to adapt to new and difficult situations.
It is not accidental that the intermittent political systems still
in existence in the modern world are located on the periphery

of the habitable parts of the globe. The Eskimo bands are to be found in the relatively inhospitable areas of the Arctic; the Bedouin in the Arabian desert; and the Bergdama bands in the mountains of southwest Africa. The capabilities of these societies are small in terms of the resources which they can control and mobilize. And they are unable to compete effectively with and to defend themselves against more complicated societies and political systems.

The anthropologists tell us of a somewhat more complex type of intermittent political system, the segmentary system. A segmentary political system consists of a number of autonomous kinship or lineage units, all belonging to a common tribe. The tribe itself has no explicit political organization or structure, and each one of the component lineage segments is a self-governing unit. However, when conflicts arise between members of different segments of these tribes, some informal political machinery becomes available which makes it possible to resolve disputes and conflicts of this kind without too serious a disruption of safety and order. There may be a meeting of headmen or of elders from the two disputing segments, and a solution of the dispute may be recommended and in some sense enforced.[6]

The segmentary lineage system is more complex than the simple band which may or may not be patriarchal in form. Apter distinguishes another level of intermittent political structure, which is more differentiated than the segmentary system. This is what he calls the pyramidal system, in which there are several layers of authority (chiefs and subchiefs), but in which the local units tend to have the same powers as the central, paramount chief. Apter gives the kingdom of Ashanti as an example.[7] This contrasts with the hierarchical system of authority, which is more centralized and is the same as Weber's

[6] Lucy Mair, *Primitive Government* (Baltimore: Penguin Books, Inc., 1962), pp. 61 ff.

[7] David Apter, *The Political Kingdom in Uganda* (Princeton: Princeton University Press, 1961), pp. 86 ff. Apter cites Aidan Southall's study *The Alur* (Cambridge: W. Heffer & Sons, Ltd., 1953) for a discussion of this type of political system.

patrimonial system of authority. Apter uses the kingdom of Buganda as an example of hierarchical, or patrimonial, authority.

(II) DIFFERENTIATED GOVERNMENTAL-POLITICAL STRUCTURES:

(A) PATRIMONIAL SYSTEMS

Patrimonial political systems are those in which there are specialized political elites such as kings, subchiefs, and a relatively specialized officialdom. They are called patrimonial because all, or most, of these offices are located in the ruler's household. Some of these systems have been very large, as was that of Egypt under the Pharaohs. "Thus the whole country and its government were constituted as one vast patriarchal household of the Pharaoh . . . the army was equipped and maintained out of the royal storehouses. . . . Originally Egyptian officialdom appears to have been recruited from the personal dependents of the king. . . ." [8] In recent times the kingdoms of East and West Africa were of this patrimonial type.

The founding myths of many patrimonial systems suggest that they developed out of situations in which a particular lineage group would establish control over other clans in the same area, or out of situations in which a wandering, militarily powerful band would conquer less powerful groups and subject them to permanent control.

THE KINGDOM OF OUAGADOUGOU

It may be useful to take a closer look at a patrimonial political system of the kind encountered by the European powers in their drive for the control of Africa in the nineteenth century. We choose the kingdom of Ouagadougou because its political system has been described effectively and in great detail.[9] According to myth this kingdom was founded some forty generations ago (sometime in the fourteenth century) by a small

[8] Reinhard Bendix, *Max Weber: An Intellectual Portrait* (New York: Doubleday & Company, Inc., 1960), pp. 334 ff.

[9] F. P. Skinner, *The Mossi of the Upper Volta* (Stanford: Stanford University Press, 1964).

conquest group which subjected native tribes in the Upper Volta area of West Africa to their control. The system which evolved had four levels of authority hierarchically subordinated to the royal court. The basic unit was the extended family living in a village compound and subject to the authority of the oldest male. The compounds were organized in villages under the authority of a village chief. These, in turn, were under the authority of district chiefs, who were subject to the control of provincial ministers under the ultimate control of the king.

Conversion Functions. Let us examine first the conversion processes of this patrimonial kingdom — the pattern of flow of inputs and outputs. Demands for political action, which we call interest articulation, were made by the elders of the extended family compounds to the village chiefs. The chiefs, in turn, could request action of various kinds of the district chiefs, who could respond to these demands or transmit them to the provincial ministers and the royal court. At each level of authority, there were councils which might be viewed as performing aggregative functions as they heard complaints and deliberated over appropriate courses of action. Thus, the flow of demands into the political system was not handled by specialized political structures such as interest groups or political parties, but rather by the governmental officials, or family or lineage heads at each level of the political system. It is important to keep this in mind, since the lack of differentiation of political infrastructure is the major distinction between traditional systems (Classes I and II in our typology) and modern or modernizing political systems.

Ouagadougou was a traditional political system in the sense that law making or rule making was not viewed as a legitimate function of the political system. It tended to be a derivative of the rule-application and rule-adjudication functions. In the course of the deliberations of the councils in the villages, the districts, and the central organs of the political system, and through the application of custom to specific cases, general rules emerged and slowly were elaborated and changed as the kingdom encountered and coped with novel problems.

There was some slight differentiation of a communications structure. When it came to transmitting official orders and messages from the higher levels of authority to the lower levels, specialized communicators or messengers were employed. Thus, in the royal court there was a group of servants who were used for the purpose of transmitting information and orders from the center to the districts and villages. The existence of this corps of specialized messengers served the purpose of avoiding face-to-face contact between powerful men. The use of a messenger had the effect of saving the face of the recipient of the communication when it involved a direct order or a punishment. In other words, the development of this primitive specialized system of communication was a device intended to neutralize the political communication process. It is said that the king sometimes executed messengers when they brought bad news, which suggests the difficulty of separating the channel of communication or the instrument of communication from the particular message that it conveyed. But if neutralization of communication was a difficult problem for the kingdom of Ouagadougou, we should appreciate the fact that such neutralization has not been fully attained in the most modern of political systems, where political leaders constantly appraise the source of information before giving it credibility. The communications function in Ouagadougou was also handled by compound and lineage elders, village chiefs, district chiefs, and the central administration.

The enforcement of rules in this kingdom was handled through a relatively specialized officialdom consisting of police officers, tax gatherers, treasurers, military officers, messengers, the various officials responsible for the maintenance of the court, and the attendants on the king. The adjudication of rules was handled by the chief officials at each level of authority. Thus, in the village compounds the family heads acted as judges of their members. The village chief acted as judge, as did the district chief, the prime minister, and the king himself. In other words, the same officials handled the political and the adjudicative functions. Adjudicative tasks were differentiated from political ones not by the appointment of special officers, but rather by shifting the location of the action and by employing a different kind of procedure.

Capabilities. The capacity of the kingdom of Ouagadougou to mobilize and extract resources from the kingdom, to distribute these resources, and to regulate behavior, though substantially higher than that of the simpler systems we have already described, was not so high as that of the larger scale empires or of the modern political systems, which we shall treat below. One of the reasons for this was the absence of a standing army and of a well-organized system of police. Thus, the ability of the central government to enforce its demands on the districts and villages of the kingdom was relatively limited. This was, at least in part, due to the mixture of household and bureaucratic forms of organization and control which is characteristic of patrimonial political systems. Needless to say, in this particular case it was also attributable to the fact that this was a preliterate society, which meant that effective records could not be kept. Then, too, the absence of a money economy made it difficult to accumulate resources. Much of the tax revenue was in the form of agricultural produce, which had to be distributed and consumed quickly.

Nevertheless, this and other patrimonial kingdoms had quite elaborate extractive, regulative, distributive, symbolic, and responsive capabilities. In addition to the produce of his own royal estates, the king received a portion of the harvest and of the livestock from all parts of the kingdom, forwarded to the central government through the district chiefs; fees for the performance of his judicial functions; gifts from vassals; inheritance taxes on the estates of district chiefs, and taxes on caravans and foreign traders; slaves taken from slave-raiding expeditions or captured in war; and labor levies on his own population for the maintenance and repair of the royal estates and palaces. While the number of objects which were taxed was high and the sources of revenue were quite varied, the efficiency of the taxing system was relatively low. At each level the appropriate authority would take his "administrative slice" as produce moved from the compounds to the villages, to the districts, to the royal court. Limits were set on the extraction of resources from the society. Tyrannical district and village chiefs could be removed from office or even executed for excessive exploitation or taxation.

The regulative capability was quite extensive. Marital relations were subject to regulation. Persons and property were protected by the political system. Market relations were subject to regulation. Respect for elders and for governmental officials was enforced by the political system. All four levels of the political system were involved in the performance of the regulative function in Ouagadougou society. Thus, the family head in the compound had the duty of settling all family quarrels and of punishing persons for theft within the compound, for acts of disrespect toward elders, or for the crime of incest. The compound elder had the power to reprimand, to flog, and even to banish members of the compound for violation of any of these rules and customs.

At the village level the chief would pass on all cases involving theft, quarrels, trespassing, adultery, indebtedness, and abuse which could not be settled at the level of the compound. At the same time, serious injury and homicide cases had to be sent up to the district chief for decision along with disputes between villages and cases that the village chief could not himself resolve. At the level of the central government, only the most serious cases were heard or cases which were appealed from the decisions of the district chiefs.

While in a formal sense the regulative capability was completely in the hands of the Ouagadougou king, in actual fact it was substantially decentralized. Transportation and communication were primitive and costly; gifts and fees to the court were high. Consequently, there was a premium on settling disputes at the lowest possible level. Thus, while one can say that there was an effective regulative capability in Ouagadougou it was widely diffused throughout the political system and not concentrated at the center. This meant that the responsive capability of the system was greater than it appeared from its formal place in the system. The mere fact that most regulative issues were settled at the lowest possible levels made regulative decisions more responsive to the interests of the parties, who lived in the immediate village or district. The rule seems to be that the smaller and more intimate the group and the smaller the administrative staff, the greater the dependence of the ruler on the participation and the support of the rank-and-file members of the group. Thus, these centralized, regulative, traditional systems had more responsiveness in them than would seem to be the case from a description of the formal powers of the central authorities.

There were other practices and institutions that contributed to the responsive capability of this kingdom. Sometimes kings would disguise themselves and visit the wards of the capital city in an effort to learn things that did not ordinarily come to their attention. In addition, the heads of lineages, the elders of compounds, and the village chiefs could petition and complain against maladministration and injustice. There were councils at the central, district, and village levels which provided opportunities for the articulation of complaints and demands. There was also a custom that if one wished to complain against the tyranny of a district chief, one could make application to another district chief who might be persuaded to transmit the complaint to the royal court. From the foregoing discussion we can say that the scope of regulation of the Ouagadougou was relatively limited because of the primitiveness of the institutions and of the technologies available to it. And we might say that the responsive capability in this type of political system was greater at the local levels than at the central level. In both cases, it may be noted that the limited development of the communication function was a major factor, suggesting the interdependence between capability and structure as well as the prerequisite nature of communication performance.

Some evidence would seem to suggest that the kingdom of Buganda had a more effective and more centralized regulative capability than did the kingdom of Ouagadougou. Thus, though the evidence is quite inadequate, we might say that the Ouagadougou system was a more traditional kind of patrimonialism, while that of Buganda corresponded to Max Weber's category of "sultanic patrimonialism." There appears

to have been more arbitrariness, more violence, and more disregard of tradition in the kingdom of Buganda than the kingdom of Ouagadougou.

The distributive capability of Ouagadougou was in part tied
up with the extractive capability and in part with the symbolic
capability. Thus, as revenues, fees, and gifts would pass from
the periphery to the center of the political system, each authority was entitled to take a share. It was also the traditional
practice of the courts of the village chief, of the district head,
of the provincial ministers, and of the king himself to dispense
generously the perishable goods which constituted a large
proportion of the total revenue. Thus, beer and kola nuts were
always available for distribution at the village, district, and
royal courts. Much of the revenue actually was expended in
this form of hospitality. But it should be remembered that this
hospitality was mainly available to governmental and administrative officials and to members of the aristocratic strata of the
population.

The commoners were the beneficiaries of what one might
call nonmaterial distributions. Among these psychological
distributions were the show of pomp, rite, symbolism, and
ceremony, particularly at the royal and at the district courts.
One of the chief ministers of the king had the duty of praying
every night to the ancestors of the society to protect the subjects of the king through the night, to maintain the peace, and
to insure health, prosperity, and fertility. There was an annual
festival at which all the authorities, central and local, would
pray to the ancestors, thereby linking the whole of the society
together and establishing its relation to its sacred origins.

The symbolic capability of Ouagadougou seems to have
been quite substantial. The population was on the whole loyal
and submissive. There was an effort to make the king appear
to be a man of extraordinary power and sacred virtue. It was
forbidden to touch his hand, or to speak to him save in a kneel-
ing position with the forehead touching the ground. He was
constantly attended by pages ministering to him. His first appearance in the morning was marked by a royal drummer who
would rub his drum to imitate the growl of a lion. Every king

had to be of the blood of the original and mythical founders of the regime, who constituted the chief dieties of the Ouagadougou. The king and his officials through their prayers were able to maintain contact with and ensure the benevolence of these supernatural powers. The district chiefs imitated the ceremonies of the king, but on a less elaborate scale.

A note may be in order regarding the international capabilities of Ouagadougou. While the kingdom had a strong military tradition, prior to its subjection by France in the latter part of the nineteenth century, it was living in relative harmony with neighboring kingdoms. On the periphery there were a number of political systems which might be viewed as fiefs of the king of Ouagadougou. Though they were governed by independent chiefs, they owed tribute and military support to Ouagadougou. But it appears that the kingdom was unable to exercise effective control over these peripheral political systems, and that it was not always able to extract the tributes and services it demanded. Ouagadougou lacked a standing army, and as a consequence its ability to extract and regulate declined significantly toward the periphery of the kingdom.

Most of the wars which occurred seem to have been administrative actions against feudal princes behind in their payments of tribute, or against district chiefs who had contravened orders or violated customs. Small-scale raids and intervillage wars were endemic and were rarely interfered with from the center unless they took on major proportions. Another type of warfare characteristic of Ouagadougou was the slave-raiding expeditions into non-Mossi territories. Major wars were rare and had to be based on special levies of troops and supplies from the various districts and principalities. Military services were limited to the dry season and were terminated in the rainy season.

System Maintenance and Adaptation. The political rulers at the various levels of the Ouagadougou political system were recruited from the royal and aristocratic lineages. The king by custom was selected from the immediate descendants of the mythical founders of the regime. The district chiefs were chosen from the nobility of the local ruling lineages, and the village chiefs were chosen by the district chiefs from among all the eligible members of the appropriate lineages. On the other hand, the administrative officialdom was selected from commoner administrative families and lineages. The five provincial ministers were selected hereditarily from these specialized administrative lineages. One interpretation of the origins of this class of administrators is that they were originally slaves but that they acquired the status of freedom. The theory is that the king sought to insure himself of the loyalty of his administrative staff by drawing them not from the nobility, who might have competed with him, but rather from lineages which by custom were ineligible to hold high political office.

This pattern of recruitment made it possible in the Ouagadougou political system to avoid the necessity for a specialized socialization into the particular roles of the political system. Socialization of the males in the royal and aristocratic families and in the specialized administrative lineages could combine political role socialization with general socialization. This arrangement avoided the necessity of providing specialized political training or administrative training. Nevertheless, this combination of general socialization with political socialization stood in the way of a more effective development of political and administrative skills which might have resulted from specialized training institutions and processes.

The political culture of Ouagadougou tended to be divided into subcultures on the basis of political and social status and of religious differences. The attitudes, expectations, and values of the aristocratic, commoner, and slave strata differed one from the other, and each of these strata had different roles to play in the political system. The political culture was of a "subject" type, oriented to output structures but with limited distinction between social and political roles. The Moslems constituted a powerful minority in the kingdom of Ouagadougou. Their political influence was in part based on their contacts through religious affiliation to areas outside the kingdom. Their superior knowledge of and role in trade and commerce made them especially valuable as advisers to the political elite.

Were we to generalize about the capacity and adaptiveness of the Ouagadougou political system, we might first say that in a positive sense it was able to maintain its integrity and cohesion as a political system over a period of several centuries. Furthermore, it was able to penetrate neighboring societies and at least to reduce them to temporary vassalage. In addition, it could draw on simpler societies on its border for occasional supplies of slaves and spoils, but the limits of its capacities are reflected in the fact that it could expand so far and no farther, and that toward the periphery, the effectiveness and the cohesion of the system declined. When the Ouagadougou political system finally confronted the conquering French, it collapsed quickly for lack of effective military organization and technology.

(II) DIFFERENTIATED GOVERNMENTAL-POLITICAL STRUCTURES:
(B) CENTRALIZED BUREAUCRATIC SYSTEMS

The category of "bureaucratic empires" is a new one in schemes of political classification; Max Weber does not single it out specifically as a distinctive type of political system. Eisenstadt devotes a whole book to the analysis of this class of political system and compares some twenty-seven cases including the Roman, Byzantine, and Ottoman empires, and the great European powers in the Age of Absolutism — Britain, France, Germany, Spain, and Russia. The criteria he uses for this class of political systems are as follows: (1) the development of autonomous political goals by the ruler and to some extent by those who participate in the political struggle; (2) the development of specialized political and administrative roles and agencies; and (3) more or less effective attempts to organize the society into a centralized unit.[10]

A variety of political systems is included in Eisenstadt's classification. At one extreme, the Inca empire of South America fulfills Eisenstadt's criteria only in a minimal sense. At the other extreme, Britain under the Tudor monarchy, and

[10] S. N. Eisenstadt, *The Political Systems of Empires* (New York: The Free Press of Glencoe, 1962), p. 18.

particularly under the reign of Henry VIII, fulfills his criteria to a very substantial extent. In our discussion of bureaucratic empires we will use these two cases as illustrations.

THE INCA EMPIRE

The Inca empire reached its apogee in the first decades of the sixteenth century, immediately prior to the Spanish conquest. At that time it extended some 2500 miles along the western coast of South America from Peru down to the present location of Santiago, Chile. Its population is estimated as somewhere between five and seven-and-one-half million. Though it was a preliterate, predominantly agricultural society with only the llama as a beast of burden, it was extraordinarily effective in expansion and in centralization.

The social structure of the Inca empire included an aristocratic class consisting of members of the imperial clans, an administrative hierarchy and a priesthood, and commoners consisting of the great bulk of the population. The empire was divided into four quarters, with the four roads leading into and dividing the capital serving as borders for these quarters. The four provinces of the empire were administered by viceroys, usually relatives of the emperor who lived in the capital and served as his advisory council. The role of viceroy represented a combination of administrative, political, and judicial activities.

The provinces were subdivided into units by number of families. Thus, there were administrative districts for 10,000 families, for 1,000 families, for 500 families, and so on. The more inclusive units were governed by members of the nobility. Officials at the lower levels were commoners in origin, but they acquired a low aristocratic rank on their appointment. The topmost levels of the administrative hierarchy were appointed by the Inca, and those below were appointed by the district officials.

Conversion Functions. The Inca political system was highly authoritarian and paternalistic, and specialized political input structures were conspicuously limited or absent. The interests of the commoners were articulated through their clan heads and district chiefs, and through an imperial inspectorate which traveled through the empire to report on conditions and problems in the various areas. Another form of interest articulation among the common Indian was occasional rebellions. Interest articulation among the nobility principally took the form of informal demands for offices, privileges, and benefits. This was said to be one of the primary forces accounting for the continued territorial expansion of the empire. Each expansion provided opportunities for additional offices for members of the nobility. This struggle for power became most intense at the time of the death of an Inca. Though there were rules of succession, the usual case apparently involved civil war, palace intrigue, and conspiracies by pretenders to the throne.

Interest articulation and aggregation seem also to have been among the primary functions performed by the councils which existed at the various levels of the Inca system. The Inca's own council consisted of the four viceroys and four scholars who were the repositories of the history and custom of the empire as well as sources of statistical information regarding the country. At the regional and local levels of the Inca system, there were similar councils performing articulative, deliberative, legislative, and adjudicative functions. But in theory, the Inca was the sole, legitimate lawmaker of the empire.

The central bureaucracy was relatively specialized. Records were kept by an ingenious system of knots on strings (*quipus*) which recorded events, population data, military campaigns, crimes, and agricultural yields. A group of special officials made scale models of the various areas of the empire, which facilitated governmental planning and administration. There was also a central inspectorate which toured the empire periodically to report on conditions. The military responsibility seems to have been somewhat diffusely distributed in the various organs of the administrative staff, which provided officers for military campaigns. All males were given military training and were subject to draft for military purposes. In addition there were officials and teachers for the central schools, and a priestly heirarchy. The functions of the various offices of the central administrative organization were only partially differentiated.

Most officials performed aggregative, deliberative, administrative, and adjudicative functions as well as military ones in time of war.

The Inca did not have a specialized system of courts. The Inca's council constituted a tribunal to try high officials and to hear cases involving serious crimes. Less serious offenses were handled at the local levels by the regional heads and their councils. But when cases were being tried by these political and administrative bodies, a judicial procedure was employed which involved the presentation of cases by the disputing parties and an impartial tribunal.

One of the most impressive aspects of the Inca system was its extraordinarily effective communications network. The maintenance of an effective system of roads was one of the most important activities carried on by the political system. This made it possible for information to be transmitted effectively throughout the empire through specialized couriers as well as through the imperial inspectors. Despite the fact that the Incas lacked a system of writing, and despite the enormous expanse of the empire and the primitiveness of transportation, communication was relatively rapid; apparently a substantial degree of centralization was possible. However, the extent of centralization may be somewhat idealized, based as it is on the accounts of Spanish priests who in turn received their information by talking to older Inca informants after the fall of the empire. The rapid expansion of the Inca empire and the inclusion of ethnically and linguistically foreign elements must have created centrifugal and pluralistic tendencies of some importance. The normal practice after the conquest of a new area was to include it as a subregion in the empire and to co-opt its rulers into the Inca bureaucracy. Despite such measures, the extent of the empire and its ethnic heterogeneity would suggest centrifugal political tendencies.

Capabilities. The extractive capability of the Inca empire took the form of services and tribute. Those parts of the land which were set aside for the emperor and the priesthood had to be cultivated by the local population. The produce of these lands was kept in storehouses located throughout the empire and in the temples. These supplies were available for officials traveling throughout the empire as well as for armies on the march. The population was also obliged to perform a number of labor services, such as working in the national mines and on the maintenance and construction of public buildings, roads, warehouses, fortresses, irrigation projects, and bridges. There was constant appraisal of performance and yields on the basis of estimates which were made by the central bureaucracy. Levies on the population or on produce could be checked on the basis of census statistics.

Women were selected from the population by the imperial officials for religious purposes or for concubinage. There were also levies on artisans and skilled workmen for the construction of public buildings, furniture, costumes, and jewelry.

The resources of the empire as well as its extractive capability are suggested by the story of the speed with which a whole roomful of gold was accumulated in order to ransom the emperor during the Spanish conquest. In view of the state of Inca technology and the enormous scale of the empire, its extractive capability must be viewed as exceptionally large and unusually well organized.

The Inca political system also performed an important distributive function. Land for cultivation and subsistence was made available to the common Indians, and adjustments were made to raise their income to subsistence level where necessary. The basic items of clothing worn by the common Indian were distributed from state storehouses. In periods of poor crops or famine, entire districts might be supplied by the state storehouses. The nobility and the officialdom were rewarded with substantial grants of land, servants, and wives.

There were important service distributions among the Inca. The Indians were given technical help for the cultivation of their land. In addition, they were provided with elementary schools where they were taught the common language. The nobility were taught in special schools located in the capital.

The granting of status was also an instrument of distribution controlled by the political system. Thus, commoners who were selected for local chieftainships acquired a low noble

rank, and their sons might become military officers or administrative officers and thus be co-opted into the privileged Inca
status. Honors and awards were distributed for military service,
for the construction of public buildings, or for purely political
reasons.

The regulative capability of the Inca political system was
unusually penetrative and extensive, covering almost the whole
range of personal and social activity. The penetrativeness and
extent of the control makes one think of modern totalitarian
systems. Individual behavior, family relations, clan structure
and responsibilities, and the entire economy of the empire were
subject to regulative control. The performance of the bureaucracy in exercising its regulatory powers was subject to review and appraisal by inspectors. The central bureaucracy
could control the whole system of regulation by virtue of its
effective communication system and its maintenance of statistical records in the capital.

Production quotas were assigned to the various regions.
Seeds and labor were made available where necessary, and provision was made for the storage of crops. Population was moved
from overpopulated areas to those which were underpopulated.
Newly conquered tribes whose loyalty was still in question
could be moved to areas nearer the capital, and more reliable
populations might be transferred to the frontier lands.

The Inca elite deliberately set out to create a single, homogeneous nation, speaking one language and submissive to the
imperial institutions and to the religious and legal systems.
The forms of dress appropriate to the various status groups
were prescribed by law, and persons found improperly dressed
were subject to punishment. Personal movement was limited.
People found outside their own region without authorization
were subject to punishment. In some cities curfew hours were
imposed. Sexual behavior was rigorously controlled.

The symbolic capability of the Inca empire was intended to
create awe and submissiveness to authority among subjects.
The evidence suggests that it was largely successful in accom-
plishing these goals, although the effectiveness of the flow of
symbolism seems to have varied at different times in the devel-

opment of the empire. Thus, it might be at a low point at times of conflict over succession to the throne.

The emperor was treated as a divinity, and as the symbol of the unity and power of the empire. He could not be looked at face-to-face, nor was it possible to talk with him directly. Conversation had to take place through a screen. The costumes of the high officials; the lavish use of gold in the palaces and temples; and the pomp, ceremony, and rites were all designed to develop and maintain a feeling of awe among the subjects of the empire. Celebrations for military victories, royal anniversaries, and burials were used as occasions to consolidate the authority and the legitimacy of the political system through lavish displays and ceremonies. The capital city of Cuzco was viewed as a sacred city.

It might be said that the Inca political system responded more to needs imputed to the population by the leaders than to demands of the people themselves. The flow of information from the periphery of the empire to the center was effective. The network of roads made it possible for relay runners to bring information within a few days from the most distant regions. Such unrest or demands as developed were handled through the governmental officialdom and structure. The bureaucracy at the various levels of the empire transmitted information regarding needs and conditions to the center. The regional inspectors, who watched over the performance of the regular bureaucracy, might be viewed as important articulators of interests and demands. In addition, the chiefs of the various districts and subdistricts were required to come to the capital at festival periods. This might have been another device which contributed to the responsive capability of the Inca system. The emperor made frequent trips to various parts of the empire with his retinue, and was thereby able to inform himself directly about conditions. The over-all pattern of capability of the Inca political system was one of high extractive, regulative, distributive, and symbolic capability, and of low responsive capability.

Recruitment and Socialization. In describing the system maintenance processes in the Inca empire, we have to distin-

guish between the recruitment and socialization of the population in general into the roles of subjects, and the recruitment
and socialization of elites into the more specialized roles of
the political system. All males were trained for military service
and were inducted at an early age into other forms of imperial
service, such as work on building construction projects and on
the maintenance of roads. Teachers sent from the capital were
supposed to train all elements of the population in the use of
the national language. Although we cannot be sure how effective this recruitment and socialization into subject roles actually was, the goal sought was the creation of a population of
submissive subjects, accepting the divinity of the emperor, and
the plenary powers of the emperor and his officials, over all
phases of individual and social behavior.

Recruitment into higher levels of regional administration
and of the central bureaucracy was confined to the Inca aristocratic stratum. At the lower levels, recruitment among commoners offered effective channels of social mobility. The
district governors and officials and the central bureaucracy were
trained in special schools in the capital under the control of an
educational hierarchy. These schools involved training in
religion, the arts, the official language, and the techniques for
keeping records and accumulating information. The norms
of recruitment represented a mixture of ascriptive and achievement criteria with a heavy emphasis on the latter. Outstanding
military and governmental service was rewarded by promotion
to higher ranks.

One of the great riddles of the Inca civilization is its quick
and complete collapse. Why did this enormously complex and
effective system of regulation and control disintegrate so
quickly on the invasion of Pizarro and his one-hundred-seventy-
odd soldiers? It may be in part explained by the fact that
centralization in the system was extreme, and that once the
Emperor himself had been hanged and Cuzco captured, the
heart and the brain of the system were destroyed. In other
words, the very success of the effort at centralization, regulation, and the development of a submissive mentality throughout the empire may account for its quick collapse. In addition,

at the time of the Spanish conquest there was a civil war over the question of imperial succession. Thus, the legitimacy of the empire may very well have been at a very low point at this period,[11] its symbolic capability undermined and system support weakened.

THE TUDOR MONARCHY

We take as our second example of bureaucratic empires Britain in the period of Tudor absolutism during the reigns of Henry VII and Henry VIII. At the beginning of the sixteenth century the population of Britain was less than three million. The ratio of rural to urban population was on the order of 10 to 1, and the various regions of Britain still showed marked differences resulting from different ethnic origins. The dialects spoken in various parts of Britain could be barely understood from one region to the next. In Dorset and Somersetshire the language still showed the marks of the Saxon origin of the population. In Kent the influence of the Jutes was still apparent, and in the north the dialect reflected Danish origins. It was during the Tudor period that London English began to spread more rapidly and became standard English throughout the realm. It was during this period that the older dialects based on ethnic origins began to attenuate, and differences in pronunciation based on class became increasingly marked. The dominantly rural class structure of England included an aristocracy, a gentry, and a peasantry. The aristocratic peerage authorized to sit in the House of Lords numbered under fifty. Prior to the Tudor period many of them lived as patrimonial rulers with their own courts and their own governing powers. The War of the Roses thinned the ranks of the aristocracy. During the Tudor monarchy their powers were substantially

11 This analysis of the political system of the Inca is based on three research papers prepared by members of a graduate seminar in the Department of Political Science at Stanford University, Antonio Ugalde, Robert W. Gage, and Lois Swirsky. They drew on the following studies *inter al.*: L. Baudin, *A Socialist Empire: The Incas of Peru* (Princeton: D. Van Nostrand Co., Inc., 1961); J. Bram, *An Analysis of Inca Militarism* (New York: Columbia University Dissertation, 1941); Eisenstadt, *Political Systems, op. cit.*; B. C. Brundage, *Empire of the Inca* (Norman, Okla.: University of Oklahoma Press, 1963).

reduced. But during these times, intermittent rebellions led by local magnates reflected the persistence of the earlier pattern of feudal particularism.

Below the level of the aristocracy were the gentry, or country squires, who lived on the rent from their lands. There was substantial mobility in the gentry class, which was drawn from the younger sons of the aristocracy on the one hand, and from merchants, manufacturers, and professional men on the other. The peasantry included a top stratum of freeholders and of tenants with secure tenure. This top stratum of peasants owning land or holding secure tenures enjoyed the right to vote. Below them was a class of tenants more dependent on the whim of their landlords, and a small surviving stratum of villeins bound to the land.

The social structure of English towns consisted of freeholders and tenants who had the franchise and were called "burgesses." During the Tudor period urban stratification increasingly took on the structure of a governing class consisting of merchants, industrialists, lawyers and professional men, and a larger unfranchised class of craftsmen and artisans, small traders, and dependent servants.[12]

The significance of the Tudor period for British political development lies in the fact that it established the control of the central government over the aristocratic magnates and over the church hierarchy. The assimilation of the aristocracy into the central governmental system made possible the penetration of the regions of England by the central regime. The separation of the Church of England from the Vatican contributed to centralization and to independence from external control.

It is of great significance that this centralization of England took place under the legal, and to a considerable extent the real, auspices of the "king in Parliament." British centralization was carried out by statute enacted through Parliament.

[12] See S. T. Bindoff, *Tudor England* (London: Penguin Books, Ltd., 1950); F. W. Maitland, *The Constitutional History of England* (Cambridge: Cambridge University Press, 1963); and G. R. Elton, *England under the Tudors* (London: Methuen & Co., Ltd., 1955).

In effect, this meant for British political development the rise of an explicit rule-making power located in an agency broadly representative not only of the king, but of the aristocracy and the middle classes.

Elton argues that modern centralized government in England, in the full sense of the term, dates back to the Tudor period, with the full legitimation of the statutory power of the king in Parliament:

> The essential characteristic of medieval government was that it discovered the law and then administered it, while modern government first makes and then administers laws; thus the 1530's marked quite definitely the end of the medieval constitution and the beginning of the modern.[13]

The fact that the central power of England represented a partnership between king, lords, and commons meant that British centralization stopped short of continental European absolutism. The fact that the House of Commons was an active and important body during the Tudor monarchy meant that some of the earlier autonomies of urban and rural England could survive and carry on an effective articulation of local and oppositional interests and demands. Similarly, the power of the House of Lords preserved some of these earlier particularisms and autonomies. While strong kings — and the Tudors were almost all strong kings — could play a dominant role, they were never able fully to suppress these pluralistic tendencies. The political art of the Tudor monarchs and their ministers was to make effective coalitions out of these components. They could carry through the separation from the Church of Rome by virtue of the support of the House of Commons and of a substantial part of the lay peerage. They could draw upon the gentry and the professions to staff their growing ministries and bureaucracy, and could use these new institutions to suppress the rivalry of local magnates and competing institutions.

The Tudor revolution was carried through by the legal and legitimate political institutions of England. It assimilated

[13] Elton, *ibid.*, p. 168.

and modified pre-existing elements; it did not destroy them. This fusion of traditional and modern institutions in the period of absolutism was one of the more important reasons that the British political system could continue to grow incrementally in the centuries that followed in the direction of more centralization and more popular participation. A secularized political culture gradually emerged without the sharp breaks and divisions which lead to subcultural fragmentation.

The accommodation of the centralization process in England to local and particularistic interests is reflected in the growth in importance of the justices of the peace under Henry VII and Henry VIII. Every locality in England had its justices of the peace; there were some six or seven hundred of them during the reign of Henry VII. These important officials were drawn from the gentry, which also contributed largely to the membership of the House of Commons. The powers of the justices of the peace were fixed by central statute and regulation; but since they were men of independent means and local reputation, and were well represented in Parliament, they could not be viewed as the obedient arm of a centralized bureaucracy. They were originally established in the thirteenth century as a local judiciary; they gradually acquired greater powers, including the fixing of wage rates, control over the sheriffs, regulation of weights and measures, and the exercise of a general censorship over economic activities, family life, and morals. By virtue of their possession of this combination of social and governmental powers, they enjoyed a general moral authority in their communities.[14]

While Tudor England saw a substantial centralization of power, local, corporate, and particularistic tendencies retained vitality. In addition, a judiciary with an independent common-law tradition and a legal profession with a strong vocational ethic monitored the growing political power of the central agencies.

Conversion Functions. The two houses of Parliament were vital institutions during this period, and both houses represented local interests. The knights of the shires and the bur-

[14] Maitland, *op. cit.,* pp. 206 ff.

gesses of the towns elected to Parliament were viewed in some sense as delegates of these corporate entities. In the deliberations of the House of Commons, members could and did speak in the name of local and special interests. The presence of members of the church hierarchy in the House of Lords also insured some representation of the interests of the church. However, during the period of the Tudor reformation the ecclesiastical members of the House of Lords were by and large a submissive lot, and it was the lay peerage and the Commons which were the articulate components of Parliament.

Thus, it would perhaps be accurate to say that the chief articulators of local and special interests in Tudor England were the members of the houses of Parliament, and in particular of the House of Commons. The primary source of parliamentary bills was the government rather than Parliament. Thus, the primary functions of Parliament were the articulation and the aggregation of interests rather than the actual formulation of legislation.

Another significant instrumentality for the articulation of local interests was the justice of the peace, who, though appointed by the king, was selected from among the local gentry. Thus national statutes and orders, in all probability, were enforced in the light of local needs and interests. During the Tudor period, and especially during the reign of Henry VIII, the formulation of statutes came to be the responsibility of the great officers of the realm, and in particular of the king's principal secretary. This office was turned into something comparable to the modern prime ministership during the reign of Henry VIII by his principal secretary, Thomas Cromwell. Statutes were formulated by the top officials of the bureaucracy and then modified and authorized by Parliament. Regulations and orders were drafted and adopted by the Privy Council, which was limited in membership and became an effective rule-making body during the period of Cromwell's dominance.

The enforcement of statutes and orders during the reign of Henry VIII was lodged in an increasingly rationalized bureaucratic structure. Cromwell took steps toward the rationalization of the collection of revenue by setting up separate agencies to handle the various sources of income. Cromwell also introduced a hierarchical pattern of organization into the central bureaucracy by elevating his own role of the king's principal secretary to that of the role of chief executive and coordinator of the various administrative agencies.

It was also during the Tudor period that the adjudicative process was nationalized. It was under Cromwell that all judges and justices throughout England first came under the appointment of the king. At the national level the King's Bench and the Courts of Common Pleas were specialized courts, having been divested of their administrative duties. The local justices of the peace, on the other hand, combined adjudicative with administrative duties. Traveling justices from London periodically visited all parts of the kingdom and held court for those offenders whose cases could not be dealt with by the justices of the peace, or who were bound over by the justices for trial. The institution of grand juries for indictments and *petit* juries for trying cases had already been established in the Tudor period. This differentiated judiciary, backed up as it was by an influential legal profession, carried on the bulk of important adjudication in Tudor England. However, the Court of Star Chamber and the Privy Council could intervene in the adjudicative process, particularly in connection with political matters. One can only say that in Tudor England the British were well along on their way to establishing a fully independent judiciary.[15]

There were beginnings in Tudor England of a specialized system of political communication. Though newspapers had not yet developed, there was a religious pamphlet literature. Street ballads lampooning political leaders were sung in the streets of London and of other cities. "Broadsheets" reporting particular events, or advocating causes, were printed and hawked intermittently in city streets. The significance of these early forerunners of the specialized media of communication is reflected in efforts on the part of Henry VIII, Queen Mary,

[15] *Ibid.,* pp. 240 ff.; and Elton, *op. cit.,* pp. 175 ff.

and Queen Elizabeth to control the printing and stationers' trades.

The growth of industry and trade brought some improvements in roads, and increased the frequency of travel and the speed of the mails. The older forms of face-to-face communication at manor courts and county fairs continued, of course, to be important parts of the system of political communications. One important way by means of which communication between the center of the political system and the periphery was maintained was through the movement of members of Parliament to sessions at Westminster. The growth of central bureaucracy in London meant a sharply increased flow of information to and from the towns and counties of England.[16]

Capabilities. The capabilities of the British political system grew enormously during the Tudor period. Henry VII began his reign in debt, but ended it as a creditor of kings and of his own aristocratic and merchant subjects. He reclaimed the royal lands which had been alienated by his predecessors, and added to them the estates of his defeated aristocratic opponents. He enforced the tax on land with thoroughness, and sold knighthoods at high prices. Increasing trade resulted in enlarged income from customs duties. Heavy fines were imposed for resistance and rebellion. While the extractive capability continued to grow under Henry VIII, the rate of expenditure for military purposes, for an extravagant court life, and for the construction of new palaces resulted in an empty treasury in the closing years of his reign.

The yield from direct taxes under Henry VIII grew to more than a million pounds in the last years of his reign, from an average of less than fifteen thousand pounds under Henry VII. The dissolution of the monasteries brought vast properties into the possession of the king. The sale of these church lands brought increased income to the crown; but more important, they ended up in the possession of the gentry and greatly increased the number and influence of the holders of medium-sized estates. Henry VIII was also able to increase his income

[16] Frederick S. Siebert, *Freedom of the Press in England* (Urbana: University of Illinois Press, 1952), Chap 1.

by a debasement of the coinage, which contributed to the price inflation which troubled the period.[17]

The distributive capability under the Tudor monarchs — both intended and unintended — was quite substantial. The seizure and sale of church lands under Henry VIII greatly enlarged and strengthened the gentry class. A series of statutes intended to limit the enclosure movement, which was drawing land away from farming into the support of the rapidly expanding sheep and wool industry, were only partially successful. However, they were intended to protect the economic interests of the agricultural landowners and peasantry.

The development of industry and the growth of towns during the Tudor period stimulated efforts to limit urbanization and industrialization and to cope with some of the welfare problems resulting from these changes. Poor relief, on a minimal basis, was provided for by the introduction of a compulsory collection law. Houses of correction were established for vagabonds. The Statute of Artificers was intended to control the movement of labor into the various trades and professions, and, in particular, to protect agricultural labor from competition. A number of the larger cities developed more elaborate systems of welfare legislation and institutions — hospitals, orphan homes, asylums, and relief for the aged and the incapacitated. It is quite clear that Tudor England viewed welfare and the distribution of goods, services, and status as legitimate functions of the political system.

The growth of the regulative capability in Tudor England has already been implied in what has been said above. The growth and differentiation of the centralized bureaucracy meant that the regulative capability was substantially intensified. Elimination of the feudal courts, the nationalization of the court system, and the strengthening of the justices of the peace also contributed to centralization of the regulative capability. The emergence of a secular statutory power brought with it a great increase in the extent of central regulation — in the objects and relationships which were subject to regula-

[17] Bindoff, *op. cit.*, pp. 64 ff. and 113 ff.

tion. In particular, many aspects of economic and religious behavior were effectively regulated during the Tudor period.

The economic, social, and political development of the Tudor period provoked a whole sequence of anomic movements. The conflict of Henry VIII with the Vatican and the Church provoked risings in the north and in other parts of England, particularly in reaction to the destruction of monasteries and shrines. These anomic tendencies became increasingly economic in motivation as rising rents and prices, and the encroachment of sheep pasturage affected the interests of peasants and landowners. These resentments culminated in two major risings, the so-called Western Rebellion, based in Cornwall and Devon, and the rebellion in Norfolk. The rising at Cornwall was an essentially religious reaction against the introduction of the new Prayer Book, and was largely led by priests and peasants. The rebellion in Norfolk was more purely economic. The rebels were mainly peasants with economic grievances and an agrarian-reform ideology. These rebellions were put down ruthlessly, and resistance to enclosure was suppressed. They triggered off an increase in the regulative capability. A standing army, primarily for the maintenance of internal order and officered by selected noblemen and gentlemen, was instituted at public expense.[18]

Even though these anomic movements were suppressed, resistance and opposition continued to be articulated in Tudor England. These were fed by resentment against rising prices and against unemployment attributable to the fluctuations in the wool trade, and to the spread of Protestantism. While Puritanism had its origins during the reign of Queen Elizabeth (among those Englishmen who had returned from the Continent, where they had fled from the persecutions of Queen Mary), Puritanical tendencies were already present during the earlier Tudor period. These were beginning to produce, particularly among the British middle classes, a newly aware and independent elite — men who relied on their own reading of the Scriptures and on their own consciences in interpretation of the scriptural and the moral law. Their voices were heard

[18] *Ibid.*, pp. 137 ff.

in local governmental affairs and in the House of Commons; thus, the later development of democratic infrastructure in England was already foreshadowed in the Tudor period. There was the beginning of an oppositional pamphlet literature. A broad socialization process had begun, which was to produce the stronger democratic tendencies of the seventeenth and eighteenth centuries.

The breaking of religious ties with the Vatican and the establishment of a church subordinate to governmental authority resulted in a secularization and a centralization of the symbolic capability in the Tudor political system. The symbolic capability of the aristocracy was reduced by its subordination to central authority and its assimilation into the central governmental institutions. The development of an active and legitimate statutory power in the monarchy and Parliament effected a significant secularization in the symbolic capability. The symbolism of the religious system was weakened in a period during which sacred and traditional matters could be openly and explicitly regulated by means of a rational, deliberative, and legal administrative process. If matters of theology, the content of the Prayer Book, and forms of religious worship could be legislated, they must obviously have lost some of their sacredness and immutability.

However, two qualifications are in order regarding the centralization and secularization of the symbolic capability. In the first place, the power of the Roman Church persisted among a very large part of the population. In addition, the local aristocracy and gentry still were in a position to cow and edify the peasant population with threat of sanction and with ceremonial display. Indeed, a considerable extent of symbolic pluralism persisted into later centuries. Add to this the fact that all this modernization, secularization, and centralization was accomplished within the framework of traditional offices, agencies, and roles.

Like frugal housewives, the architects of Tudor absolutism never threw anything away. The verbal forms were only slightly changed even though practice might change substantially. Rods, maces, costumes, verbal formulas, rites, and cere-

monies all persisted to evoke primordial memories. Thus, the
secular constitution retained the sacred legitimations, and the
peculiar mixture of magic and reason which lies at the root
of the British symbolic capability was preserved. Thus, one
might say that the incremental pattern of British political development was established during the crucial nation-building
era under the Tudor monarchy.

Socialization and Recruitment. During the Tudor monarchy
the ethnic particularisms of the regions of England were atten-
uating, and the process of nationalization and class stratification of culture was acquiring momentum. As the powers of
the central government penetrated the countryside and reduced the powers of the aristocratic manors, a "national subject" culture began to spread. But the rebellions led by local
aristocrats during this period reflected the continued resistance
of these particularistic subcultures in some parts of England.
The rebellions against the enclosure of land, and in particular
the "commonwealth" movement (a radical drive for moral
reform and the restoration of Christian virtues against the
"decay" of contemporary life), might be viewed as incipient
tendencies toward a participant culture.

The spread of a subject culture in England did not go so far
as was the case in the continental European absolutisms. The
vitality of Parliament — and the representation of the gentry
and the middle classes in it — the autonomy of the towns, and
the vigor of the local notables produced what might be referred
to as a "mixed subject-participant" culture, at least among the
urban upper classes, the rural gentry, and the upper strata of
the peasantry. We see the beginnings in Tudor England of a
process of political resocialization resulting from the Protestant
Reformation and from urbanization and industrialization. In
addition, the spread of the Renaissance and the revival of
learning in England during this period resulted in the spread
of education and its secularization. The sons of the aristocracy
and the gentry were increasingly coming to be educated in
secular and classic culture, and literacy was spreading among
the lower classes.

As far as recruitment into political roles was concerned, the right to vote in local and parliamentary elections brought a part of the middle class and of the upper strata of peasants into the political class. While voting was done in public and under considerable pressure from local landlords, the rebellions and unrest of the period, as well as the stress on individual conscience resulting from Protestantism, were beginning to produce some political independence among these elements.

Parliament drew its members from among the aristocracy and the country gentry, and from the business and professional men of the towns. The growing bureaucracy was recruited primarily from among the gentry, the merchants and professions, and the younger sons of the aristocracy. The local officialdom, whether elective or appointive, was also recruited from among the gentry, and from the merchants, manufacturers, and professional men of the towns.

The members of the political and bureaucratic elite were increasingly drawn from among those who had attended schools and universities. Many of the great public schools in England were founded in the Tudor period, and new colleges were founded at Cambridge and Oxford. In these schools, and in particular in Oxford and Cambridge, there was an increasing stress on the training of accomplished gentlemen for the service of the state, and less stress on the training of scholars and members of the clergy. The great emphasis placed upon the classics in the curriculums in these schools and universities tended to produce a cosmopolitan mentality. The homogeneity of the British political elite is in part the consequence of common training in the public schools and in Oxford and Cambridge. This process began in the Tudor period.

(II) DIFFERENTIATED GOVERNMENTAL-POLITICAL STRUCTURES:

(C) FEUDAL POLITICAL SYSTEMS

The term "feudalism" has been used with a wide variety of meanings.[19] It is not the same thing as a political system in

[19] This discussion of the feudal political system is based on Max Weber, *Theory of Social and Economic Organization* (New York: Oxford University Press, 1947), pp. 373 ff.

which an aristocracy owns large landed properties and performs some governmental functions in relation to these lands and their populations. It is not the same thing as Apter's pyramidal system in which a group of subchiefs control their villages under the authority of a paramount chief. Feudalism is different from an aristocracy because the feudal vassals perform all or almost all of the governmental functions within their fiefs. At the same time they are in a contractual relationship with a feudal overlord requiring the exchange of services and an oath of fealty. Feudalism is different from Apter's pyramidal system in that the component units are larger and more complex, and the relations among the units are more explicit and specific.[20]

In an analysis of the main historical examples of feudal systems Coulborn concludes

> Feudalism has been found here to be a mode of revival of a society whose polity has gone into extreme disintegration. The disintegrating polity was in every known case a great empire, but feudal institutions may occur either in territory which belongs to the old empire or in territory which was outside its own limits. Feudalism is by no means a necessary stage in political recovery. It occurs, in fact, only in regions in which recovery has been slow and weak. The nuclear, usually the larger, part of the old empire recovers its political vigor without resort to feudal methods. Feudalism is thus a phenomenon of the margin of a civilized society which has fallen into decline, not a necessary development even there however. But the margin of the society may be quite extensive: it may be as extensive as the larger part of western Europe, or as Japan, Korea, Tibet, and parts of Manchuria, perhaps all of Mongolia.[21]

The typical historical origins of feudal systems help us explain their characteristics. Since they occur at the margin of disintegrating civilizations, the forms of government tend to be more advanced than those of primitive and tribal systems. The

---

[20] David Apter, *Political Modernization* (Chicago: University of Chicago Press, 1965).

[21] Rushton Coulborn (ed.), *Feudalism in History* (Princeton: Princeton University Press, 1956), pp. 364–365.

component units of these systems tend to be patrimonial in character; each vassal tends to be the lord over his lands and peasants.

> His position was based on his military strength. He had a group of trained fighting men in his service; he held fortified strategic positions throughout his lands; he possessed sufficient economic sources to pay for both the army and the fortifications. There might be lesser lords within a sphere of influence who had accepted his leadership in order to gain protection or because his military power left them no choice but submission.[22]

These lesser lords might function more or less as subpatrimonial rulers within their own fiefs. The superior lord controlled his own lands and people directly, and his subfiefs indirectly.

The forms of feudalism are extremely mixed. What we were just describing is represented by Strayer as being characteristic of northern France around the time of the twelfth century. Strayer describes a second stage in western European feudalism in which the smaller vassals had become more assimilated into the central political system. While these local lords still continued to perform important functions, the military, administrative, and adjudicative power of the higher lord had penetrated into the local domains. This transition to the more centralized form of feudalism was accomplished through the expansion of the patrimonial characteristics of the polity of the higher feudal lord. His military power increased relative to that of his vassals, his administrative officialdom became larger and more differentiated, and he developed expansionist and centralizing political goals.

If, as the historians tell us, feudal systems are to be understood as arising out of previously existing centralized bureaucratic empires, the fate of some was to give way to the re-emergence of centralized bureaucratic empires. Thus the feudal systems of Britain, France, Prussia, Austria, and Spain gave way in the sixteenth and seventeenth centuries to the bureaucratic empires of the Age of Absolutism.

[22] Joseph R. Strayer, "Feudalism in Western Europe," in *ibid.*, pp. 18–19.

From one point of view, feudalism may be viewed as an international political system, as a kind of hierarchically ordered alliance of patrimonial kingdoms. The ideal conception of feudalism would imply a great deal more than this, but the historical reality of many forms of feudalism would suggest their international character. Indeed the transformation of these feudal systems into bureaucratic empires in the Age of Absolutism was associated with war and diplomacy, as the capabilities of the more powerful components became greater and the feudal vassals were either destroyed or assimilated into an aristocracy and a court nobility.

CHAPTER X

Types of Political Systems:
Modern Democratic and
Authoritarian Forms

THIS CHAPTER is devoted to modern political systems: those in which there is a specialized political infrastructure consisting of associational interest groups, political parties, and media of communication. The emergence of a secularized political culture and an awareness of the role of government in changing human conditions are also common features. As the classification scheme introduced in the previous chapter has suggested, these systems differ among themselves according to the degree of autonomy of the structures and according to the degree of differentiation and secularization. They are, for the most part, the systems of the twentieth century; their common characteristics are bound up with their presence in a world of economic, cultural, and technological change.

It may be useful to have in mind the general classification scheme used in this and the preceding chapter. We reproduce, on page 256, the classification of modern systems from Chapter IX.

THE SECULARIZED CITY-STATE

The class of systems with differentiated political infrastructures includes, principally, systems of the contemporary world.

III. MODERN SYSTEMS:
   DIFFERENTIATED POLITICAL INFRASTRUCTURES
   A. Secularized City-States:
      Limited Differentiation (*Athens*)
   B. Mobilized Modern Systems:
      High Differentiation and Secularization
      1. Democratic Systems:
         Subsystem Autonomy and Participant Culture
         a. High Subsystem Autonomy (*Britain*)
         b. Limited Subsystem Autonomy (*Fourth Republic France*)
         c. Low Subsystem Autonomy (*Mexico*)
      2. Authoritarian Systems:
         Subsystem Control and Subject-Participant Culture
         a. Radical Totalitarian (*U.S.S.R.*)
         b. Conservative Totalitarian (*Nazi Germany*)
         c. Conservative Authoritarian (*Spain*)
         d. Modernizing Authoritarian (*Brazil*)
   C. Premobilized Modern Systems:
      Limited Differentiation and Secularization
      1. Premobilized Authoritarian (*Ghana*)
      2. Premobilized Democratic (*Nigeria prior to January 1966*)

But before considering the main varieties of modern political systems, we ought to look briefly at the secularized city-state, an ancient form of polity which has some of the components of a political infrastructure and of a secularized political culture. It bridges, in some sense, the traditional and the modern.

When we speak of city-states in this context, we refer to autonomous towns and cities having relatively complex social structures. Some of the Greek city-states, republican Rome, and some of the city-states of medieval Europe were relatively complex, stratified societies, based on economic, professional, and status differences. They were affected by a commercial revolution, if not an industrial one. These urban societies usually had patrician and plebian strata as well as specialized trades and professions. In the medieval European city-states groups of artisans, merchants, and professionals were organized in guilds, the forerunners of the modern associational interest groups. In some city-states the guilds were represented as professional bodies in the city assemblies. They also enjoyed important self-governing powers. In addition, these cities were characterized by a political phenomenon which may be viewed as the ancestor of the modern organized political party — the "faction." In Florence, for example, the *Popolo Grasso* and the *Popolo Minuto* were coalitions of guilds of the entrepreneurial and professional elements, and of the small tradesmen and artisans, respectively, which competed with one another for power over the municipality during the fourteenth and fifteenth centuries.[1] Interest groups and political parties, which in fully differentiated form are the marks of what we can call modern political systems, were already latent, and sometimes more than latent.

One can perhaps say that the secularized city-state was the prototype not only of the modern polity but of the modern society, and that the two emerged together. Thus, it was commerce, trade, and the changes in attitude that went with these economic-social patterns that produced a complex system of social stratification and the beginnings of a rational secular culture. Struggle over political goals, the development of explicit policy alternatives, and the emergence of an active and explicit lawmaking and law-enforcement function were characteristic of these city-states. As a consequence, the infrastructure of political struggle, of explicit interest articulation and interest aggregation, had to emerge in some form. It is important to keep in mind that rational lawmaking is as old as Greece and Rome. Max Weber points out:

> The creation of laws reached such a fluid state that eventually in Athens the question was directed yearly to the people whether existing laws should be maintained or amended. Thus it became an accepted premise that the law is artificially created and that it should be based upon the approval of those to whom it will apply.[2]

The phenomenon of party (in the form of a relatively stable faction) is at least as old as the tyranny of Pisistratus, who organized a movement called the "Hill" consisting of a coalition of poor mountaineers from the highlands of Attica and

[1] Max Weber, *The City*, ed. and trans. Don Martindale and Gertrude Neuwirth (New York: The Free Press of Glencoe, 1958), pp. 172–173.
[2] *Ibid.*, p. 183.

many impoverished and discontented members of the upper class.

The city-state as a political form is now primarily of historical interest, and there would be little purpose in exploring the various categories which might be employed to order the examples of this type of system. But this particular type of system serves as an important reminder of the relationship between polity and society. It was those features of ancient city life which seem so strikingly contemporary — the economic differentiation and specialization and the emergence of a pragmatic, manipulative orientation to life — which provided impetus for the development of the nearly modern political forms. As a consequence of the inherent limitations on this process, and perhaps because of the small scale of political action, the city-state seldom fully developed the highly organized and differentiated structures which are prominent in contemporary politics.

The political systems to which we now turn are all characterized by a larger size than that of the city-states, by a more differentiated political infrastructure, and by some form of a participant political culture. The first major class, the *mobilized modern systems,* is marked by both a high degree of structural differentiation and a secularized political culture. Secularization, as a widespread societal phenomenon, is found in societies which have begun the process of transition to modernity: societies in which traditional orientations and ties have begun to be broken down and large numbers of individuals have become available for new patterns of life and thought. These societies are capable of attaining a much higher level of economic productivity, and, hence, material resources are more likely to be readily available to the political system. At the same time that the capacity for increased extraction, regulation, and distribution is expanding, however, the processes of differentiation and secularization flood the political systems with new demands for distribution and/or participation. Highly differentiated political infrastructures are necessary, therefore, to enable the political elites either to respond to the demands and develop support for various activities or to manipulate and control them, thereby either directing the system toward new goals or preserving system stability.

Mobilized modern systems may be divided into two subclasses: those which have autonomous infrastructures and participant cultures, and those in which the infrastructure is not autonomous and in which the political culture is of a mixed subject-participant variety. We usually speak of the first category as democratic political systems, and of the second as authoritarian. We must keep in mind, of course, that all these classes of systems grade off into one another. Thus, we have already pointed out that the Tudor monarchy, like the city-state, had the beginnings of a differentiated, autonomous infrastructure and the beginnings of a culture of political participation.

MOBILIZED MODERN SYSTEMS:
(A) DEMOCRATIC POLITICAL SYSTEMS

Democratic political systems can in turn be divided into three subclasses. The first of these has *high subsystem autonomy*.[3] This is a type of political system, such as the British or the American, in which political parties, interest groups, and the media of mass communication are relatively differentiated one from the other, and in which there is a relatively well-developed and widely distributed participant culture. The second subclass is characterized by *limited subsystem autonomy*. This category might include France of the Third and Fourth Republics, Italy after World War II, and Weimar Germany. These are systems in which political parties, interest groups, and the media of mass communication tend to be dependent one upon the other. Thus the Catholic Church in these countries does not simply function as an interest group, but has its own more or less controlled system of interest groups, a Catholic political party and trade union, and Catholic media of mass communication. These systems are also characterized by fragmentation of political culture. There are relatively large persisting subject and parochial subcultures, and the partici-

[3] Robert A. Dahl, *Modern Political Analysis* (Englewood Cliffs: Prentice-Hall, Inc., 1963), pp. 35 ff.

pant subculture is, at least in part, an alienated subculture. The third class of democratic political systems is made up of those with *low subsystem autonomy*. These have been referred to as one-party-dominant systems, or as hegemonic party systems. Mexico would provide an example of this type of democratic system. Since each one of these subclasses of contemporary political systems will be treated in detail in individual country studies in this series, our discussion of them will be relatively brief and schematic.

BRITAIN: HIGH SUBSYSTEM AUTONOMY
AND HOMOGENEOUS CULTURE

We shall use Britain as an illustration of our first subclass of democratic political systems. In the case of Britain we have to speak of subsystem autonomy in relative terms. Most of the British trade unions are affiliated with the Labour party. But the parliamentary Labour party, when in power, is relatively independent of trade union pressure, and the British trade unions tend to exercise self-discipline in attempting to influence the policy of a Labour cabinet. Similarly, trade associations and chambers of commerce in Britain are aligned with the Conservative party. But here again, Conservative cabinets and the Conservative parliamentary party are relatively autonomous vis-à-vis these influential interest groups. Similarly, with regard to the press, though there are both Labour and Conservative newspapers, these are not simple organs of the party leadership.[4]

The British political culture is a relatively homogeneous participant one. This political culture has been described as a "deferential participant" culture:

. . . The development of the participant orientation in Britain did not challenge and replace the more deferential subject orientations, as was the tendency in the United States. Despite the spread of political competence and participant orientations,

4 Samuel Finer, "Interest Groups and the Political Process in Great Britain," in Henry Ehrmann, *Interest Groups on Four Continents* (Pittsburgh: University of Pittsburgh Press, 1958), pp. 133 ff.; Martin Harrison, *Trade Unions in the Labour Party Since 1945* (London: George Allen & Unwin, Ltd., 1960), Chaps. 4 and 5.

the British have maintained a strong deference to the independent authority of government.[5]

The *conversion* characteristics of the British political system are related to these structural and cultural conditions. Associational interest groups play an active and regulative role in relation to the formulation of demands for public policy and enforcement. The two major parties in Britain are able to aggregate demands into alternative programs of public policy. Both parties, in competing for a parliamentary majority, attempt to appeal to the maximum range of interests in British society. As a consequence, the differences between party programs are relatively small, and either party can tolerate being in the opposition.

The media of mass communication in Britain — even though in part government owned, and in part oriented toward one or the other of the political parties — are relatively neutral in performing their function of disseminating information about political events. The flow of political decision and action in the British system is relatively continuous. Aggregation, decision, and implementation are relatively responsive to the flow of demands. We are, of course, simplifying here. There have been periods of immobilism in British political development. Nevertheless, fluctuations in the rate of flow of demands and outputs are less extreme than in the case of Fourth Republic France, which we shall discuss below.

Associated with these structural, cultural, and conversion patterns is a relatively high level of political *capabilities*. The extractive and regulative capabilities in Britain have been consistently high. For more than a decade during and after World War II, Britain imposed and effectively enforced stringent taxation and rationing. During the second part of this same

[5] Gabriel A. Almond and Sidney Verba, *The Civic Culture* (Princeton: Princeton University Press, 1963), p. 455. See also Richard Rose, *Politics in England* (Boston: Little, Brown and Company, 1964), Chap. 2; Richard Rose, "England: The Traditionally Modern Political Culture," in Lucian W. Pye and Sidney Verba (eds.), *Political Culture and Political Development* (Princeton: Princeton University Press, 1965); Harry Eckstein, "The British Political System," in Beer and Ulam, *Patterns of Government* (New York: Random House, Inc., rev. ed., 1962), pp. 73 ff.

decade, Britain carried through a program of nationalization of industry and extension of social services, all of which reflected a relatively high level of distributive capability. In more recent years an increasing rate of public investment in the expansion of the British educational system indicates a continued capacity to redistribute opportunities and rewards among the various strata of British society. All these patterns reflect a very high level of support for the British political system, as well as a high level of adaptive responsiveness on the part of the British political elites. A high symbolic capability reinforces this support level. We shall refer to this kind of profile or pattern of political capability as a "versatile" one, meaning that the British political system can respond more flexibly to internal and external demands than many, perhaps most, other systems. This is not the same as saying that all the capabilities are of an equal level. Over time the levels of the individual capabilities fluctuate, but the fluctuations are limited and broadly responsive to the flow of demands from the various components of British society and from the international political system.

The *system maintenance* patterns of the British polity — recruitment and socialization — are congruent with its conversion and capability characteristics. In recent decades recruitment into British politics has begun to reflect the increasing effectiveness of the distributive capability. Membership in the House of Commons and the House of Lords has become somewhat more open to recruitment from the middle and lower classes, and the spread of social welfare and of educational opportunity has begun to increase the rate of this mobility. Similar changes in recruitment into the upper levels of the British civil service may begin to acquire momentum with the development of new universities and the increased size of the university-educated population.[6] However, we should avoid exaggerating the rate of change in British political recruitment processes. One of the most interesting things about British

---

[6] W. L. Guttsman, *The British Political Elite* (New York: Basic Books, Inc., Publishers, 1963), Chap. 11.

politics is the persistence of its older system of status and deference.

The changes in recruitment patterns reflect significant trends in the development of British political culture. Evidence suggests a declining deferentialism and a broader spread of participant orientations in British society. But such changes in British political culture seem to be widely distributed throughout the various strata of British society. In other words, while the relative balance of the deferential and participant components seems to be changing, the over-all homogeneity of the British political culture does not seem to be significantly affected by these developments. This would suggest that family, peer group, school, work place, and the socialization processes of the political system itself, all seem to be adapting in the process of political culture change. Perhaps the slowness of the process of change is related to these simultaneous changes toward participation. There do not appear to be significant tendencies in the direction of cultural fragmentation or of political alienation.

FRANCE: LIMITED SUBSYSTEM AUTONOMY AND FRAGMENTED CULTURE

France of the Fourth Republic may be used as an illustration of the second class of democratic political systems, those in which there are specialized associational interest groups, organized political parties, and well-developed mass media of communication, but where these agencies have limited autonomy. Interest groups, political parties, and the press during the Fourth Republic in France tended to be divided into three main ideological families or subcultures. The Communist subculture included the Communist party, the C.G.T. (the Communist-dominated general trade union), and the Communist press, including *Humanité* and a host of regional and specialized Communist newspapers and periodicals. The Socialist system consisted of the Socialist party (S.F.I.O.), the trade union organization Force Ouvrière, the newspaper *Le Populaire,* and a number of regional and specialized Socialist newspapers and periodicals. The Catholic system consisted of the church hierarchy and clergy; Catholic Action with its network of specialized groupings based on age, sex, occupation, and profession; a Catholic trade union (C.F.T.C.) and political party (M.R.P.); and a number of Catholic journals and periodicals including the newspaper *L'Aube* (during the early period of the Fourth Republic) and periodicals such as *Le Temps Présent, La Vie Intellectuel,* and *Esprit.*

We do not suggest that the relationship between the different components of the Communist, Socialist, and Catholic systems was one of complete dependence and control, but the fact that the agencies were coordinated in ideological families made it difficult for them to perform their specialized functions as interest groups, political parties, and media of mass communication. The Communist, Socialist, and Catholic trade unions had difficulties in coming to agreements on policies regarding the specific interests of the various sectors of the working class; political parties had difficulties in forming stable coalitions because of sharp ideological differences and distrust; and the media of mass communication were unable to function effectively in disseminating unbiased information regarding social and political problems. Thus, the conversion processes in the Fourth Republic were often blocked. Demands, so to speak, piled up and were not converted into policy alternatives or enacted into law.

In the early years of the Fourth Republic a political pattern became established in which there was the Communist party on the left with substantial popular support, a diffusely antirepublican party or movement on the right (the Gaullist movement), fluctuating in strength, and a center coalition consisting of the Socialist, Radical Socialist, and moderate Catholic (M.R.P.) parties. The center coalition of parties was a heterogeneous coalition. They could agree on the defense of the Fourth Republic from threat from the left and the right, but could not agree on a number of fundamental economic, social, religious, and foreign-policy issues. Thus, center coalition cabinets fell again and again. They were unable to find effective compromises and to respond to the pressure of demands coming from social groups on the one hand and from the international political system on the other. The Fourth Republic collapsed on the issue of Algerian independence.

The conversion processes of the Fourth Republic followed a fluctuating course with long periods of immobilism followed by occasional "crisis-liquidation cabinets," which were able to deal with one or two issues and then disintegrated as a consequence of ideological and political differences among the member parties of the coalition cabinet.

This alternation of periods of immobilism with brief periods of crisis-liquidation summarizes the capability profile of the Fourth Republic. One would have to say that in comparison with the level of capabilities of Great Britain or the United States, that of the French political system was relatively low. French evasion of taxation, cynicism regarding law enforcement and noncompliance with the law, and general alienation from the institutions of the Fourth Republic suggest low support levels and limited extractive, regulative, and symbolic capabilities. The distributive capability of the French Fourth Republic is a more complicated problem: A relatively ineffective cabinet and legislative structure meant that powerful interest groups such as big business, and politically effective agricultural and small-merchant groups, could make their voices heard in both the National Assembly and in the bureaucracy. Less powerful interests or less well-represented groups in the population were neglected in the process and became alienated from the political system as a whole. Thus, there was considerable distribution of subsidies and regulations favoring some groups, and none favoring others. In general the responsive capability of the system was relatively low and intermittent, as the distributive pattern might suggest.

The agencies of political socialization — family, neighborhood, peer group, work situation, voluntary associations, political parties, and media of mass communication — tended to perpetuate the fragmented and alienated nature of French political culture. Thus, a Communist might spend his whole life in what might be thought of as an ideological enclave in the French political system. Family, neighborhood, peer group, work associates, trade union, party, and newspaper might seal him off from effective contact and communication with Frenchmen having other political views. The same might be said of French Socialists and French Catholics, although the homogeneity of their experience would be substantially less than that of someone growing up in Communist France.

The political structure instituted by the Fifth Republic has substantially reduced the importance of French political parties, interest groups, and the media of mass communication in the conversion processes of the French political system; in other words, it has reduced their autonomy and limited their access to decision making. In effect, the input structures and processes, while still in existence, have been blocked off, and the authority of President de Gaulle and his cabinet has been rendered secure by the extraordinary powers given to the presidency and by the general public support which De Gaulle has received from a large majority of the French population. The consequences of the experience of the Fifth Republic for the future of the French political system is a matter of some mystery. A recent book on French politics bears the title *In Search of France: Economy Growing, Society Changing, Political System in Doubt*.[7] The authorities are not ready to commit themselves as to whether the fundamental changes in the French economy and the French society in recent decades, along with the Gaullist experience with a partial suspension of politics, have resulted in any permanent changes in French political patterns.

MEXICO: LOW SUBSYSTEM AUTONOMY AND FRAGMENTED CULTURE

In Mexico the dominant political party, the Institutional Revolutionary Party (P.R.I.), typically receives about 80 per cent of the total popular vote. Its candidates dominate state and federal elections in almost all areas, and its presidential candidate has never failed to win. To become a legally constituted political party, an organization must register with a central government agency dominated by the P.R.I. to receive

---

[7] Stanley Hoffman (ed.), *In Search of France* (Cambridge: Harvard University Press, 1963).

formal acceptance. Election returns are counted by officials who are sympathetic to the P.R.I. There is no doubt that the P.R.I. holds the whip hand over opposition parties in Mexico. Interference with opposition political activity has become less frequent, however, and in recent years such activity has come to be effectively tolerated.

The P.R.I. has within its rather hierarchical structure a coalition of interest groups. Its ruling body, the Central Executive Committee, is in part made up of representatives of agrarian, labor, and middle-class organizations. Each sector within the hierarchy formally operates as a single, functional organization, although in fact each contains a variety of groups which are in competition with one another on matters of public policy. Most complex of all is the "public" sector, which includes government employees, small business men, artisans, members of professional organizations, and intellectuals.[8]

There are, in addition, interest groups which operate outside the framework of the P.R.I. These include, among the most prominent examples, powerful business and industrial elements, Communist trade unions, and the Catholic Church together with the organizations which it sponsors. Although many of the most prominent and powerful interest organizations in Mexican society are constituent units of the P.R.I., informal access channels to the president and to top-level bureaucracy are available to almost all groups. Given the hierarchical nature of decision making, these channels may be as important or more important than the formal party channels.[9] Moreover, the mass media in Mexico are fairly well developed, and, with relatively few exceptions, in the last twenty years the media have functioned in a relatively open and autonomous fashion.

Thus, although it would be correct to speak of the political infrastructure in Mexico as having low antonomy, there is

[8] For an excellent, brief account of the party organization, see Robert E. Scott, *Mexican Government in Transition* (Urbana: University of Illinois Press, 1959), pp. 130–135 ff.

[9] See the discussion above (in the note on page 85, Chapter IV) of the disagreement on this question.

nevertheless a considerable degree of pluralism and competition. There is a constant struggle among the interest groups and factions within the framework of the P.R.I. There is also competition with and among these groups and the strong middle-class and industrial elements which find their strongest voice through informal presidential contacts. The shifting specific policies of Mexican leaders over the years have found support in different coalitions of these interests. However, the elites have made great efforts to sustain a consensus of general support through unifying symbolic outputs and formal involvement of major groups in the P.R.I. The tendency in Mexican politics in the last decade or two has been in the direction of increasing subsystem autonomy and political pluralism.[10]

We have reported elsewhere (Chapter III, page 54) that Mexican political culture has undergone substantial change and secularization since the Mexican revolution. Scott has estimated that at the onset of the revolution in 1910, nine out of ten Mexicans were parochial in their political orientations. That is to say, they were diffusely oriented toward village authority and toward the powers of landlords and clergy. To the extent that they were oriented at all toward central authority, they were alienated from it. Scott goes on to estimate that as of 1960 the proportion of surviving parochials, who were found primarily in the rural and remote areas of Mexico, was only 25 per cent, while 65 per cent of the Mexican population were oriented to the national political system as subjects, and 10 per cent, primarily concentrated in the urban areas and among the educated middle classes, could be viewed as political participants in Mexican politics. These parochial, subject, and participant components may be viewed as political subcultures. However the processes of culture-change in a secular and participant direction seem to be going forward quite rapidly, and these subcultures should probably not be viewed as stable and self-sustaining.

[10] Scott, *Mexican Government, op. cit.,* pp. 145 ff.; Martin C. Needler, *Political Systems of Latin America* (Princeton: D. Van Nostrand Co., Inc., 1964), pp. 9 ff.

In addition, Scott points to considerable alienation in Mexican political culture. A substantial proportion of the Mexican population distrusts governmental authority and views it as corrupt and arbitrary. At the same time, there is strong national loyalty and positive feeling for the Mexican nation and for the ideals of the Mexican revolution.[11] Another aspect of Mexican cultural fragmentation would be the partial alienation of some parts of the Catholic Church hierarchy, clergy, and laity. In addition, that part of the working class which is organized in the Mexican Communist party and the Communist trade unions, as well as part of the Mexican intellectuals and students, would also have to be viewed as alienated components in the Mexican political culture.

Political socialization in Mexico has been moving increasingly in the direction of modern forms and content. Urbanization, industrialization, the development of the middle classes and the professional classes, and the growth of voluntary associations and media of mass communication have increased the impact of secondary institutions on Mexican political attitudes. Tendencies toward the emancipation of women and toward the breakdown of the diffuse ties of an extended family system contribute to the reduction of the parochial component in the Mexican political culture. At the same time, recruitment into the political elite has become more open, and recruitment into the bureaucracy is increasingly based on achievement and performance criteria.

The conversion processes of the Mexican political system grow out of these structural and cultural characteristics. Thus, the relatively small size of the stratum of the population which is politically competent and the much larger proportion which is generally submissive to governmental authority (though distrustful of it) tend to give considerable power to political elite groups. The elite groups in turn are coordinated within the

[11] Robert E. Scott, "Mexico: The Established Revolution," in Pye and Verba, *op. cit.;* Almond and Verba, *op. cit.,* pp. 414 ff.; Sidney Verba and Gabriel A. Almond, "National Revolutions and Political Commitment," in Harry Eckstein (ed.), *Internal War* (New York: The Free Press of Glencoe, 1964), pp. 205 ff.

structure of the dominant political party and the presidency. Thus, interest articulation and aggregation is often a partially covert political process, a process of bargaining within the P.R.I. and with the informal presidential advisers. The president is the chief rule maker in the Mexican system and the chief monitor of the enforcement of rules. Although access to the president through informal channels is limited, and hence the bureaucracy and the P.R.I. play powerful roles in the aggregation process, the orientations of the president and those close to him are decisive in determining which groups and interests receive priority in the decision-making choices. Although the agrarian and labor interests are most prominent in the P.R.I., and are represented in the informal presidential councils as well by such figures as ex-President Cárdenas, it has been argued that "decision-making in Mexico has been dominated by the urban middle sectors since the early 1940's." [12] Studies of Mexican policy clearly show that industrialization received first priority in the years following World War II, often at the expense of considerable lower-class suffering.[13]

The authoritarianism of the Mexican political system has, however, been subsiding as opposition movements have become increasingly effective and as the interest associations within and without the framework of the revolutionary party have become increasingly autonomous. Urbanization and industrialization in Mexico have produced a growing stratum of politically competent citizens and powerful interest-group elites. The army, which dominated Mexican politics and was represented as an organization in the P.R.I. in its earlier stages, no longer bulks as large as was once the case.

If we consider the development of the capabilities of the Mexican political system in the course of the half century of its revolution, we would have to say that the first decades were marked by increasing regulative and extractive capabilities as

[12] John J. Johnson, *Political Change in Latin America* (Stanford: Stanford University Press, 1958), p. 129.

[13] See in particular, Oscar Lewis, "Mexico Since Cárdenas," in Richard N. Adams *et al., Social Change in Latin America Today* (New York: Random House, Inc., 1960), p. 325; and Frank Brandenburg, *The Making of Modern Mexico* (Englewood Cliffs: Prentice-Hall, Inc., 1964), p. 144.

the central government consolidated its position in the 1920's vis-à-vis the army and local factions. In the 1930's, there was real development of the distributive and symbolic capabilities, as land reform, expropriation of foreign property (particularly in the oil industry), and the formal incorporation of labor and agrarian interests in the political party built genuine system support and made the revolution a living and popular symbol. In the 1940's and early 1950's, the emphasis returned to the extractive capability and to economic development as the Mexican elites undertook a massive industrialization effort (and later attempted to build up agriculture as well) at the cost of welfare and land redistribution programs. Drawing upon its symbolic capability and formally co-opting the masses in the P.R.I., the elite managed to enlist informal business support and to carry out social mobilization without totally alienating the masses of disadvantaged Mexicans. The system's responsiveness has been limited, undertaken in a real sense mostly at the discretion of the elite, although a great show of formal access has been made. In recent years a more balanced pattern of response to various interests has appeared as land redistribution, for example, has been reintroduced. Through a judicious use of symbols, of unifying hierarchical bargaining mechanisms, and of response to the interests of different sets of groups, the Mexican elites have managed to expand all the political capabilities and to move Mexico from a traditional bureaucratic system (1910), to a premobilized authoritarian (1925), and eventually to a partially mobilized democratic system, though one with a still relatively low level of subsystem autonomy.

MOBILIZED MODERN SYSTEMS:
(B) AUTHORITARIAN POLITICAL SYSTEMS

The systems described above are all characterized by a measure of both legal and actual pluralism or autonomy in the political infrastructure. We chose three cases which illustrate different levels of autonomy. In the last system discussed — the Mexican — we were still dealing with a kind of political system in which there was both formal autonomy and freedom of competition, and some real autonomy and competitive process.

In the authoritarian and totalitarian systems, to which we now turn, we are not shifting to nonautonomous systems, but rather to systems in which formal autonomy is eliminated but in which some measure of real pluralism and competitive process still persists. In actual fact, a fully nonautonomous system is unthinkable. There are different kinds of interests and demands in any society, and there must be some way for these interests and demands to be communicated and transmitted into the political system. So when we move from democratic to authoritarian and totalitarian systems, we are grading off, so to speak, from the one to the other; and even the most extreme form of totalitarianism — for example, the Soviet Union under Stalin — still contains pluralistic tendencies and what we might call a political process.

The forms of authoritarianism with which we deal here are contemporary twentieth-century forms. They are political systems which have come into existence after the industrial revolution, after some urbanization has actually taken place or after the impact of Western industrialized society has been felt through the diffusion of the ideas, aspirations, and some of the practices of Western society and politics. It is important to keep these points in mind, for all the systems with which we are here concerned — the Russian, the Chinese, the eastern European Communist, the German Nazi, the Italian Fascist, and Spanish and Portuguese authoritarianism — had no choice but to develop some kind of political infrastructure. We are dealing with regimes which came into existence in societies which were already in the process of industrialization and urbanization and in which some political infrastructure of political parties, associational interest groups, and media of mass communication had already emerged. Thus, the political elites which shaped these authoritarian and totalitarian regimes had to cope with already existing infrastructures.

The authoritarian and totalitarian systems may be classified into four subtypes according to their structural and cultural characteristics: radical totalitarian (the Communist countries), conservative totalitarian (Nazi Germany), stabilizational conservative authoritarian (Spain), and modernizing authoritarian (Brazil).

Adam Ulam has argued that the Leninist revision of Marxism was in real fact the ideological basis for a thoroughgoing and militant industrialization and modernization of society, rather than a simple revolutionary movement directed against the evils of capitalism.[14] Since the main aim of the Communist elites was the maximization of industrial and military power, the political infrastructure of party, interest groups, and media of mass communication was turned into a kind of specialized "mobilizational bureaucracy." The elites sought to turn agencies which were generating disruptive demands and resisting programs into devices which could mobilize active support and instill not only compliance with the programs of the elite but a willingness to participate actively in these programs. Thus we speak of the political cultures of the Communist systems as "participant-subject" cultures. In the case of Nazi Germany we have a second variant to totalitarianism. Here the elites were concerned with the maximization of national and ethnic identity and with aggressive international power as well as with a solution to internal unemployment problems. But economic modernization and mobilization was not a necessary goal — Germany was already a modern society. The elites sought to control or destroy an internal pluralism in order to attain the other goals.

The differences in the starting points and the elite goals of the radical and the conservative forms of totalitarianism may help explain the differences in their structural and cultural characteristics. Thus, in Russia all the strata and institutions were either penetrated or eliminated in favor of a centrally controlled system of political and economic mobilization. In Nazi Germany left-wing and moderate political parties were eliminated, and the various associational interest groups were assimilated into the National Socialist party. But some autonomy persisted — at least a greater degree of autonomy than in

[14] Adam Ulam, *The Unfinished Revolution* (New York: Random House, Inc., 1960).

the Russian system. The Catholic Church and some parts of the Protestant Church in Germany were able to maintain their separateness during this period. Big-business interests were also able to function autonomously to some extent. It is this more limited societal penetration which distinguishes the conservative branch of totalitarianism. The media of communication and political organization, however, became the monopoly of the Nazi elites. If we were to compare the political cultures of the Communist and Nazi versions of totalitarianism, we would have to say that although the two systems are characterized by similar participant-subject patterns, Nazism included an especial accent on ethnic-racial nationalism. Surely it is not accidental that Germany prior to its totalitarian phase was a new nation with an uncertain sense of national identity.

Spanish and Portuguese authoritarianism is yet another variant. In its earlier stages Spanish authoritarianism looked as though it was moving in the direction of totalitarianism. It also had a political party — the Falange — which at least on paper and in its earlier years sought to penetrate Spanish society, to assimilate all political tendencies and interest groups in the interest of a general mobilization of Spanish society. But the Spanish elite was not motivated by the impulses toward aggressive expansionism which characterized Nazi Germany or by the modernization drive of the Soviet elite. It was what one might call a "traditionalist" regime. It was opposed to the social revolutionary and the secularizing tendencies of the left-wing and moderate parties of the earlier Spanish regime. The Falange party never effectively penetrated Spanish society. The Church preserved a powerful position, and the professions and the business community have been able to maintain some independence. Spanish authoritarianism is not a mobilizational regime; it is rather a conservative regime. Existing in a society already mobilized to some degree, it tolerates, rather than coerces, pluralistic tendencies and bargains with some of the interest groups of Spanish society.

TOTALITARIANISM: THE SOVIET UNION

As compared with the conservative authoritarianism of Spain, the Soviet political system has reduced subsystem autonomy in at least two respects. There is a much more thoroughgoing penetration of economic, religious, cultural, and family life by the political system as a whole. While the penetration is by no means complete, particularly in the sphere of family life, the aim of assimilating the economy into the polity, of undermining the influence of the Church, and of assimilating non-Russian ethnic groups has been in considerable part successful.

Along with this subordination of social processes and groups to the political system goes an extremely elaborate and effective apparatus of social and political mobilization. The Communist party performs two major roles: first, that of setting the goals of the system and of overseeing and monitoring the implementation of these goals; and second, that of mobilizing Soviet society in carrying out the goals. Thus, the political infrastructure of the Soviet political system is a thoroughly elaborated one, encompassing organizations intended to mobilize the energies of all the strata and groupings of Soviet society. But this effort at assimilating and mobilizing all elements is only partially successful.

A constructive polemic is now raging among specialists on Soviet politics on the question of pluralism versus totalitarianism as an explanation of Soviet politics. Those who have been arguing against too complete an acceptance of the monolithic or totalitarian model of Soviet politics cite a variety of political groups and bases of conflict within the Soviet political system. One analyst lists some twelve categories of competitive relationships.[15] Among the groups struggling over power and policy in the Soviet Union are cliques competing for control of the top instrumentalities of the party apparatus; bureaucratic groups in conflict with groups in the party apparatus; groups within the governmental bureaucracy such as the army and the various branches of civil and economic administration in conflict with each other; regionally based groups in conflict with each other and with the central government and the party bureaucracy; professional groupings such as artists, writers, and scientists in conflict with the party bureaucracy and top party elite. In addition, there are conflicts between different occupa-

[15] T. H. Rigby, "Crypto-Politics," *Survey*, January, 1964, Chap. 10, p. 30.

tional and skill groupings over their share of the national product, and conflicts between the regime and such groupings as the peasantry and non-Russian ethnic groups which resist efforts of the regime to assimilate them and mobilize their energies.

It would be a mistake to distort the picture in the opposite direction, to give too great stress to the extent of pluralism and subsystem autonomy in the Soviet political system. It is important to recognize that pluralism and political conflict is not an overt and legitimate political process. Tendencies that oppose the regime must operate within the framework of the party and its system of organizations, and in the background there is always the menace of direct coercion and of powerful socio-economic sanctions. Perhaps equally significant, the system has maintained its control over the mass media. Even in the course of the recent relaxation, the elites have been very sensitive to any hint of criticism of the society, let alone the regime, by writers and intellectuals. The mass media do not function as internal interest-articulation channels except in the form of channels for individual complaints regarding lower level bureaucratic officials.

The pattern of political culture in the Soviet Union corresponds to this mixed pattern of central mobilization and pluralism. Thus the overt political culture of the Soviet political system is the doctrine of Marxism-Leninism as this is formulated and communicated by the party at any given time. The ideology of the Soviet Union is inculcated through centralized and powerful agencies, through a monopoly of the media of mass communication and of political organization, and through a centrally controlled educational system. Through all these instrumentalities the Soviet citizen is provided with a comprehensive set of beliefs, political feelings, and values. It provides an explanation of the past, beliefs and predictions about the future, and a definition of the mission which each individual and group in the system is supposed to fulfill. Underneath this official political culture there are attitude patterns persisting from the pre-Bolshevik regime and other attitude patterns that have resulted from the social transformations which have taken place in the Soviet Union in the last half century.

It is among the peasantry and the unskilled workers that one finds political and religious attitudes characteristic of pre-revolutionary Russia. In the modern sector of Soviet society — the skilled workers, clerical employees, technical-managerial personnel, scientists, engineers, professional men of various kinds — one encounters interest-group tendencies similar to those encountered in the industrialized societies of the West. Scientific, professional, and artistic interests are articulated and affect the outputs of the Soviet political system. Thus, there are covert political subcultures in Soviet politics which intermittently break through the surface and which are in conflict with the official political culture.

These cultural and structural characteristics give us some clues to the nature of the political conversion processes in the Soviet system. Demands in some form are made by the peasantry, by non-Russian ethnic groups, by industrial workers, by professional and technical personnel, by groups within the bureaucracy, and by groups within the party, but the aggregation of these demands into alternative policy proposals is carried on largely through a covert political process in which the legitimacy of conflict over policy is never explicitly acknowledged. Interest articulation by such nonassociational groups as consumers, wage earners, and collectivized farmers is primarily latent and diffuse. It may take the form of such cues as high production in individual kitchen garden plots and low production on collective plots, or the flourishing of a black market in various consumer goods. These cues may be read by individual elite members and represented by them, or may to some degree be reported through the institutions, such as the secret police, which are engaged in gathering information for the elites. In recent years adaptive response to latent and diffuse forms of interest articulation has seemed to increase markedly. It would appear, however, that it is primarily at the very top levels of party and government bureaucracy that policy alternatives are explored and decisions made. The high echelons of the party — the Politburo and the Central Committee — monitor the implementation of policies through the Soviet bureaucracy and the lower levels of the Communist party.

The Soviet political system has a level of regulative, extractive, and distributive capability perhaps greater than that of any other human experiment in political rule. It exceeds the capabilities of historical tyrannies by virtue of the extraordinary technical and organizational apparatus available to modern man and the ideology which legitimates their use. Modern transportation, communication, and weaponry, and modern bureaucratic organization give a new dimension to centralized and arbitrary rule.

The symbolic capability of the Soviet political system has gone through an interesting history. At the outset of the Soviet regime and during the era of Stalin, the fact and the threat of terror and coercion as a means of attaining compliance was surely as important, if not more so, than propaganda and indoctrination. In recent decades indoctrination, military successes, and industrial-scientific accomplishments have created substantial support among most groupings in Soviet society. At the present time it may very well be that the symbolism which stresses the power and industrial-technical accomplishments of the Soviet Union constitutes the more effective part of the symbolic output of the Soviet regime and that the more ideologically oriented part of the symbolic output is less significant. But it would be a great mistake to overlook the fact that perhaps the great majority of Russians accept the ethical validity of their ideology. Those Russian artists and writers who are cited as evidence of alienative tendencies in the Soviet Union more often than not accept many of the basic premises of the regime and its ideology.

The model of totalitarianism would suggest that there is little or no responsive capability in the Soviet system. In fact there is a flow of demands into the political system and a kind of bargaining process among unorganized interest groupings and factions. Peasants on collective farms and workers in factories bargain with their rates of output. Artists and scientists can in some sense withhold their creativity. Bureaucrats and party officials can switch their support from one top party clique to another. The top political elites in Communist nations are constantly confronted with the problem of creating and maintaining coalitions on which their power is based. The very mobilizational system which the Communist elites develop generates not only support for the aims of the regime, but demands that the aspirations of the mobilized groups be in some measure gratified. The resistance of the Russian peasantry and the failures of Soviet agricultural policy are only the more dramatic illustrations of the interplay of demand and response in Soviet politics.

In analyzing political socialization in the Soviet political system, we have to distinguish between the apparatus of party control and related agencies which seek to create a homogeneity of political orientation, and the institutions and agencies which are responsible for the development of conflicting tendencies. The party organization, its youth groups, and its professional and occupational associations seek to inculcate a homogeneous point of view, limiting or suppressing conflicting attitudes and orientations. On the other hand, the family, work, and professional groups, and regional and ethnic groups, often perpetuate conflicting attitudes, aspirations, and beliefs. There is some evidence that the socialization experiences which occur outside the framework of party control are being accorded an increasing toleration. What actually seems to be happening is that the regime is no longer confronted with a crisis of mobilization. Consequently there is an increasing accommodation of differences in attitude and orientation. As these conflicting tendencies challenge the aims of the party leadership, however, there are intermittent repressive responses taking the form of coercion and socio-economic sanctions.

Recruitment into the Soviet political system generally involves a combination of ideological conformity, and abilities and achievements of a variety of different kinds. Recruitment into the top political elite is predominantly through a prior experience in the party apparatus. Technical competence and professional achievement in the various spheres of Soviet life may lead to membership in the soviets at the central or local levels, or in unusual cases in the Central Committee of the Communist party, but not in the Politburo and the Secretariat.

The Communist systems of eastern Europe and Cuba, it

should be noted, are by no means identical with that of the Soviet Union. The eastern European systems have stopped short of the social penetration of the Communist movement in Russia. They are in this respect more representative of the conservative totalitarian type of system. Religious bodies have not been so thoroughly subordinated, and the economy has not been so thoroughly penetrated. There is greater artistic and intellectual freedom. In general there is a more overt bargaining process in these moderate Communist systems. But the question of how great these differences are among Communist countries must await careful research and the development of a comparative politics of communism.

AUTHORITARIANISM: SPAIN

Juan Linz speaks of the Spanish authoritarian regime as having a limited pluralism which contrasts with the monopoly imposed by a totalitarian party on the one hand, and with the formally complete pluralism characteristic of democratic systems on the other. He argues,

> The authoritarian regime may go very far towards suppressing existing groups or institutions inimical to the social order . . . and the threat of control is always present; but due to a number of circumstances the control process is arrested.[16]

Linz's picture of the Spanish system is one in which the top leadership under Franco balances the pressures of such institutions as the army, the bureaucracy, the Church, and professional and business organizations. These interest groups are legitimate, and the bargaining process which takes place is at least in part an overt one. Little or no effort is made to mobilize the population:

> Membership participation is low in political and parapolitical organizations and participation in the single party or similar bodies, whether coerced, manipulated or voluntary, is infrequent and limited.[17]

[16] Juan J. Linz, "An Authoritarian Regime: Spain," in E. Alardt and Y. Littunen (eds.), *Cleavages, Ideologies and Party Systems: Contributions to Comparative Political Sociology* (Helsinski: Westermarck Society, 1964).
[17] *Ibid.*, p. 304.

The regime does not seek enthusiasm or support; it is ready to settle for passive acceptance. It even tolerates opposition as long as it is not overtly and publicly expressed. Linz is, of course, speaking here of the later years of the Spanish authoritarian regime. His description would be less applicable to the first years after the civil war, when a program of suppression of opposition was carried through aggressively and some effort was made to mobilize the population through the Falange party.

Linz also comments on a study he and colleagues made of youth attitudes in contemporary Spain. What is most striking in this study is the report that a substantial proportion of the younger generation is alienated from the Spanish authoritarian regime and speaks of its opposition with relative openness.[18] From this and other works it would appear that the alienative and fragmented nature of pre-Franco political culture still persists to a considerable extent. Alienation seems to be particularly widespread among the workers and farm laborers. Political participant tendencies are widespread in the larger cities and particularly among the urban middle classes. Submissive or subject and parochial orientations are widespread among the rural population and the believing Catholics. Broadly speaking, there is compliance with governmental authority, or at least not active resistance to it. The elite seems to be prepared to accept this kind of apathetic, nonpolitical orientation among large strata of the population; it does not seek to mobilize Spanish society or to increase significantly the capabilities of the political system either for purposes of internal change or for external expansion.

Linz also discusses the approach of Spanish authoritarianism to the media of mass communication. He points out that even while the freedom of the press is curtailed and the press is centrally controlled, the impact of this control is less intense than in a totalitarian regime because of the absence of mobilization goals in the political elite. The Spanish regime has not sought to interfere with informal communication

[18] Juan J. Linz and Amando de Miguel, "Intra-National Differences and Comparisons," unpublished manuscript, 1964.

processes, and one is allowed to express opposition sentiments in writing as long as he does not make more than five copies of his opinions.[19]

Linz makes a number of illuminating points in contrasting Spanish authoritarianism with democratic systems on the one hand, and with totalitarian and traditional authoritarian regimes on the other. He argues that the authoritarian regime, unlike the democratic one, limits its legitimate pluralism to interest-group activity. There is no party system, and there can be no open, competitive process in the selection of the political elite. Unlike the totalitarian regime, the authoritarian regime does not seek to penetrate and mobilize the society. Thus, the single political party in an authoritarian regime is not used as a means of assimilating other political interest groups, but simply comes to be a political faction and interest group of a special kind along with the others. In recent years in Spain the Falange has tended even to lose this function. It seems to have taken on more of the character of a patronage organization, a basis for recruitment into some kinds of public offices.

In contrast with traditional regimes of the types discussed in the preceding chapter, conservative authoritarian regimes seem to be "a likely outcome of the breakdown of such traditional forms of legitimacy." [20] What Linz is getting at here is that conservative authoritarian regimes such as the Spanish and Portuguese systems seem to have arisen in some traditional political systems where there has been a partial penetration of economic, social, and political modernization which has shaken the traditional system. These regimes are "traditionalistic" rather than traditional. In other words, they use some of the modern techniques of organization, propaganda, and control in order to limit the disruption of the traditional order by modernizing forces.

The conversion processes of Spanish authoritarianism reflect its cultural and structural characteristics. There is an overt interest articulation and aggregative process based upon asso-

[19] *Ibid.*, p. 316.
[20] *Ibid.*, p. 321.

ciational and institutional interest groups. The Catholic Church hierarchy, and business and professional interest groups bargain overtly and legitimately with the top political elite and the bureaucracy. The working class manifests its discontent primarily through occasional illegal strikes. The rule-making function is performed by Franco and his cabinet along with the top levels of the bureaucracy. The bureaucracy also performs important articulative and aggregative functions.

Compared with the capabilities of effectively functioning democratic systems, one would have to say that the responsive, extractive, distributive, and symbolic capabilities of the Spanish regime are lower, while its regulative capabilities are higher. In comparison with totalitarian systems, on the other hand, one would have to say that Spanish extractive, regulative, distributive, and symbolic capabilities are lower, but that its responsive capability is higher.

Recruitment into the political elites of the Spanish authoritarian system reflects the system's pluralistic character. Linz points out that only 25 per cent of the Spanish cabinet members during the period from 1938 to 1962 were men actively identified with the Falange party. Twenty per cent of the cabinet members were recruited from traditional Spanish institutions such as Catholic Church or monarchist groups; 39 per cent were recruited from among military officers, and another 15 per cent from among the technical professions or the civil service. In other words, political recruitment processes into the cabinet reflect the power of major interest groups and the political tendencies in Spanish society. The peasantry and labor are not represented; and the secular intelligentsia is less well-represented than in the days of the Republic.

Political socialization in authoritarian Spain is a fragmented process. Linz speaks of depolitization, of deliberate efforts on the part of the regime to discourage ideological indoctrination and political activism. Substantial portions of the working classes and of the educated strata of the population are alienated from the regime. And one would suppose that family socialization, peer group socialization, and work place socialization contribute to this alienation. Similarly, among those

social strata oriented favorably toward the regime, the socialization agencies of family, Church, and voluntary associations
would contribute to the formation of positive attitudes. But
one would have to say that both the alienative and the supportive components of Spanish political culture are moderate
in tendency. There is little extreme alienation, and little
enthusiastic support. In recent years the political system of
Spain seems to have been moving in the direction of the more
overt expression of dissent and toward greater toleration of
limited political activity.

PREMOBILIZED MODERN SYSTEMS

All the modern systems which we have discussed have been
more or less "mobilized" political systems, characterized not
only by a differentiated infrastructure, but also by a rather
widespread secularized political culture. Although traditional
values and structures may be important in these societies, their
political systems rest on a base of considerable social and economic development. Large numbers of individuals have been
urbanized, have become literate, and have been exposed to
differentiated economic enterprises. The spread of instrumental and participatory attitudes creates both problems and potential for the political systems.

In premobilized modern systems the trappings of political
modernity — parties, interest groups, and mass media — have
been imposed upon highly traditional societies. Mobilization
and exposure to modernity have been confined to a small
elite. Although political awareness may have been aroused
through independence movements and through the gradual
diffusion of the idea of economic improvement, political attitudes remain for the most part caught up in a web of traditional family and community ties. Knowledge of the means and
skills of political action, or even the desire for autonomous
participation, are virtually absent. The modern political party
is penetrated by traditional elites and is forced to appeal to
traditional and communal loyalties. The demands stemming
from such loyalties and from the vague aspirations for eco-

nomic betterment are in sharp conflict.[21] Traditional and modern elites manipulate mass activity in both democratic and authoritarian variants of premobilized systems, yet the fragmentation among the elites and the ultimate inability to satisfy aroused mass aspirations create a continuing spiral of frustration and instability.

It is a difficult process to break out of the vicious circle of social, economic, and political underdevelopment. Thus, to speak of a system such as Ghana's as a "modernizing oligarchy" or of that of Nigeria as a "tutelary democracy"[22] confuses potentiality with actuality. These are political systems in the very early stages of growth, engaged in instilling some national consciousness into their primarily parochial populations, in attempting to transform their locally oriented villagers into subjects of national or even regional authority, and in seeking to recruit competent and loyal incumbents into the roles of their political systems, their economies, and their societies. It is for this reason that we speak of the premobilized modern systems as a distinct class. They are, at least in a sense, historical accidents, systems provided with a modernized elite and a differentiated political infrastructure because of the impact of colonialism or because of the diffusion of ideas and practices from more developed parts of the world long before they would have had the need or the impetus to develop such structures and cultures on their own. Although this accident has opened up a vast new future for their citizens, it has also created political systems the infant institutions of which are subject to a tremendous load of pressures and problems at a time when their capability to meet them is quite limited.

Of course these classes of political systems "grade off" into one another. Such is true of the degree of mobilization and secularization as well as of subsystem autonomy or structural

[21] See James S. Coleman and Carl G. Rosberg (eds.), "Conclusion," in their *Political Parties and National Integration in Tropical Africa* (Berkeley: University of California Press, 1964), especially pp. 656 ff.

[22] Edward A. Shils, *Political Development in the New States* (The Hague: Morton & Co., 1960), pp. 393 ff. See also James S. Coleman, "Conclusion," in Gabriel A. Almond and Coleman (eds.), *The Politics of the Developing Areas* (Princeton: Princeton University Press, 1960), pp. 572 ff.

differentiation. However, if we compare Ghana and Nigeria with Spain and Mexico, the two least developed systems discussed above, it is quite clear that the former societies are predominantly premodern, and that their political systems are just in the process of being created. In the *World Handbook of Political and Social Indicators*,[23] for example, Ghana is listed as a "transitional society"; but this category is quite inclusive, and Ghana is at the less developed end of the scale. Nigeria is classified in an even less developed category. Thus, Ghana has a literacy rate of only 22.5 per cent as compared with 50 per cent for Mexico and 87 per cent for Spain. Nigeria's literacy is an even more limited 10 per cent. The following table summarizes some comparative statistics for the four nations, and suggests why we can clearly class Ghana and Nigeria in the premobilized group and Spain and Mexico in the mobilized group:

	Literacy [24]	Percentage in towns over 20,000 [24]	Percentage receiving wages and salaries in employment [24]	Radios per 1,000 [24]
Nigeria	10.0%	10.5%	2.6%	4.0
Ghana	22.5%	6.4%	9.5%	22.2
Mexico	50.0%	24.0%	28.0%	96.9
Spain	87.0%	39.8%	38.2%	90.0

Of course, social and economic indicators provide only one perspective on the process of mobilization. Political experiences such as a revolution or a struggle for independence do indeed mobilize people and change their attitudes and orientations. Economic determinism is too simple an explanation for the events of the real world. Nonetheless, as the following brief capability profiles should illustrate, there are limits in the degree to which political mobilization "from the top" can bypass economic development in creating new secularized atti-

[23] Bruce M. Russet *et al.*, *World Handbook of Political and Social Indicators* (New Haven: Yale University Press, 1964), p. 296.
[24] *Ibid.*, pp. 295–296.

tudes. The particular configurations of problems and factors facing premobilized systems such as Ghana make it imperative that we view such systems distinctly from those in more developed societies and possessing more secularized political cultures. Mexico is an example of a system which has recently left this category, and even a brief comparison of her system with those following should illustrate the impressiveness and difficulty of the development achievement.

PREMOBILIZED AUTHORITARIANISM: GHANA

Prior to the recent military revolt, Apter divided the history of Ghana's political infrastructure into five stages. During the first period, roughly from 1870 until 1940, the organization of the native population largely took the form of ethnic and tribal associations, and of literary and discussion groups among the educated strata of the population. A second stage, running approximately from 1920 until 1950, was a period during which interest groups and nationalist groups began to come together in more inclusive associations. This was the period during which taxpayers' associations were formed and the West African National Congress was established. Apter's third stage, running from the end of World War II until 1956, was the period of political party formation. During this decade the conservative nationalist parties such as the United Gold Coast Convention (U.G.C.C.), and radical nationalist parties such as the Convention People's party (C.P.P.) were formed. These first three stages overlapped somewhat, both chronologically and organizationally, as later patterns emerged out of earlier ones. During the fourth period (beginning in 1957) the C.P.P. sought to destroy the opposition by interfering with their local organizations and harrassing their leaderships. The fifth period began in December 1963, when a referendum was held which made Ghana into a one-party state and gave to President Nkrumah "the right to dismiss judges of the Supreme Court and the High Court at any time." [25] (In February 1966,

[25] David E. Apter, "Ghana," in Coleman and Rosberg, *op. cit.*, pp. 259 ff. See also Apter, *Ghana in Transition* (New York: Atheneum Publishers, 1963); F. M. Bourret, *Ghana — The Road to Independence* (Stanford; Stanford University Press, 1960).

Nkrumah's C.P.P. regime was overthrown by officers of the military and an interim government established which promised a more "democratic" and less centralized regime. It is, of course, too early to predict the future course of the military's intervention.)

In establishing its political monopoly, the Convention People's party fought against a coalition of chiefs and traditional rulers, and against the educated strata of the population, who favored a moderate democratic course of modernization. The C.P.P. sought to undermine the strength of traditional ties and values by an intensive program of recruitment and organization among all elements in the society, by the development of centralized party organization, and by the cultivation of a charismatic cult around the leadership of Nkrumah, and a diffuse ideology of nationalism, pan-Africanism, and socialism.

As the C.P.P. under Nkrumah sought to develop a mobilizational political party penetrating the whole of Ghanaian society, it assimilated oppositional tendencies within its own organization. At the local levels opposition groups were admitted to membership in the C.P.P., and in the Ghanaian legislature opposition members joined the C.P.P. parliamentary organization. In order to counteract the tendencies toward localism that resulted from this pattern of assimilation, the C.P.P. sought to develop an apparatus similar to that of totalitarian regimes. Thus, it assimilated the trade union movement and the agricultural cooperatives and sought to use these occupational associations as means of counteracting local and particularistic tendencies. It also sought to penetrate and assimilate the churches, and formed or assimilated youth and women's organizations. The press was also almost entirely subjected to party control.

Two years before the coup Apter argued that while these groups and agencies were swallowed, they had not been digested:

> By elevating the functional organizations, the party created a dualism that was to have almost disastrous results. Excessive pressure brought to bear on local branches and regional groups, which

had become extremely localized and parochialized, and even oppositionists, resulted in a disenchantment with the party in local areas. The functional groups which provided a new power base against constituency and local organizations stimulated competition between the leaders of the functional and ideological groups and those of the constituency organizations. At the same time it intensified conflict between ethnic and regional branches, on the one hand, and newer and centrally controlled functional groups, on the other. This would be difficult enough under ordinary circumstances, where the desire of local and regional groups to enlarge their autonomy creates antagonism between them and the central party organization. In Ghana it resulted in tension between functional and other party groups, between ethnic and national loyalties, and between secretariat and field organizations all within the party itself.[26]

The lack of homogeneity and the intense conflict within the party brought about an increase in suppressive tendencies and great stress on the creation of a kind of political religion with Nkrumah cast as a kind of messiah. The leaders of the C.P.P. did not have available to them an effective political party apparatus capable of mobilizing the population to attain the goals of the regime. Holding the party together and giving it focus and direction was itself a major problem for the leaders.

In addition, the C.P.P. had still to come to grips with the problem of gaining effective control of the instrumentalities of formal government. The process of replacing the old civil service, trained under the British and largely conservative and hostile to the C.P.P., was just beginning, and in the interval the effectiveness of government was being undermined. In spite of its efforts of societal penetration, the Ghanaian political system remains a premobilized authoritarian system. It has not as yet taken full hold of Ghanaian society, nor is it fully clear that it will succeed in doing so. Apter pointed out before the coup:

The politics of faction which predates political parties in Ghana are now inside the *C.P.P.,* nor is tradition destroyed. Chiefs will

[26] David E. Apter, "Ghana," in Coleman and Rosberg, *op. cit.,* p. 301.

never recover their position, but perhaps chieftancy already has. Clearly Nkrumah is more than ever like a chief. The drums beat when he makes his appearance; libation is poured. These are not empty symbols. The traditionalization of authority has begun. Under the socialist slogans are the thousands of practical translations that ordinary people make in ordinary ways in terms familiar and comfortable. It is with these ordinary people and their ideas that the *C.P.P.* and its leadership must make their peace.[27]

The political system of Ghana appeared to be mobilizing demands at a rapid rate, and attempting to satisfy these demands by symbolic responses — the imputation of extraordinary qualities to Nkrumah and the diffuse symbolism of nationalism, pan-Africanism, and socialism. There seemed to be, however, declining support for the regime and increasing resort to suppression. Despite the establishment of a centralized single-party apparatus, the regulative and extractive capabilities had not acquired much effectiveness. No one really knows the extent of corruption in the system. Widespread cynicism suggested that it was very high indeed.

Although the decision to discuss Ghana and Nigeria as examples of premobilized systems was made before the recent military coups in the two nations, these events emphasize the degree to which the recently imposed modern political structures have failed to penetrate the societies. A small army, scarcely mentioned in most analyses of Ghanaian politics, was able to overturn the supposedly monolithic C.P.P. with hardly a struggle, except from Nkrumah's personal bodyguard. In spite of the regime's efforts to mobilize support and build an effective set of leadership symbols, the abrupt transition was received by the people with enthusiasm or with indifference. The charge that Nkrumah had failed to solve Ghana's economic problems was emphasized. In spite of official emphasis on unity and centralization, the young army officers apparently received no opposition from other components of bureaucracy or from the police. These structural shifts are features common to premobilized contemporary systems, as events of the past

27 *Ibid.*, p. 311.

twenty years have exemplified. Whatever the "stance" taken to development, whether authoritarian or democratic, pre-mobilized systems face a host of extremely difficult problems in developing their capabilities, and a host of pressures upon their political structures. Neither the adoption of authoritarian nor of democratic forms of modern political structures can cause these pressures and limitations to vanish. Although the mass political party may have a great potential for mobilization and unification, it is a long and difficult task to translate that potential into reality. And the molding of the instruments of change themselves — party and bureaucracy — is among the most difficult tasks. Ghana's new leaders, whatever their intentions and whatever the strategies they adopt, will face problems similar to those that confronted Nkrumah and the C.P.P.

PREMOBILIZED DEMOCRACY:
NIGERIA PRIOR TO JANUARY 1966 [28]

Nigeria, before the military coup of 1966, was a federation governed at both regional and national levels through large-scale, mass-supported, formally democratic political parties. The parties operated through the formal Western structures of legislature and cabinet, and competed with one another in more or less free elections open to all citizens (except women in the Islamic North). The parties were subjected to widespread criticism from an unusually lively and autonomous press, and from a considerable diversity of autonomous interest groups including trade unions, student unions, independent politicians, and intellectuals.

But these surface characteristics revealed only one facet of the Nigerian system. Nigerian politics are dominated by the politics of community and traditional authority, by a political culture and a social system which is only beginning — in a strikingly diverse and uneven fashion — the process of secularization. The differentiated political structure and the awareness of the possibilities of economic improvement through govern-

[28] Though at the time of writing the fate of the Nigerian political system is in doubt, we present it as it was during the brief years of its first constitution as an independent nation. It is an excellent illustration of the problems of democracy in a new nation.

ment action, which are the heritage of independence and the
accident of a twentieth-century international environment,
have penetrated the traditional, premobilized society in a
complex and uncertain fashion. The different political patterns
of Nigeria's regions suggest ever more clearly that, as Sklar and
Whitaker conclude:

> . . . the political form of the democratic political party seems
> able to sustain vastly different types of political regimes. In
> southern Nigeria the political party has served as an instrument
> of the political ascendency of new elites produced by the com-
> plementary processes of Western education, urbanization, and
> commercial development, whereas in northern Nigeria the politi-
> cal party has served equally well as the instrument of an ancient
> regime that has controlled and limited the political thrust of
> the "new men." The role of the political party in Nigeria has
> been determined, it would seem, less by the nature of the norms
> and the rules that formally govern the institution than by the
> nature of the underlying social and economic conditions in
> which the institution operates.[29]

Structural and Cultural Patterns. Nigeria's first constitution
established a federal governmental structure which was a deliberate reflection of its most basic patterns of structural and
cultural fragmentation. The constitution reserved or permitted many types of government performance to be carried
out at the regional rather than at the national level. The federal government was run by a parliament and cabinet system
based on nationwide elections. The N.P.C., the dominant party
of the Northern Region, dominated the federal parliament,
usually in coalition with one of the other parties. (Slightly
more than half the population resides in the north.) There
were at least three major political parties, each resting primarily on the ethnic base of the dominant people of one of
the regions.[30]

[29] Richard L. Sklar and C. S. Whitaker, Jr., "Nigeria," in Coleman and
Rosberg, *op. cit.*, pp. 648–649.

[30] This description in general focuses on the situation prior to 1963. In
the next two years the party structures shifted with the destruction of the
Action Group and the emergence of N.N.D.P. from its ruins, and a new
region (the Mid-West) was formed. The complexity of these developments

Although the regional systems had formally similar structural arrangements, in reality they presented at least two very different cultural and structural patterns. To understand Nigerian national politics, it is necessary to consider these major regional differences.

The Northern Region has been relatively untouched by the changes of social mobilization. Its political culture was — and is — highly traditional. The social system is dominated by the Islamic culture, emphasizing obedience and rigid social stratification. The traditional rulers — the emirs — were sustained by the British policy of indirect rule. The emirate remains the fundamental political sub-unit of the region. The major political party, the N.P.C., was a highly decentralized structure whose organization reflected and acknowledged "the traditional status of the emirates as virtually autonomous states." [31] The independence movement and the introduction of party and elections had the effect of bringing about a greater awareness of the polity. Subsequent government development projects increased expectations of the benefits of government outputs. But these developments took place within the framework of obedience to immediate traditional authority. Thus, although voting turnout was relatively high, the majority of the people of the north supported the traditional elites.

In the southern regions a much more participatory political culture had emerged. This may be in part the consequence of a traditional political culture among the Yoruba peoples which emphasized the rulers' responsibility to the people, and of a strong tradition of government by discussion and consent among the Ibo and Ibibio tribes of eastern Nigeria.[32] However, political activism in the southern areas resulted also from a more vigorous participation in the independence movement

precludes full analysis here, but the general points made regarding this type of system are hardly affected. The original regions were the Northern, Eastern, and Western regions, and were in each case dominated by, but not exclusively populated by, a separate ethnic group.

[31] Sklar and Whitaker, *op. cit.*, p. 625.

[32] Pendleton Herring, "The Future for Democracy in Nigeria," in Robert O. Tilman and Taylor Cole (eds.), *The Nigerian Political Scene* (Durham: Duke University Press, 1962), pp. 255–256.

and from the processes of mobilization and secularization which had commenced in these areas. It is not so often conflict between traditional communities, but conflict between indig enous groups and new arrivals to the growing towns, or class conflict between new groups such as manual and clerical workers and other new or traditional groups, which underlies the maze of group strife. The heterogeneous traditional groups, combined with the diverse effects of demographic and occupational change, produced a level of cultural fragmentation of disturbing depth. The appeal of the parties to these different groups, an appeal based more on patronage than on ideology, greatly increased communal tensions.[33]

System Maintenance and Adaptation Functions. The processes of socialization and recruitment in Nigeria reflected these regional differences. The party leaders in the southern regions were largely self-made men of one sort or another. They were educators, lawyers, and businessmen of the Westernized elite. The achievement orientations of the Ibo and Yoruba peoples' traditional cultures no doubt contributed to this tendency. In these areas the traditional chiefs were checked and controlled by the political parties. In the Northern Region, on the other hand, an ascriptive process of recruitment into leadership roles was most common. Sklar and Whitaker found that in 1959, 87 per cent of N.P.C. parliamentary members from emirates belonged to the traditional ruling class.[34]

The Conversion Functions in Nigeria. The patterns of interest articulation and aggregation showed regional differences which corresponded to the fragmented structural and cultural patterns. In the Northern Region the traditional elites were the primary and dominant interest articulators. The N.P.C. provided a useful mechanism for the reinforcement and coordination of these traditional interests. The N.P.C. parliamentary party came to exercise unquestioning control over the rank-and-file membership in deciding party policy. The control was based largely on the traditional hierarchical relationships and expectations which pervaded the region. The N.P.C.

33 Sklar and Whitaker, *op. cit.,* p. 648.
34 *Ibid.,* pp. 617–618.

sought to maintain maximum regional autonomy and to sustain the traditional social and political structure of the northern area. It stressed the traditional community of Islam in its appeal to the masses for unified support. Although the party accepted the innovations of free election and secret ballot when introduced in the national elections, and proclaimed its dedication in principle to democracy, it simultaneously supported traditional theocratic authority. The patterns of regional policy emphasized maintenance of the status quo. A small opposition party demanding social change, the N.E.P.U., was allowed to operate — appealing mostly to minority ethnic elements — but its activities were limited and subject to harassment by the authorities. The communication structures in the north were dominated by traditional patterns and informal interaction. Mass media were quite undeveloped.

The parties of the two southern regions grew during the struggle for political independence. They were led by the Westernized intellectual elite which emerged in the urban areas. However, during the independence struggle these elites attempted to organize the traditional peasantry in the rural areas. Each party became rooted in the major ethnic group of its home region and attempted to contest elections in the other regions by appealing to local minority groups. The parties themselves were internally competitive and "freewheeling," although dominated by the relatively small Westernized elite. General party strategies were based for the most part on electoral considerations, rather than on ideological issues, and emphasized the politics of patronage and communal conflict.

Prior to January 1966, a growing number of associational interest groups emerged in the southern regions and constituted political access channels of growing importance. Business associations tended to support the dominant political party of each region, but the labor unions were "relatively independent of formal party relationships, owing partly to the disaffection of radical unionists from the major political parties and partly to tactical considerations of collective bargaining." [35] In the two southern regions the traditional authorities, the chiefs,

[35] *Ibid.*, p. 636.

were of limited importance, although traditional communal and ethnic ties were powerful. While traditional communication structures were important, a strong and autonomous press constituted an active source of information and criticism, though primarily confined to the urban areas.

The conversion processes at the national level reflected these very considerable regional differences, as well as the peculiar complexities of the internal politics of the two southern regions. The government was dominated by the party of the more populous Northern Region. Although overtly espousing development, welfare, and democracy along with the parties of the south, the N.P.C. in fact followed a conservative approach, seeking to protect its traditional institutions. This conservatism was particularly frustrating to many of the modernizing elements in Nigerian society. But both because of the less developed socio-economic structure and because of the hierarchical pattern of political structure and culture in the north, the articulation of opposition to the government came mainly from the southern regions. As an analyst of Nigerian foreign-policy making observed before the military coup of January 1966:

> The articulate pressures against the Government exist mainly in Southern Nigeria, northerners maintaining an almost contemptuous silence on many of the issues. It is here that one form of federal strain enters the picture. Most of the articulate critics of Government must work through one of the southern parties . . . and/or through such social groups as the Nigerian Youth Congress. Yet it is the conservative north, with its almost universally-supported *N.P.C.,* which controls the Federal Government and in fact has now an absolute majority in the Parliament. The Government, therefore, faces no threat to its control from the articulate pressures as long as the present federal structure is maintained. On the other hand, there is no doubt that the federation itself does face the threat of dissolution from such pressures; that is, if the articulate southern opposition groups are constantly frustrated in their demands, the temptation to win their way by non-democratic means will undoubtedly increase.[36]

36 Claude S. Phillips, Jr., *The Development of Nigerian Foreign Policy* (Evanston: Northwestern University Press, 1964), p. 87.

However, even without the resistance of the conservative northern elites, the high levels of demand and expectation, generated by the vote-seeking efforts of the politicians, were to a large extent impossible to aggregate satisfactorily given the limited development of the system. The scarcity of desired rewards — education, community development, employment, higher wages — as well as the ethnic form the demands often assumed, intensified the level of conflict. Discontent, sharp party strife, and such modes of direct protest as the general strike of 1964 (which was somewhat successful in forcing the government to improve wage and salary conditions) were frequently manifested in the conversion process. These were the conditions which lay behind the military takeover.

Capabilities of the Nigerian System. Nigeria's capabilities remain largely undeveloped. Her exceedingly low level of economic production places very real and immediate limitations on the extractive capability. In 1959 Nigeria had a per-capita income of only $78, less than half that of Ghana and one third that of Mexico. Moreover, her rate of annual growth in the 1953–1957 period was among the world's lowest.[37] With this sort of base it is impossible for the Nigerian system to create an extensive extractive capability by drawing on her internal economy. The weakness of the bureaucracy and low levels of popular support intensify the problem.

Needless to say, these limitations also sharply curtail the distributive capability of the system. Although some very notable economic development and educational projects have been initiated, largely with the help of foreign assistance, the over-all distribution levels have been low. In 1960, for example, only some 25 per cent of the population between the ages of five and nineteen was in school, as compared to 81 per cent in the United States and 41 per cent in Mexico.[38] However, the absolute expenditure level of the federal government more than doubled between 1959 and 1962.[39]

[37] Russett *et al., op. cit.,* pp. 156–161.
[38] *Ibid.,* pp. 218–220.
[39] P. N. C. Okigbo, *Nigerian Public Finance* (Evanston: Northwestern University Press, 1965), p. 180. See Chap. 7 for an economic analysis of problems and prospects of increasing revenue and growth.

The regulative capability of the former Nigerian system remained relatively undeveloped and decentralized. In the Northern Region formal and informal coercion was a prevalent pattern when the traditional elites were faced with any threat to their position, but freedom of communication and association was maintained in the Eastern and Western Regions. In 1963 an all-party conference called by the prime minister considered and rejected — under intensive pressure from the Nigerian press — a proposal to introduce a preventive detention act which would have allowed the government to imprison suspected subversives without trial, as in Ghana.

The symbolic capability of Nigeria is perhaps one of its most serious weaknesses. Lacking the experience of a deep and unifying struggle for independence, the Nigerian peoples entered nationhood with a greater consciousness of their regional and ethnic than of their national identities. The effective symbols in Nigerian politics have been those of tribe and local tradition, not of modern nationhood. Although the major elites and the parties generally proclaimed their allegiance to the federation, in recent years the calls for its dismantling had been growing louder with each successive crisis.

Under its first constitution Nigeria was faced with a set of conflicting demands which were virtually impossible to aggregate. The divisiveness of ethnic and community ties, the excessive expectations aroused by politicians seeking electoral support, the low level of capabilities to meet even a moderate flow of demands from an aroused populace, and the resistance of the traditional northern elites to widespread socio-economic change, placed the Nigerian system in a position where it could not respond effectively to the pressures placed upon it. The autonomous and differentiated infrastructure introduced into this premobilized society had the effect of arousing conflicting expectations without disciplining them, and of creating aspirations long before the system could possibly fulfill them.

CHAPTER XI

Toward a Theory of Political Development

THE CONCEPT OF development has run consistently throughout this study.[1] In our treatment of political structure we have emphasized role differentiation and subsystem autonomy as criteria of development, and in our treatment of political culture and socialization we have stressed the concept of secularization as a criterion of development. Similarly in our treatment of the conversion processes of politics, the themes of differentia-

[1] See the *Studies in Political Development* series (Princeton: Princeton University Press, 1964–1965): Vol. I, Lucian W. Pye (ed.), *Communication and Political Development;* Vol. II, Robert Ward and Dankwart Rustow (eds.), *Political Modernization in Japan and Turkey;* Vol. III, Joseph La-Palombara (ed.), *Bureaucracy and Political Development;* Vol. IV, James Coleman (ed.), *Education and Political Development;* Vol. V, Lucian W. Pye and Sidney Verba (eds.), *Political Culture and Political Development.* See also David Apter, *The Politics of Modernization* (Chicago: University of Chicago Press, 1965); Lucian W. Pye, *Aspects of Political Development* (Boston: Little, Brown and Company, 1966); A. F. K. Organski, *Stages of Political Growth* (New York: Alfred A. Knopf, Inc., 1965); Gabriel A. Almond, "Political Systems and Political Change," *American Behavioral Scientist,* June, 1963; Gabriel A. Almond, "A Developmental Approach to Political Systems," *World Politics,* January, 1965; Harold D. Lasswell, "The Policy Sciences of Development," *World Politics,* January, 1965; Samuel P. Huntington, "Political Development and Political Decay," *World Politics,* April, 1965; Robert A. Packenham, "Political Development Doctrines in the American Foreign Aid Program," *World Politics,* January, 1966.

299

tion, structural autonomy, and secularization have served to distinguish the varieties of ways in which these functions are performed. In our treatment of the capabilities of political systems we have argued that particular levels and patterns of system performance are associated with levels of structural differentiation, autonomy, and secularization. Finally, our classification of political systems is a developmental one in which the variables of structural differentiation, autonomy, and secularization are related to other aspects of the functioning of particular classes of political systems — their conversion characteristics, capabilities, and system maintenance patterns.

Thus in this study "level of development," specified in terms of differentiation, autonomy, and secularization, is used as a starting point for description, explanation, and prediction. The problem of generalization and prediction — surely a most hazardous and difficult task — is of particular concern for two reasons. First, we are ethically concerned with the problems of political development and political change in the contemporary world. The prospects for democracy and human welfare in many parts of the contemporary world are unclear and troubling. We regard the confusing and often threatening events of the last twenty years, and the search for solutions to the problems of instability and internal warfare as challenges to us as citizens and as political scientists. They are a part of the challenge to all the social sciences to help men describe, explain, and predict the events of social life in order that they may grapple with their problems in a rational manner.

But regardless of these normative concerns, there is a second reason to turn to the difficult task of generalization and prediction. We believe that the ultimate test of the strength of a scientific theory is its ability to generalize and predict. Indeed, unless a theory designates relationships between variables in such a way that predictions can be made about the consequences of their interaction, it is hard to establish whether the theory is valid or invalid, whether it should eventually be discarded, revised, or accepted. The advancement of knowledge comes through the testing and reformulation of theories. We can evaluate the theories of Marx, for example, in terms of the predictions he made about the future of class and conflict. If his insistence that economic events would shape the form of political interaction has become in part accepted, it is also true that his predictions about the nature of class warfare in developed countries has by and large proved wrong. Yet it is in part the strength of Marx's contribution that he could make such predictions, and that his work has stimulated some of the great sociologists of our time to devote themselves to reformulating his analysis to take account of new information.[2]

We have, in short, emphasized political development because we believe that this approach enables us to lay the basis for prediction as well as for description and explanation. The forces of technological change and cultural diffusion are driving political systems in certain directions, which seem discernible and susceptible to analysis in terms of increasing levels of development. The developmental approach also enables us to classify political systems according to one of the most powerful sets of constraints and limitations which shape their future — their political past. The processes of political change are extremely complex and rest upon a very large number of interacting factors. Yet, the hope for prediction and, indeed, for any kind of reasonably parsimonious explanation, lies in the fact that every system is the prisoner of its past. The way in which a system faced certain types of problems, and the nature of its present characteristics as they bear the mark of those efforts, limit and constrain the alternatives which lie before it. History does not, of course, determine the future, but it may well limit or foreclose certain alternatives.

Suppose, for example, we were to try to predict the future career of a young high school graduate. In order to make explicit predictions about his future we should have to know a great deal about his capabilities, needs, beliefs, resources, and environment. Even with such knowledge, our predictions would be at best probabilistic. Yet, on the basis of very few facts we could make some very strong predictions about the limitations and constraints shaping the courses open to him.

[2] Much of the work of Max Weber, for example, can be interpreted in this light.

If he has failed to study any mathematics beyond elementary algebra, for example, we can rather safely predict that (a) the probability of a career in science, mathematics, or engineering is very low and (b) if he is to embark upon such a career, he must choose a strategy of action which will make it possible to gain this requisite background. We also know that if faced with certain kinds of problems he will be incapable of solving them.

Similarly, if we know about a set of important variables among the large number of characteristics of political systems, and have equally strong generalizations about the limits or potentials they imply, we can make similar strong predictions about political change. Thus, we know that the ruler of a traditional empire simply cannot attain some of the system goals for which a totalitarian dictator might reasonably strive. And we can predict some of the fundamental changes which would be required if the traditional empire were to seek such goals. We shall assert that the utility of the developmental approach of classifying political systems as we did in Chapters IX and X is not merely that it groups systems according to factors of normative or historical interest, but that it groups them according to the kinds of *futures* which they face. As we shall see, systems at different levels of differentiation and secularization, or at different levels of subsystem autonomy, face substantially different sets of constraints, pressures, and potentialities. Our classification contains elements of prediction and generalization, as well as a basis for more refined developmental theory — that of specifying relationships between more and more complex system and environmental factors — towards which political science can build. However, before we can extend this analysis to the problem of predicting political change and development, we must discuss the role of a developmental approach in describing, comparing, and explaining the characteristics of political systems.

DESCRIPTIVE ANALYSIS AND A DEVELOPMENTAL APPROACH: PRIMITIVE AND TRADITIONAL SYSTEMS

In Chapter IX we described examples of various types of primitive and traditional systems. The emphasis on levels of development in comparing such systems refers us to the different degrees of structural differentiation and cultural secularization. These in turn are related to different kinds of conversion processes, system capabilities, and system maintenance and adaptation processes.

The typology contains some generalizations about different system characteristics. Thus, if we begin with our first category of intermittent political systems, we can discriminate primitive bands, segmentary lineage systems, and pyramidal systems, one from the other, according to the specialization of political roles and the instrumentalism or rationality of their cultures.[3] While at this level the differences in structural differentiation and secularization are small, they are there; and making these discriminations is of some importance for a theory of political development. In some of the new nations political systems of these kinds are still to be found, and it is important to understand their characteristics if we are to explain their problems of assimilating into the larger and more complex systems.

As we move from this so-called primitive category to the traditional one, we take a large jump on the scale of differentiation and secularization. At an earlier point we spoke of the transition from primitive political systems to the "hierarchical" and patrimonial systems as being based on a political invention, that of a differentiated officialdom. The concept of "invention" is only partially appropriate in this context. Historians and sociological theorists point out that it is one of the characteristics of the patrimonial political system that the officialdom represents an extension of the roles encountered in the simpler patriarchal system. Many of the founding myths of patrimonial kingdoms refer to a conquering clan as the origin of the patrimonial system. What seems to have happened in many cases is that a clan or tribe has moved into an area, constituted itself as a ruling clan, and subordinated the indigenous social groupings to itself. These kingdoms appear often to have been the result of a kind of primordial mobilization process resulting from the movement and struggle of primitive peoples.

The formation of patrimonial kingdoms seems often to have

---

[3] See David Apter, *The Politics of Modernization, op. cit.,* Chap. 3, for an excellent treatment of primitive and traditional political systems.

involved the pressure of political systems on one another. The early patrimonial kings have usually been conquerors, integrators, and extractors of resources. In order to accomplish these goals they have had to recruit and train officials with special skills and loyalties to themselves. The development of such officialdoms has usually been associated with an increased capacity to regulate behavior, to compel obedience, and to gain compliance with the goals of the ruling group. And this in turn has been associated with an increase in the human and material resources which the political system has been able to extract from its society and from its international environment.

Thus we can speak of the patrimonial kingdom as representing a higher level of political development than the primitive bands and the segmentary and pyramidal systems to which we have referred. The higher "level" of development refers to differences in structural differentiation and in secularization, and these are related to differences in conversion patterns, in levels of political system capability, and in socialization and recruitment processes.

The bureaucratic empire can be compared with the patrimonial kingdom in structural and cultural terms. On the structural side we observe a separation of the officialdom from the household of the ruler, and the development of bureaucratic departments and offices which have some autonomous base, some independence of the control and immediate supervision of the ruler. Thus, if the ruler dies, the government can in some sense continue. If his energies decline, or if his attention is diverted, some continuity of the political and governmental process is assured. Along with this development toward a more rational type of bureaucratic organization goes a more effective penetration of the periphery of the society and a more effective centralization of control. The development of a relatively autonomous bureaucracy creates a more complex political process, with conflict developing over political goals, as between the component parts of the bureaucracy and the ruler and his household. Other structural components in the political process of the bureaucratic empire are the persisting aristocratic and lineage elites, which tend to resist centralization, regulation, and extraction.

Thus, the political conversion processes of the bureaucratic empire are usually much more complicated than those of the patrimonial kingdom. In some cases adjudicative agencies become differentiated and acquire some independence of the ruler and the bureaucracy (note the case of Tudor England). The greater scale and heterogeneity of the component parts of the bureaucratic empire may occasion a more clearly demarcated structural differentiation between policy-making and policy-implementing agencies. Some of these bureaucratic empires, in other words, begin to show the characteristics of "separation of powers."

On the cultural side, as the political system becomes differentiated from other social systems, the rulers begin to develop secular goals, and a rational sense of the relationship between means and ends and of one set of ends as over against other ends. Rule making comes to be viewed as a goal-setting process, and rule implementation is directed toward the attainment of these goals and policies. The need for accountability and responsibility is reflected in the development of record-keeping devices and inspectorates of one kind or another, and reflects the spread of rational choice, calculation, and control. Corresponding changes begin to take place in the mass political culture. Thus, in those bureaucratic empires in which rule-making and rule-adjudicating structures become differentiated, we begin to get the development of "subject competence." That is to say, the subjects of the governmental system become aware of the specific laws or rules governing their conduct; and if they have access to courts where the application of the rule to the specific case has an opportunity for an independent check, they develop a kind of competence, a form of participation in output processes.

Along with cultural and structural changes goes an increase in the extractive, regulative, and symbolic capabilities of these political systems. The distributive and responsive capabilities of the systems differ substantially from case to case, as was brought out in our descriptions of the Inca empire and the Tudor monarchy.

Eisenstadt points out, and the evidence largely supports him, that the bureaucratic empires seem to have grown out of patrimonial kingdoms, feudal systems, or city-states.[4] In the European context the sequence seems to have involved either a challenge or threat from the international environment, with a resulting effort to reduce feudal particularism in order to increase capabilities at the center, or — reversing the process — an opportunity for expansion into the international environment, which led to a reduction of feudal particularism in order to take advantage of the situation. The flows of international pressures and of elite inputs interact one with the other.

Thus, in our first two major classes of political systems, it appears that the chief proximate causes of political change have been international system inputs (*e.g.*, threats from the international environment) or centralizing policies initiated by the political elites. The chief structural changes which have been associated with the increasing levels of political development involve bureaucratization, and in some cases the differentiation of rule-adjudicating structures and rule-making structures. The chief changes in capabilities take the form of increases in extractive, regulative, and symbolic capabilities.

THE COMPARISON OF MODERN POLITICAL SYSTEMS

When we speak of level of political development, we really are dealing with three interrelated variables–role differentiation, subsystem autonomy, and secularization. There is a tendency for these processes of change to vary together. Thus if a new subsystem of roles develops in a political system, there is a tendency toward a more instrumental or rational political culture; but the relationship between role differentiation and secularization is not a necessary and invariant one. If a political system introduces suffrage, the adult population or a part of it in some sense becomes "voters." But we are all familiar with the situation in which voters cast their ballots according to traditional norms, as do tribesmen, villagers, or tenants under the control of a tribal chief, village headman, or landlord. Actually, this lag between structural and cultural change is one of the distinctive characteristics of the class of pre-

4 S. N. Eisenstadt, *The Political Systems of Empires* (New York: The Free Press of Glencoe, 1962), p. 11.

mobilized systems referred to in Chapter X. They have introduced some of the formal roles of modern political systems, but the orientations to these roles continue to be traditional.

Similarly, structural differentiation — the development of new roles and subsystems — is related to increasing subsystem autonomy, but the relationship is not a necessary and invariant one. Needless to say, there can be no subsystem autonomy without role differentiation, and once a new set of roles is established, there are pressures toward the autonomous performance of these roles. But it is also clear that relatively differentiated and secularized systems such as the totalitarian ones use their great organizational capabilities to keep subsystem autonomy at a minimum and thereby penetrate and regulate their societies more effectively.

In the table on page 308 we have plotted the types of political systems discussed in Chapters IX and X according to degrees of differentiation and secularization (on the ordinate scale) and of subsystem autonomy (on the abscissa). Two points may be made in the interpretation of the table. First, at the level of relatively undifferentiated political systems, subsystem autonomy has a quite different significance than in modern systems. In pyramidal and segmentary systems the sub-units are not specialized components of a larger and relatively integrated whole, but come very close to being independent political systems. Feudal systems also, though at a higher level of differentiation and secularization, tend to be loosely related aggregations of relatively independent patrimonial systems. A second point is that in modern democratic systems, subsystem autonomy increases with structural differentiation and secularization, but that in authoritarian systems, it decreases. In this sense increasing structural differentiation seems to force a more and more clear-cut choice between authoritarian and democratic relationships of system and subsystem.

Thus, in comparing the characteristics of modern political systems or classes of them, we find patterns of performance and capability associated with these powerful variables: level of differentiation and secularization, and subsystem autonomy. There are, of course, other important factors which shape the

Relationship between Autonomy of Subsystems
and Degree of Structural Differentiation
and Cultural Secularization of Political Systems *

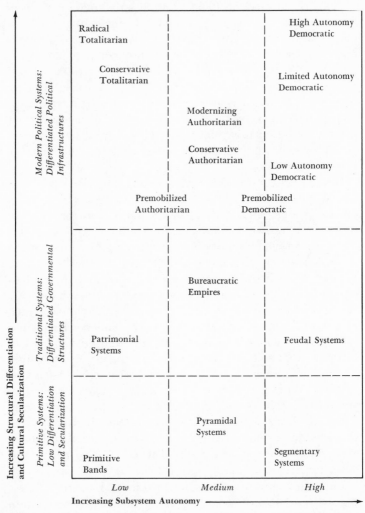

*In this table differentiation and secularization are combined in a single scale. Needless to say, these two properties of political systems, while related, may vary independently.

characteristics of any political system. The level of economic development, for example, is obviously very closely related to the level of structural differentiation, and constitutes one of many important environmental variables. But a comparison of the political systems themselves can be undertaken independently of environmental factors, although, as has so often been stressed, they have great influence on explanation and on prediction of change.

The decision to classify systems in terms of the level of differentiation and secularization and the degree of subsystem autonomy is based upon the utility and meaningfulness of this classification in comparisons. It is, of course, possible to compare any two political systems utilizing the functional concepts which we have been discussing throughout this book: capabilities, performance of process functions, and performance of socialization and recruitment. However, by structuring the comparison around the three developmental variables, it is possible to compare systems which are alike in respect to one set of major characteristics, while different in another. Thus, political scientists have generally recognized that in some important respects the United States and the Soviet Union are more similar than are the United States and Mexico. In other respects the opposite is true. The capacity to extract resources from the environment is more similar in the highly differentiated systems of the United States and Russia. But the relative openness of the flow of information and travel of the United States and Mexico contrast with that of the much more "closed" totalitarian system.

The utility of the approach suggested here is that it becomes possible to compare systematically the characteristics associated with one type of system to those associated with another. If one wishes to focus upon one type of configuration or one type of problem, it is possible to select the most appropriate comparison. And this systematic comparison prepares the way for the formulation of general hypotheses about the kinds of associated relationships. We shall illustrate this approach to comparative analysis by a brief sketch of the following: (1) comparison of characteristics associated with democratic systems at different levels of development; (2) comparison of characteristics associated with authoritarian systems at different levels of development; (3) comparison of characteristics associated with the most highly developed democratic and authoritarian forms; (4) comparison of characteristics of premobilized systems with those of more mobilized systems.

It is interesting to observe, by the way, that most comparative studies have implicitly settled upon one of these types of comparison. One finds textbooks dealing with "modern European systems," both democratic and totalitarian, or dealing with "underdeveloped nations," or dealing with "democratic systems" at various levels of development. The point is not that the variables of secularization, differentiation, and autonomy are unfamiliar to political scientists, but that it is useful to make explicit the grounds of classification and comparison. This is what makes it possible for us to deal, though in a very brief and schematic fashion, with such a wide variety of historical and contemporary systems.

(1) A comparison of the three varieties of democratic political systems in our classification scheme according to level of political development suggests several points. Those political systems in which there is high subsystem autonomy represent a higher level of differentiation and secularization than do those classified under the limited and low autonomy categories. In capability terms, those with high subsystem autonomy have relatively versatile and continuous capability (*i.e.*, they have the capability both of adapting to their environments and of shaping them), while those characterized by limited subsystem autonomy tend to have a fluctuating pattern of capability. What this means is that periods of immobilism (in other words, blockage of the conversion processes) appear to alternate with brief "crisis-liquidation" regimes, or with authoritarian interludes in which the responsive capability is repressed. In immobilist periods political systems can neither adapt to their environments nor alter them. Finally, if we compare democratic systems which are characterized by low subsystem autonomy, such as the Mexican, with the Anglo-American type of

political system, we would have to say that along with low subsystem autonomy goes a suppression of the responsive capability and a swelling of the regulative capability. In other words, these systems reduce their responsiveness to their environments in order to increase their capacity to shape and alter them.

(2) If we turn to authoritarian systems and compare them according to the type of capability associated with differentiation, we would have to say that both the conservative authoritarian systems and the modernizing authoritarian systems have limited responsive capabilities, but that they differ according to the groups or strata in their societies to which they are responsive. Conservative authoritarian regimes are responsive in a limited way to the demands of traditional and conservative interest groups such as the Church, landowners, and perhaps certain sectors of the business elites. In the modernizing authoritarian system, there is a limited responsiveness to the more modern elements in the society, such as Western-trained army officers, technically trained elements in the bureaucracy, and perhaps some of the components of the modern economy such as business entrepreneurs, managers, and technicians.

Totalitarian regimes differ from the other authoritarian ones in the lower level of their responsive capabilities and in the higher level of their regulative, extractive, and symbolic capabilities. Along with this is a more thoroughgoing structural differentiation and penetration of the society. The differences between conservative and radical totalitarianism are in the level of the responsive capability and in the impact of the regulative, extractive, and distributive capabilities. If we take as our examples Soviet Russia and Nazi Germany, it is clear that there was some limited responsiveness in Nazi Germany to demands coming from business and conservative elements. Similarly, the impact of the repressiveness and of the distributive patterns of the regime favored business and conservative elements. Soviet totalitarianism, on the other hand, is more universally differentiated and penetrative.

(3) Turning to a general comparison of democratic and au-

thoritarian forms, we may illustrate our approach to comparison by examining the extreme varieties — the democratic systems with high subsystem autonomy at one extreme, and radical totalitarianism at the other. We deal here with the chief political protagonists of our age — Anglo-American democracy and Soviet totalitarianism.

A structural comparison of these political systems leads us to the following conclusions. A totalitarian system in a nominal sense has all the structures and subsystems of roles that exist in a democratic system, but rather than being autonomous, the interaction of these political substructures is hierarchically controlled. In conversion or process terms, the flow of inputs from the society is suppressed or strictly regulated. Consequently, we cannot speak of interest groups, media of communication, and political parties as constituting an autonomous political infrastructure. They are to be viewed more as mobilization structures contributing to the regulative, extractive, and symbolic capabilities than as substructures creating the basis for a responsive capability.

A comparison of the political cultures suggests the following conclusions: The dominant and legitimate culture of totalitarian systems is ideological in its intellectual characteristics. There are limits on rational calculation and analysis. The ideology sets certain ends as absolute, and treats the Communist party as the sole interpreter of ends and selector of means. Decision making, thus, tends to be relatively rigid in comparison with the more open process of balancing and combining ends and means characteristic of the political process in fully differentiated and secularized democracies. While there has surely been a decline of ideology in the Soviet version of the totalitarian system, particularly in recent years, the ideological form of political calculation and analysis still enjoys great influence. There are at the same time ideological rigidities in the democratic political process but in the high-subsystem-autonomy version of democracy, there can be little question that we are dealing with a more open and secular form of political process.

A comparison of political performance patterns suggests the

following conclusions: The profile of capability of the most developed democracies is more versatile and adaptive. What this means is that *all* types of capability are developed in both the input and the output phases of the political process. The political system can respond to or adapt to the demands that are being made upon it from its own social environment or from the international environment, and at the same time it can cope with and manipulate its social and international environments.

When we use the terms "versatile" and "adaptive," we do not mean "better" or "worse." Ethical appraisal of these structural, cultural, and capability characteristics is a complicated problem. Some political systems in the course of their growth have had the good fortune of being less heavily loaded by international pressure and threat than others. Some political systems have had the advantage of large natural resources. Late-developing political systems were unable to take a more leisurely route towards political development. They have confronted a world in which the only way to compete, and perhaps to survive, called for a kind of boot-strap political development operation, involving the swelling of the regulative and extractive capabilities and the suppression of the responsive and distributive ones.

(4) We have separated out the class of contemporary systems which we refer to as "premobilized" political systems. What we have sought to convey here is the idea that though in form these may appear to be democratic or authoritarian systems, they are in fact in only the beginning stages of the differentiation and secularization processes. What modern political structure and culture they have is usually concentrated among certain strata in the cities. The modern structures and cultures have not as yet effectively penetrated and transformed the traditional or primitive structures and cultures. Furthermore, the levels of capability are generally so much lower than those of the other systems in our classification that these premobilized systems need to be separated out. When one calls a political system at this stage of development "democratic" or "au-

thoritarian" one refers not to a functioning political system, but rather to what might be thought of as a "stance" at the beginning of a developmental process, and one that may change quickly and without much prior warning.

SYSTEM DEVELOPMENT PROBLEMS: THE "WHY" OF DEVELOPMENT

Now that we have shown how the structural and cultural characteristics of a political system are associated with its process and performance characteristics, we turn to the problem of explanation, the question of why a system developed along particular lines. In Chapter II we spoke of system development problems and how the manner in which they are experienced affects the differentiation and secularization of a political system, as well as its degree of subsystem autonomy. We suggested a fourfold classification: state building, nation building, participation, and distribution. By state building we refer to the problem of integration and control; by nation building, the problem of group identity and loyalty; by participation, the involvement of members of the society in the decision-making processes of the system; and by distribution, the problem of the allocation of goods, services, and other values by the political system. There are undoubtedly other ways of categorizing these persistent political system problems. At this stage in our development of a theory of political growth, it may be useful to take this tentative coding device and see how much it will help us in discriminating different patterns of development.

The primitive political systems we have discussed cope with system development problems largely in diffuse and intermittent ways. They may be compared to unicellular organisms which deal with problems by means of *ad hoc* or minimal structural differentiation and specialization. Traditional systems are to be distinguished from the primitive ones in that they have encountered state- and nation-building problems either through a threat from the international environment, or through the emergence of elites with expansionist goals. These systems are characterized by specialized regulative and extractive structures, and by a symbolic capability intended to create loyalty among its members and identity with the larger political system. In these more differentiated and secularized political systems, the problems of participation in the political system and of distribution of its products continue to be handled diffusely and intermittently by undifferentiated structures.

In dealing with contemporary political systems we can go a long way in explaining their present capability patterns and their structural and cultural characteristics by examining how they have confronted, experienced, or resolved the four system development problems. Suppose we begin with the category of stable democracies, which we have described in our classification as having high subsystem autonomy and homogeneous, secular political cultures. Taking Britain as our example, we observe that the British solution of the problem of integration and penetration — what we can call state building — had a number of unique features. Most striking was the fact that the centralization of government and control in the Tudor period stopped short of the destruction of the varieties of particularism characteristic of the preceding epoch. Thus, the feudal lords ceased being rulers of what in effect were autonomous dukedoms and earldoms, but they continued to enjoy both local and central power through their activities in the parliamentary bargaining process, in which they had both means of resisting central authority and opportunities for participation in its decisions. Similarly, the Church and religious movements were subordinated by the political system without being completely assimilated. Municipal corporations also preserved some autonomy. An independent judicial system along with a powerful legal profession enjoyed some autonomy and could mitigate the rigor and arbitrariness of central control. Britain in the Age of Absolutism, consequently, became an accommodative system, a bargaining system, within a framework of a relatively effective central authority and control. Feudal pluralism persisted and provided the structural and cultural basis for the later development of democratic pluralism.

Problems of national identity and nation building in Britain were solved incrementally and continuously over a period of several centuries. During the Tudor period ethnic particularism began to give way to a homogeneous national culture. Though Scotch, Welsh, and Irish resistance continued to trouble British politics, only the Irish problem persisted as a crisis into the nineteenth and twentieth centuries. Immigration into Britain has been on a small scale, but it is of interest that whenever Britain has been confronted by serious problems of ethnic and cultural conflict, its unity and stability have been affected in much the same way as that of nations confronted with these problems on a more serious scale. In other words, there is no magic in British political development. The continuity and gradualism of its growth have been the consequence in part of the relatively light loading of the political system by problems of cultural heterogeneity and by pressure from the international political system.

Though the British political system has been actively involved in international politics, British soil has not been invaded for almost a millenium. It could function throughout the seventeenth, eighteenth, and nineteenth centuries as a great, at times a dominant, power at less cost than could other political systems. The ability of Britain to dismantle its empire and accept a significant decline in its international position without great demoralization may in part be accounted for by its long and relatively untroubled experience of national cultural homogeneity and of successful performance in international politics. It appears in the past to have been able to accept victory without intoxication; just as in the present it can accept loss in status without demoralization. The argument that the apparently deep and stable sense of national identity among Britishers is related to this nation-building experience is a convincing one.

Problems of participation in the political system and of distribution of welfare in Britain were both confronted and solved incrementally in the course of the eighteenth, nineteenth, and twentieth centuries. It would not be correct to say that Britain was able to avoid completely the "cumulative-revolution" phenomenon which has had such unfortunate consequences in the development of continental European political systems. The disorderly mobs of London and of the industrial cities of England in the late eighteenth and early nineteenth centuries were making demands for economic and social rights as well as for political rights. The British elites gave way — partially and in piecemeal terms to be sure — to demands for both participation and welfare. Thus, the suffrage was increased incrementally through the nineteenth and early twentieth centuries. Interest groups representing the demands of the working classes became both legitimate and effective in the course of the nineteenth century, and the political parties responded to the demands of the mobilized working classes. The Liberal party was responsive to the participation demands of the working classes, and the Tory party responsive to their welfare demands. In addition, a rapidly expanding economy and international trade reduced the pressure of welfare demands on the political system itself.

Thus, while it can be said that Britain in the last few centuries of its history has been confronted by all four problems of state and nation building, participation, and welfare, it has not been confronted by simultaneous acute crises to the extent that was true on the European continent. Although we are simplifying the historical process, we might suggest that the state- and nation-building crises were fundamentally solved in the period from the fifteenth to the seventeenth centuries. The participation problem in its crisis form was solved roughly from the period of the French Revolution through the middle of the nineteenth century, while the distribution problem as a crisis occurred in the late nineteenth century and in subsequent decades. The welfare problem still constitutes the most serious challenge confronting the British political system as it gropes toward a more effective distribution of education and opportunity.

Some of the peculiar features of British political development come out more sharply when we contrast it with a radically different pattern. The German case is instructive. While the building of the German state was not completed until the second half of the nineteenth century, its pattern had already been established in Prussia in the sixteenth and seventeenth centuries. The building of the state in Prussia involved the assimilation of the feudal nobility into the central bureaucracy and army. In other words, feudal pluralism in Prussia was assimilated into a bureaucratic authoritarian structure, in contrast with Britain where it was accommodated in a parliamentary bargaining process. Furthermore, the penetration of central authority during the formative period of the Prussian monarchy was conducted under military auspices at a time when Prussia was actively and frequently engaged in warfare. The agents of centralization were the military commissars, who imparted a military quality to Prussian authoritarianism. The frequent involvement of the Prussian monarchy in large-scale land warfare during this period required the maintenance of a standing army and called for conscription of a larger proportion of the population than was the case in other countries. The pattern of authority and subordination in the state-building process in Prussia, therefore, seems to have been more thoroughgoing, more destructive of individual autonomy and independence among both the elites and the rank and file, than in other European countries.

As Prussia and the other German states entered into the nineteenth century, they were confronted by the spread of nationalism and by demands for popular participation stimulated by the French Revolution. The history of Germany in the nineteenth century might very well be written in terms of the interplay between the simultaneous problems of state and nation building, and demands for participation and welfare. Demands for political participation, particularly on the part of the middle classes in the various German states, became assimilated into demands for national integration. The statesmanship of Bismarck turned in considerable part on his skill in manipulating and combining demands for national integration and strength with demands for participation and welfare. He manipulated these problems of political system development by offering national power and substantial concessions in the field of social welfare in exchange for the moderation or the withholding of demands for participation.

Thus the Weimar Republic arose out of the defeat in World War I with a political culture marred by an insecure sense of national identity and by a pattern of fragmentation in which the dominant components were a persisting antirepublican authoritarianism on the right, the partially alienated Social Democrats and Catholics in the center, and the fully alienated Communists on the left. The ideologies of the various parties reflected Germany's system development experiences in different ways. The conservatives in different degrees rejected participant attitudes and institutions. The Social Democrats combined demands for participation and for welfare in an ideology that doubted the possibility of fulfilling these demands in anything short of a revolution and socialist transformation of society. The Communists rejected a gradual and pluralistic bargaining process completely and sought to destroy the Weimar system. The Catholics still bore the scars of persecution which they experienced in the nation-building phase in the nineteenth century. The National Socialists constructed an ideology which appealed to all these unfulfilled demands for authority, participation, welfare, and national strength; and the economic and political chaos of the great depression gave them their opportunity for power.

Thus, if we compare British and German political development, Germany has had four distinct political systems in the last century, each one discontinuous with the one which preceded it, while the British political system has experienced a continuous and incremental growth process over the last three centuries. Even at the present time one may legitimately question the degree of support among the German population for the political system of the Bonn republic. Evidence shows that a historical background of discontinuity and trauma has resulted in a political culture lacking in deep and stable system commitment and loyalty. The system is accepted in instrumental terms as long as it satisfies demands made upon it and does not impose heavy sacrifices. The psychological reserves of the British political system, on the other hand, would appear to be substantially capable of assimilating shock and crisis as well as sacrifice without threat to the stability of the system.

In the case of France the Age of Absolutism neither assimilated the feudal aristocracy into a parliamentary bargaining process (as in Britain), nor assimilated them into an efficient civil and military bureaucracy (as in Prussia). The older feudal aristocracy was in part drawn into the life of the royal court, where they were provided with sinecures, or employed in diplomacy or in the military. The newer aristocracy based on office, and primarily the higher magistrates of the provincial *parlements* (*noblesse de robe*), became the spokesmen of aristocratic privilege in the first half of the eighteenth century. They were able to do this by virtue of their control of the provincial *parlements,* which resisted the enforcement of royal legislation and the imposition of taxation which would affect the nobility.

In the decades before the French Revolution the nobility, led by the magistrates of the *parlements,* carried through a successful resistance against the central government, on the one hand, and, on the other, closed its ranks as well as high governmental office to the middle classes. The result was a cumulative crisis of state authority, identity, and loyalty, and of participation. The central government was unable to tax and regulate. The middle classes became alienated from a system which denied them access and social mobility. And the peasantry, which had to bear the main burden of taxation, military service, and surviving feudal obligations, was also alienated in substantial measure.[5]

The French Revolution resulted from a clash of aristocratic, middle-class, and Church elites, all with little prior experience in political bargaining and coalition making. The extreme measures taken by the Jacobins against the aristocracy and the Church produced a polarization and traumatization of French political culture which persist until the present day. France has had eleven constitutions since the Revolution: five republics, three constitutional monarchies, two empires, and one dictatorship (the Vichy regime). These institutional discontinu-

[5] See Alexis Charles de Tocqueville, *The Old Regime and the French Revolution* (New York: Harper and Row, Publishers, 1956); Elinor G. Barber, *The Bourgeoisie in Eighteenth Century France* (Princeton: Princeton University Press, 1955); Franklin L. Ford, *Robe and Sword* (Cambridge: Harvard University Press, 1953).

ities reflect a persistent and acute crisis of state authority. Even the longest lived of these political systems — the Third Republic — was characterized by periodic immobilism and frequent threat of authoritarianism and reaction. The instability of constitutional arrangements may in part be explained by a deep distrust of effective executive authority on the left, attributable to the imperial coups and threats of coups of the nineteenth century, and by a similarly deep anxiety over a powerful legislature on the right, fed by memories of the Convention and the Terror. Thus, all constitution making in France has been fated to alienate either the Left or the Right, and full legitimacy has never been accorded to a political system which might provide for both popular participation and effective government. The apparent legitimacy accorded the Fifth Republic seems to be given to General de Gaulle rather than to its governmental structure.

The problem of French national identity similarly does not appear to have been stably solved. The pattern in the last century has involved recurrent humiliation: defeat in the War of 1870, the tragic costs of World War I, and the defeats of 1940 and of the colonial wars in Indochina and Algeria.

French political culture was fragmented and alienated in the *ancien régime*. It was further alienated and polarized in the Revolution, and appears to remain essentially fragmented until the present day. The ideologies and propensities of French political movements in recent decades reflect these persisting crises of state authority, of national identity, and of the unresolved problems of participation and distribution. In what way and to what extent the Gaullist interlude has affected these patterns remains to be seen.

One of the central problems in the emerging theory of political development is that of relating the ways in which particular political systems or classes of political systems have encountered, experienced, and solved the four problems of system development, to their contemporary patterns of structure, culture, and performance. There is a serious problem here of the logic of proof. We cannot simply infer, using plausibility as our guide, that a particular historical experience has had particular consequences for contemporary performance patterns. This is a good way of deriving hypotheses, but it does not constitute proof. Proof will consist in actually locating what would appear to be the results of historical experience in the culture, structure, and performance of the contemporary system. Thus, for example, if we wish to relate political alienation in France to the French historical background, we shall have to ascertain just what kind of alienation toward what kind of political objects is to be encountered at what points in the French political system. The historical background may give us leads as to where to look and what questions to ask. Any effort to relate contemporary performance to past experience must look not only at the past history but also at the living history that affects the propensities of the political systems. Studies of recruitment and socialization patterns will be of particular importance in such undertakings, for these are the mechanisms which translate past experiences and memories into behavioral tendencies within the structure of the political system.

THE PREDICTION OF POLITICAL DEVELOPMENT

What we have outlined thus far may be viewed as preliminary exercises pointing toward a theory of political development. One exercise has required us to present a model of the political system — of the ways in which we can describe and compare the performance of political systems in their environments (their capabilities), their input-conversion-output patterns (conversion functions and structures), and their system maintenance and adaptation processes (socialization and recruitment). A second exercise has required us to classify and compare political systems according to basic developmental structural and cultural characteristics as these are related to different levels and patterns of performance. And a third exercise has required that we relate these various types of political systems to their historical experience with what we have provisionally called the four problems of system development — state and nation building, participation, and distribution.

In undertaking these exercises we have already moved into the realm of generalization and prediction. The classification of types of political systems constitutes in part a prediction that certain characteristics of capability, structure, and function will be associated with levels of development and autonomy.

In the opening pages of this chapter we suggested that the formation of a predictive theory of political change was likely to be a hazardous undertaking. The large numbers of variables involved and the difficulties of getting adequate information about them make it difficult to derive an encompassing theory at this level. It is easier to work with small subsystems, such as the election process, and to assume that most of the larger system variables are constant. Much of the most explicit theory construction of a detailed and predictive, or even of an explanatory, nature has indeed been carried out in such fields as voting behavior or attitude formation. But the fascination of the problem of political development as well as its importance in the light of our contemporary values remains. Moreover, as we suggested by our analogy of predicting the future career of the high school graduate, we may be able to go a good distance toward predicting the limitations, potentialities, and pressures shaping the future of a political system if we can find a few very strong relationships between fundamental variables.

The utility of the developmental approach, as it has been formulated above, is that it rests upon the initial designation of several such fundamental variables, and implies several basic theoretical relationships between these and system characteristics. The basic theoretical statement here is that the development of higher levels of system capabilities is dependent upon the development of greater structural differentiation and cultural secularization. In a more specifically structural sense, it is predicted that higher capabilities depend upon the emergence of "rational" bureaucratic organizations. Thus, we predict that a system cannot develop a high level of internal regulation, distribution, or extraction without a "modern" governmental bureaucracy in one form or another. (Although we have deliberately chosen not to include them in the present analysis, a similar predictive statement could be made about the international capabilities of a system.) Likewise, the development of something like a modern interest-group or party system seems to be the prerequisite to a high development of the responsive capability. It will be recalled that Chapter VII suggested the prerequisite nature of differentiated political communication structures for attainment of levels of capability was also suggested.

These strong relationships derive, in essence, from the sheer technical superiority in coordinating activity which "modern" organizations provide. This is a manifestation in the political realm of Weber's hypothesis about the increasing "rationalization" or "bureaucratization" of modern society.[6] There may well be upper limits to this process and to the technical advantages of this form of organization — such limits are clearly of great significance for those interested in predicting the development of the most highly differentiated contemporary systems — but the generalization holds over a wide range of capability. It sets certain boundaries and opens certain possibilities to the form of political change in any political system.[7]

Two additional generalizations have been suggested which can form the basis for a predictive and explanatory theory of political change. One of these is that political systems will encounter the system development problems of nation building, state building, participation, and distribution. This presents a particular challenge for the premobilized systems of the contemporary world. The diffusion of the "world culture," with the concomitant awareness of more highly developed eco-

[6] See Max Weber, *From Max Weber: Essays in Sociology,* ed. Hans H. Gerth and C. Wright Mills (New York: Oxford University Press, 1958), pp. 196–244; and Reinhard Bendix, *Max Weber: An Intellectual Portrait* (Garden City: Doubleday and Company, Inc., 1960), pp. 379–381, 418–425, and 450–459.

[7] Some recent sociological hypotheses have been advanced suggesting the relationship between this process of differentiation and a number of conditions and pressures in the social and international environment. However, we cannot pretend to formulate more than a few of the suggested elements of and possibilities within a predictive theory of this kind, and shall not explore these factors here. See S. N. Eisenstadt, "Social Change, Differentiation, and Evolution," *American Sociological Review,* June, 1964, pp. 375–387; and Talcott Parsons, "Evolutionary Universals in Society," *American Sociological Review,* June, 1964, pp. 339–357.

nomic and political systems, exposure to modern technology, and general impact of the realization that man's fate is subject to some degree of manipulation and control, has given rise to a set of demands for increased participation and welfare in almost every modern nation. As communication and technology continue to expand, the premobilized and the remaining traditional and primitive systems seem likely to confront system development problems in a cumulative and pressing form. Since such systems have not yet reached the level of differentiation and capability to satisfy these demands directly, the alternatives before them are severely constrained, regardless of the democratic or the authoritarian "stance" taken by the leaders.

A final generalization which has been implied relates subsystem autonomy and the responsive capability. This relationship may be seen in its clearest form in the most differentiated systems. In the analysis of highly differentiated totalitarian systems, the role of bureaucratic institutions and access channels, rule application, and communication (Chapters IV through VII), suggests that the gigantic bureaucracy-party organizational complex characteristic of these societies will dominate and shape the responsiveness of the system. This implies that *regardless* of the personal desires and ideological commitments of the political leaders, it will be very difficult for such systems to develop a broad responsive capability. We can predict that systems of this class will continue to show a limited range of responsiveness as long as subsystem autonomy remains low and differentiation high.

On the basis of these three general theoretical statements, we can move in a number of directions in formulating an increasingly specific theory of political change. In conclusion, however, we should like to suggest a particularly promising direction. A major problem in prediction is the virtual impossibility of forecasting the attitudes and policies of a given leader or of a small decision-making group. The basic generalizations suggested above are strong and powerful predictors but highly unspecific, in part because they operate regardless of the leadership policies. Weber suggested that whether a nation was run by socialists or by the capitalistic middle class, an increasing "government by bureaucracy" was extremely likely, given the need of the system to increase its capabilities to meet various problems. But clearly leadership strategies do make a vast difference in the development of many aspects of the political system. An approach to this problem in predictive theory is to view various alternative courses of leadership action, planned or not, as *political investment strategies*. The developmental theory can then suggest the implications for the system of various alternative strategies, given the present conditions of system and environment. The accuracy of such predictions would be a good indicator of the empirical soundness of the generalizations being developed at all levels in political science, since such predictions must rest on a careful and accurate analysis of system characteristics, environmental conditions, and particular components of the strategic alternatives themselves. At the same time, such an approach avoids the burden of having to predict the predispositions of a very few individuals in key positions. A particularly interesting and timely example of an area for the formulation of a theory of investment strategies is the current dilemma facing the premobilized political systems.

History seems to have confronted the leaders of these nations with challenges beyond human proportion. Thousands and tens of thousands of young men of Asia, Africa, and Latin America have come to or are now in attendance at Western seats of learning, or are being educated in Asian, African, and Latin American universities which provide educations similar to those given in European and American institutions. The sense of political history and of historic problem to which these young men are exposed is one which is appropriate in the industrializing, modernizing, and democratizing West of the twentieth century. The sense of political problem and of political value to which they are exposed has been determined by the preoccupation in Western nations with the struggle for democratization and with the spread of material and social welfare. They are told in effect through their educational experience that democracy and welfare have the highest priority in politics and public policy. But when they return to their native lands, they find in most cases that their societies lack the structural framework of the state and the cultural properties of the nation, that there is in effect no viable political system to democratize. They would have been better prepared for the tasks which confront them had they been exposed to a political theory and history which stressed the long and costly struggle in Europe over the development of the state and of the nation.

The kind of education in political theory and political history which the intellectuals and leaders of the new nations now receive almost guarantees demoralization and disillusionment. They are confronted with an image of the modern and democratic state which, given the social and cultural conditions of their societies, is unattainable in the immediate future. Their demoralization results from the fact that once it becomes apparent that a modern democratic welfare state cannot be meaningfully instituted, they have no strategy of modernization and democratization to turn to which can preserve among them some sense of being able to control or influence the developmental process toward these ends.

The study of comparative politics has an important contribution to make in this search for a more effective grasp of the processes of political change and for appropriate and effective public policies designed to affect it. It is not accidental that Marxism-Leninism took hold in those parts of Europe which had lagged behind in the industrial and political developmental process of the eighteenth and nineteenth centuries. It is not accidental that this political ideology and the movements which propagated it should have stressed the swelling of state power as a means of social modernization. And it should not surprise us that Marxism-Leninism, or more particularly the examples of it in the Soviet Union and China, should have some resonance among the elites of the new nations, for Marxism-Leninism in its operational aspects views the state in instrumental terms. It offers to political elites a conception of the state reduced to its pure power essentials and gives an ethical coloration to such a view. The challenge to democratic political leaders is to find a theory and strategy of political development which can put realism into the service of a more humane approach, which can draw from man's historical experience and from man's imagination and logical gifts some sense of how to set about on what must, in the nature of the case, be a long and uncertain voyage toward the goals of democracy and welfare.

It is perfectly reasonable to think of state building, nation building, participation, and distribution as problems of political development planning, or *investment*. The creation of a more differentiated political system out of a pre-existing, less differentiated political system or systems can be spelled out in requirement terms — what kind of bureaucracy one has to create, what kind of rule-making and adjudicative structures, and what kinds of loads these structures must be made to bear. Similarly, it is possible to spell out a program of investment in nation building, to determine what human and material resources would be needed to produce identification with and commitment to the nation and political system, what resistances might be encountered, and how to deploy educational, propaganda, and organizational inputs in order that they contribute to the creation of a culture of national identity. It would be possible to treat in investment terms the problem of introducing a structure and culture of participation and welfare — to anticipate the costs of introducing an effective political infrastructure, of providing for the autonomy of its components, and of developing a public policy of welfare and a bureaucratic structure to implement it.

Indeed, these exercises in the analysis of political investment strategies bring us to the point where we can attempt to formulate a "rational choice" model of political growth. To begin with we would have to make an analysis of the starting point of a political system. We would have to specify its structural, cultural, and conversion characteristics and its capability profile. Next we would need to specify the properties of the kind of political system we wish to introduce. The problem of rational choice is one of predicting an investment strategy among alternative strategies which will have a high probability of bringing us from the present to the given desired system characteristics with the least risk and cost.

The study of the historical development of political systems should make an important contribution to a theory of political development planning. As we examine the patterns of growth of historical political systems, our ability to make "risk," "cost," and "benefit" predictions should become more precise. Thus, we might be able to say that if we follow a Prussian strategy of state building, involving the destruction of the traditional pluralism of a society, we may gain certain immediate benefits in the raising of the extractive and regulative capabilities. However we also increase the risks and costs of investment in the development of a responsive capability at such time in the future as we may wish to invest in democratization.

Similarly, it may be possible to argue from the Indian experience as described by Weiner [8] that if one invests in a bureaucracy and in a political infrastructure at the same time, without investing in the development of a culture of bargaining and accommodation as between interest groups and the bureaucracy, it will be necessary to incur the costs of friction and conflict and to assume the risk of interest-group alienation.

The approach followed in many of the new nations, which involves simultaneous investments in the development of all the capabilities including the responsive and distributive ones, seems to be a high-risk, low-benefit strategy. The human and material resources simply are not there to produce this kind of simultaneous solution of the problems of state and nation building, participation, and distribution. There must be some scheduling, some system of priorities.

The lessons of the historical experiences of other nations facing system development problems can be of use here in suggesting the limitations imposed by certain kinds of circumstances, and the consequences of following certain kinds of strategies. The British historical experience suggests the advantages of being able to build state and nation without foreclos-

[8] Myron Weiner, *The Politics of Scarcity* (Chicago: University of Chicago Press, 1962).

ing the options of continuous structural and cultural change leading to the emergence of an effective democratic infrastructure and responsive capability. But, as the experience of the continental European countries indicates, nations which must face the system development problems in a cumulative and intense fashion cannot afford the luxury of the British model. The Mexican experience is perhaps a more relevant case in our consideration of investment strategies (see Chapter X). Here the judicious use of symbolic and limited distributive responses; the co-optation of various interest groups representing peasants, workers, and middle class, rather than the destruction of such groups; the coordination of group leadership; and the gradual but continuous growth of regulative, extractive, distributive, and symbolic capabilities, made it possible to build state and nation without destroying the autonomy of the various political subsystems. Yet, here too analysis must be cautious and oriented to all relevant variables. We must not forget that Mexico paid a heavy price in human lives during her revolution, and that her leaders felt it necessary to suppress such traditional groups as Church and landholders, at least until quite recently.

The developmental strategies which will be appropriate for the new political systems will differ one from the other. These nations will need to take into account their different starting points from both a cultural and a structural point of view. The rate of investment in political development will have to reflect differences in resource base, as well as in the ability of these societies and political systems to absorb investment efficiently. Bureaucratic, political-party, interest-group, and communications elites cannot be trained overnight. A "good" theory of political development should enable us to predict the outcome of alternative investment strategies for such goals as democracy, welfare, and stability. While much of such a theory of political development is still to be worked out, a number of points might be suggested which will certainly be incorporated into any theory focusing on these particular goals.

First, it will be a strategy which stresses the scheduling of efforts at solution of the system development problems. It will

stress state and nation building in the first stages over participation and welfare. Second, the pattern of investment in political growth will hold options open. The development of the
regulative and extractive capabilities must stop short of the
destruction of pluralism, must avoid the suppression of bargaining. Third, our theory of political development must enable us not only to devise broad investment strategies, but also
to make compensatory investments to cope with the disruptive
consequences of modernizing processes. Fourth, such a theory
of political development should enable us to cope with the
consequences for the political system of different patterns of
investment in other systems than the political. Different strategies of investment in education, in industrialization, in family
structure and organization, and in urban and community planning, affect the inputs of demand and support into the political system. We must be in a position to relate nonpolitical
development strategies to political development strategies. In
other words, an investment strategy in politics to be effective
must take into account the investment strategies that are being
followed in other components of the society and in the international political system.

Though our imagination and resolution may quail before
such challenges as these, we are compelled to move along these
lines, of elaborating the logic of public policy as it relates to
political development. The logic will provide us with an ability to handle the interaction of many variables, as well as make
us keenly aware of the structural restraints in any given starting point in political development. Such a logic should enable
us to move from an essentially ideological orientation toward
the problem of political development and modernization to an
ability to calculate the risks, costs, and benefits of different developmental strategies in secular "probability" terms.

We are confronted here with the ultimate question of the
Enlightenment. Can man employ reason to understand, shape,
and develop his own institutions, particularly those concerned
with power and coercion, to plan political development with
the least human cost and with bearable risks? Can he find solutions to the state-building and nation-building problems of the

developing areas which will not indefinitely prejudice or postpone the effective confrontation of their problems of participation and welfare? The modern political scientist can no longer afford to be the disillusioned child of the Enlightenment, but must become its sober trustee.

Index